MW01011560

Treating Post-Trauma Nightmares

Joanne L. Davis, PhD, received her doctorate in clinical psychology from the University of Arkansas, completed an internship at the Medical University of South Carolina and a postdoctoral fellowship at the National Crime Victims Research and Treatment Center in Charleston, South Carolina. She is currently an associate professor of clinical psychology at the University of Tulsa, Oklahoma, where she oversees the Trauma Research: Assessment, Prevention, and Treatment Center and co-directs the Tulsa Institute of Trauma, Abuse, and Neglect. As a scientist-practitioner, she focuses on identifying cognitive, emotional, and behavioral aspects of traumatic experience and applying evidence-based treatments to difficulties faced by victims of trauma. In addition to her research and practice, Professor Davis also teaches courses on intervention techniques, the psychology of trauma, history of psychology, and theory and practice of clinical psychology. This is her first book.

Treating Post-Trauma Nightmares

A Cognitive Behavioral Approach

JOANNE L. DAVIS, PhD
Editor

SPRINGER PUBLISHING COMPANY

New York

Copyright © 2009 Springer Publishing Company, LLC

All rights reserved.

No part of this publication may be reproduced, stored in a retrieval system, or transmitted in any form or by any means, electronic, mechanical, photocopying, recording, or otherwise, without the prior permission of Springer Publishing Company, LLC.

Springer Publishing Company, LLC
11 West 42nd Street
New York, NY 10036
www.springerpub.com

Acquisitions Editor: Philip Laughlin
Project Manager: Cindy Fullerton
Cover Design: Mimi Flow
Composition: Aptara Inc.

08 09 10 11 12/ 5 4 3 2 1

Library of Congress Cataloging-in-Publication Data
Davis, Joanne L.
    Treating post-trauma nightmares : a cognitive behavioral approach /
Joanne L. Davis.
        p. ; cm.
    Includes bibliographical references and index.
    ISBN 978-0-8261-0289-8 (alk. paper)
1. Nightmares–Treatment.   2. Post-traumatic stress disorder–Complications.
3. Cognitive therapy.   I. Title.
    [DNLM: 1. Night Terrors–therapy.   2. Cognitive Therapy–methods.
3. Stress Disorders, Post-Traumatic–complications. WM 188 D262t 2009]
    RC549.3.D38 2009
    616.85′21—dc22

                                                                2008036379

Printed in the United States of America by Bang Printing.

The author and the publisher of this Work have made every effort to use sources believed to be reliable to provide information that is accurate and compatible with the standards generally accepted at the time of publication. The author and publisher shall not be liable for any special, consequential, or exemplary damages resulting, in whole or in part, from the readers' use of, or reliance on, the information contained in this book.

The publisher has no responsibility for the persistence or accuracy of URLs for external or third-party Internet Web sites referred to in this publication and does not guarantee that any content on such Web sites is, or will remain, accurate or appropriate.

Contents

List of Figures and Tables

CHAPTER 10

APPENDIX A

Contributors

Patricia M. Byrd, MA
Graduate Student
The University of Tulsa
Tulsa, Oklahoma

Shantel Fernandez, MA
Graduate Student
The University of Tulsa
Tulsa, Oklahoma

Tera J. Langston, PhD
Private Practice
Panama City, Florida

Hannah Pennington, MA
Graduate Student
The University of Tulsa
Tulsa, Oklahoma

Kristi Ensor Pruiksma, MA
Graduate Student
The University of Tulsa
Tulsa, Oklahoma

Jamie Lynn Rhudy, PhD
Assistant Professor
The University of Tulsa
Tulsa, Oklahoma

David C. Wright, PhD
United States Air Force
Tyndall AFB, Florida

Preface

Researchers are increasingly pointing to sleep disturbance following a traumatic event as a key factor in maintaining psychological and physical problems over time. Psychological and physical effects of trauma may be particularly vulnerable to chronicity with the loss of sleep's restorative functions. This suggests the essential importance of identifying interventions that restore quality sleep. While several interventions are found to be efficacious in the treatment of posttraumatic stress disorder (PTSD), both sleep disturbances and nightmares may be resistant to such treatments that broadly target PTSD (Davis, DeArellano, Falsetti, & Resnick, 2003; Forbes, Creamer, & Biddle, 2001; Johnson et al., 1996; Scurfield, Kenderdine, & Pollard, 1990; Zayfert & DeViva, 2004). Indeed, several authors have suggested the need to target sleep disturbances and nightmares directly (e.g., Halliday, 1987). Kramer and Kinney (2003) found that Vietnam veterans with disturbed dreaming showed hyperresponse during sleep and suggest that "desensitization therapies may have their success limited if sleep responsivity is not altered" (p. 686). For some individuals, therapies that do not specifically target sleep and nightmares may not affect this aspect of trauma response.

The past decade has seen a significant increase in efforts to develop and evaluate treatments that specifically target sleep disturbance and nightmares in trauma-exposed persons. As part of this effort, this book describes a treatment that brings together literature, theory, and techniques from behavioral sleep medicine and psychological perspectives. This interdisciplinary treatment, Exposure, Relaxation, and Rescripting Therapy (ERRT), specifically targets chronic nightmares experienced by trauma-exposed persons. Several articles have been published describing ERRT (Davis & Wright, 2006) and presenting results of the research on ERRT (e.g., Davis & Wright, 2005; 2007). Information about treatment outcome for related treatments and the development of ERRT is addressed in chapter 5.

The purpose of this book is to present therapists and scientists with information that formed the basis for the development of ERRT and to describe the treatment, step by step, for those interested in the utilization and further evaluation of ERRT. The book begins with an overview of traumatic events and their impact on clients. A brief summary of information on night terrors and nontrauma nightmares is presented, including difficulties related to defining nightmares. The nature and characteristics of post-trauma nightmares are presented. Theoretical formulations of post-trauma nightmares by leading sleep and trauma experts are outlined, and a new three-factor model is proposed. Important assessment considerations are outlined, including guidance in the assessment of traumatic events, differential diagnosis of sleep events, and a review of sleep and nightmare assessment tools.

Treatments for nightmares are then reviewed and ERRT is introduced. Information is provided on the development of the treatment, including the influence of the literature from the fields of behavioral sleep medicine, trauma, and anxiety disorders. The treatment is then presented session by session. After describing the treatment in full, a special section on treatment considerations addresses potential difficulties that therapists or clients may encounter, and suggestions for handling these situations are provided. Finally, the efficacy of ERRT is reviewed, and potential critical components and mechanisms of change are discussed.

The full patient manual is presented in appendix A. The manual includes all components of the treatment explained in the book, written in layman's language. It also includes space for clients to write notes, as well as some of the assessment forms used by our research group. The accompanying patient manual may be copied for each client. In our own center, we put the manual in three-ring binders so we can add a chapter to the binder at each session. This is done so that clients do not get ahead in treatment and are able to proceed along with the therapist. Many of the homework assignments are included at the end of the chapters and can be easily removed and submitted. We generally keep the homework assignments for data analysis purposes, while the clients keep the remainder of the manual. This allows clients to maintain the information presented in the treatment in the event they want to look back and reread sections.

Case examples are provided throughout the book to illustrate various aspects of the treatment and the struggles and triumphs of the clients we have treated with ERRT. We are very appreciative of all who participated in the research trials that informed the development of the treatment.

To protect the identity of these individuals, the case examples presented in this book represent amalgamations of the many participants who were part of the clinical research that serves as the basis for this work. Often, stories of several clients are combined into one case example. Names, situations, and ages have been changed, and any resemblance to one individual person is unintended.

Given the burgeoning empirical and theoretical literature on trauma-related nightmares and sleep disturbances, the information provided must be viewed as preliminary. The proposed theory underlying the development and maintenance of trauma-related nightmares, as well as the potential critical components and mechanisms of change, are based on data where available. Thus, this work does not represent an endpoint but rather another step in the ongoing effort to better understand the nature and function of post-trauma nightmares and to assist those who suffer from them. We hope that it also serves as a point of departure for new research efforts.

The components of ERRT are drawn from the best practices across the trauma, sleep, and anxiety fields. Although the treatment is presented as a manualized approach, therapists should consider flexible administration of the treatment components depending on the presenting complaints of their clients. Considering that many individuals reporting nightmares also report other difficulties, a thorough case formulation is necessary to determine whether the treatment should be utilized as a stand-alone intervention, a concurrent intervention, or an integration with ongoing therapy. Finally, while this treatment was developed for and assessed with individuals exposed to traumatic events, similar treatments have been used successfully with idiopathic (non-trauma-related) nightmares.

Acknowledgements

The development of *Exposure, Relaxation, and Rescripting Therapy* began during my time as a postdoctoral fellow at the National Crime Victims Research and Treatment Center in Charleston, South Carolina. I would like to thank the wonderful faculty of the NCVC for their encouragement and support. Since its inception, numerous people have been involved in the ongoing research project. Dr. Jamie Rhudy has been my research partner for the past several years and has designed and conducted the physiological assessment component of the research program. Several chapters are co-authored by students and colleagues—thank you for the great contributions to this work. Three students have managed the research projects over time. Dr. David Wright was of tremendous assistance in starting the research program from the ground floor, and Patricia Byrd and Kristi Pruiksma kept it going over the years. Numerous students served as therapists and assessors, including Dr. David Wright, Patricia Byrd, Victoria Tracy, Elizabeth Risch, Dr. Cameo Borntrager, Dr. Tera Langston, Dr. Johna Smasal, Dr. Nina Schneider, Christina Cantrell, Shantel Fernandez, Kate Witheridge, Amy Nelson, Kristi Pruiksma, Hannah Pennington, Sara Mayfield, Rachel Wiedeman, and Elizabeth Avant. Our physiological assessors included Aimee E. Williams, Klanci M. McCabe, Emily Bartley, and Elizabeth Avant. Other students who assisted with the database, phone screens, and reading drafts of the book include David Richardson, Melissa Tibbits, Jennifer Allen, Julie Hill, Hayley Bastida, Marcy Elder, Donica Romeo, Julie Burch, Devra McManus, and Marsha Siebenmorgen. I would like to say a very special thank you to Dr. Elana Newman, my friend and colleague, who provided very helpful feedback on drafts of the book. Thank you to Dr. Judy Berry for her wisdom about the process. Thanks to Phil Laughlin for sticking with me and helping to shape my idea into a finished product.

A huge thank you to Sloan, Bryce, Dylan, and Caedon for their love, support, and incredible tolerance as this project continued on. Sloan, you've been my inspiration and motivation and I can't thank you enough for everything. Thanks always to my family in New York for their ongoing support and love.

Finally, I would like to thank the courageous men and women who shared their stories with us and taught us so much about the impact of trauma in their lives. Funding for the research program described in this book was provided by an OHRS award for project number HR02-002S, from the Oklahoma Center for the Advancement of Science and Technology, Psi Chi National Honor Society, and by The University of Tulsa's Office of Research and Sponsored Programs internal funding.

Overview of Trauma and Post-Trauma Nightmares

I'm lying in bed—something has awakened me, but I'm not quite sure what it is. Then I hear it again. Someone is in my house, walking through the living room. It is pitch black, and I hear whispering. It sounds like two men. I feel very scared—what if they go upstairs? I hear the bottom stair creak, and I feel paralyzed. They are going upstairs to get my kids—I have to go stop them, but I can't move. I break out in a sweat, and my heart pounds. I know that I have to get to my kids before they do. I realize that someone is coming down the hall toward my room. And I hear someone else moving upstairs in the kids' room. One is almost at my door. I slide out of bed onto the floor. I can't breathe, I feel like they must be able to hear my heart pounding—they know I'm in here. I can't move, and I am trembling so hard I can't stand up. I'm trying to move, trying to get to the door. I hear my youngest mumbling as if he's being awakened from sleep. I don't know who they are, but I know they are going to take my kids and kill me. I have to get up there, but I still can't move. I see my kids' faces in my mind . . . so little. I have to help them. I hear a hand on the bedroom door. One is coming in. One is going to kill me. I am frantic now as the door is opening. I see a hand and a foot, and then I hear my youngest scream. . . .

People have been fascinated by dreams—why we have them, what they mean—since ancient times. While we still do not understand the exact nature and function of dreams, numerous theories abound. The ancient Greeks believed that dreams were messages from the gods; Aristotle was among the first to propose that dreams were products of the mind (Gallop, 1990); and Sigmund Freud argued that dreams were disguised expressions of unconscious impulses and protectors of sleep (1900/1955). Current theories include those that focus on the neurological correlates of dreaming, such as Hobson and McCarley's (1977) activation synthesis theory, which states that dreams are epiphenomena of sleep, story lines created by the brain to make sense of signals from the brain stem and limbic system. Similarly, Seligman and Yellen (1987) describe dreams as series of primarily unrelated visual and emotional episodes and cognitive attempts to make sense of those, and Stickgold (2005) suggests that dreams are the conscious experience of memory reprocessing during sleep. Focused more on the function of the dream mentation, Revonsuo (2000) argues that dreams are defense mechanisms evolutionarily designed to help prepare the dreamer to perceive and avoid threatening events. Several researchers suggest dreams function to diffuse strong emotion (Cartwright & Lloyd, 1994; Kramer, 1991), while others suggest that they provide a means of establishing networks and recontextualizing emotions (Hartmann, 1998b).

As confusing as the current state of knowledge on dreams is, even less understood is the nightmare. Theorists and researchers have generally attempted to understand nightmares utilizing existing theories of dreams. Indeed, some researchers have considered nightmares failed dreams, as they generally awaken people, disrupting sleep processes (Kramer, 1991), or as "the dream gone 'wild' or 'bad'" (Erman, 1987, p. 668). Hartmann (1998a), however, suggests that research should actually flow the other way, starting with understanding the nightmare and extending to dreams. He asserts that the precipitator of nightmares, particularly post-trauma nightmares, is obvious. Examining the manner in which our minds process a known entity (a traumatic or stressful event) through nightmares may shed light onto the murkier waters of dreams, for which possible influences are less certain.

An extreme type of nightmare—which may actually be a phenomenon unto itself or the extreme end of a continuum—is the nightmare that follows the experience of a traumatic event. Post-trauma nightmares, often reflecting the traumatic event to varying degrees of veracity, have received increased clinical, theoretical, and scientific interest in the past 2 decades. Initiated or exacerbated by a traumatic event, these nighttime horrors may have a haunting impact on the dreamer, affecting not only the quality and quantity of sleep the individual experiences, but also the cognitive, emotional, behavioral, and physiological functioning of the individual during the day. This book explores the nature of the post-trauma nightmare, bringing together literature across various specialties in an attempt to grasp the phenomenon of the trauma-related nightmare; and describes a step-by-step approach to mitigating the frequency and severity of nightmares in a cognitive behavioral treatment. We start with a brief examination of traumatic events themselves and their impact on the functioning of adult survivors.

THE PREVALENCE AND NATURE OF TRAUMA

The third edition of the *Diagnostic and Statistical Manual of Mental Disorders* (*DSM*; American Psychiatric Association [APA], 1980) defines traumas as those stressful events that are outside the range of usual human experience. Subsequent research suggested this was not the case, however. By experiencing such events as being a victim of terrorist activity, surviving a severe car accident, hearing of the unexpected loss of a loved one, or experiencing molestation or physical abuse, far too many people will struggle through horrific events. The specific definition of a traumatic event has changed over time, and the current version of the *DSM* (APA, 2000) provides the following criteria for classifying an experience as a traumatic event: "(1) the person experienced, witnessed, or was confronted with an event or events that involved actual or threatened death or serious injury, or a threat to the physical integrity of self or others; (2) the person's response involved intense fear, helplessness, or horror. NOTE: In children, this may be expressed instead by disorganized or agitated behavior" (p. 467). This definition provides for a wide array of events to be considered traumatic (indeed, some would argue too wide of an array) and better reflects and informs the body of empirical data suggesting that approximately 60% to 70% of individuals will experience a traumatic event in their lifetimes.

Norris (1992) surveyed 1,000 adults in four southeastern cities about their experience with 10 types of potentially traumatic events. Of the respondents, 69% reported that they experienced a traumatic event in their lifetimes, and 21% experienced a trauma in the previous year. Interviews conducted with a national representative sample of 5,877 adults found that 61% of men and 51% of women reported experiencing a traumatic event in their lifetimes (Kessler, Sonnega, Bromet, Hughes, & Nelson, 1995), while 89% of adults in an urban area reported lifetime exposure to a traumatic event (Breslau et al., 1998). The most common events reported across epidemiological studies include witnessing someone being badly injured or killed, being involved in a fire or natural disaster, and being involved in a life-threatening accident (Solomon & Davidson, 1997). Prevalence rates for various events differ significantly by gender. For example, the most frequent types of events reported by women included natural disasters (15.2%), witnessed violence (14.5%), accidents (13.8%), great shock (12.4%), and sexual assault (12.3%). The most frequent types reported by men included witnessed violence (35.6%), accidents (25%), threats with a weapon (19%), natural disaster (18.9%), and great shock (11.4%; Kessler et al., 1995). Numerous investigations demonstrate that most trauma-exposed people report experiencing multiple traumatic events (e.g., Breslau, 1998).

Large scale studies of children also find that a significant proportion report experiencing traumatic events. In interviews with a nationally representative sample of 4,008 adolescents ages 12 to 17, nearly half of the sample reported experiencing some form of violent victimization, including sexual assault/rape (8.1%), physical assault (17.4%), physically abusive behavior (9.4%), and witnessed violence (39.4%; Kilpatrick, Saunders, & Smith, 2002). Other national studies reported similar findings (Finkelhor, Ormrod, Turner, & Hamby, 2005).

IMPACT OF TRAUMA

Although a response of fear, helplessness, or horror is required for an event to be considered a trauma (APA, 2000), the impact of experiencing a traumatic event may range from short-term shock and distress to a chronic struggle with emotional, psychological, physiological, and behavioral difficulties. While many assume that traumatic events typically result in long-term problems, research indicates that people are generally quite resilient in the face of potentially traumatic experiences. As Bonanno (2005) states, "resilience (not recovery) is the most common response to potential trauma" (p. 135). Increasingly, people who study trauma conceptualize resilience as a normal response to trauma, not an anomaly. Bonanno suggests that 10% to 30% of trauma-exposed individuals will experience chronic problems, 5% to 10% will have a delayed response (initial experience of moderate symptoms for some period of time that begin to increase over time), 15% to 35% will recover (moderate initial symptoms that steadily decrease over time), and 35% to 55% will demonstrate resilience (may experience mild to moderate initial symptoms that fairly quickly dissipate and do not interfere substantially with normal functioning). Indeed, even following the devastating September 2001 terrorist attack in the United States, researchers found that 65% of Manhattan residents met criteria for resilience (defined as experiencing zero to one posttraumatic stress disorder [PTSD] symptom in the 6 months following the attack); over 50% of individuals who had witnessed the attack or were in the World Trade Center buildings when the attack occurred and 33% of those injured in the attack met criteria for resilience (Bonanno, Galea, Bucciarelli, & Vlahov, 2006).

Although most people will not experience clinically significant long-term problems following traumatic events, a considerable number will. Exploring the type, nature, and predictors of negative outcome from trauma exposure has constituted the bulk of trauma studies over the past 3 decades. Numerous psychological disorders, including depression, substance abuse and dependence, other anxiety disorders, and sleep disorders, are associated with experiencing a trauma (Breslau, 1998; Breslau et al., 2004; Kessler et al., 1995; Neria et al., 2007). Among the most widely studied areas of difficulty following a traumatic event are acute stress disorder (ASD) and PTSD. These two disorders will be addressed further due to their association with nightmares.

ACUTE STRESS DISORDER

Symptoms that arise within a month of a traumatic event may fall under the category of ASD. ASD was added to the *DSM* in 1994 (APA, 1994) to describe symptoms observed in trauma survivors in the first month following the trauma. To meet criteria for ASD, a person must experience a traumatic event, experience three dissociative symptoms, one reexperiencing symptom (including dreams of the event), marked avoidance, and marked hyperarousal for 2 days to 4 weeks following the traumatic event. ASD has been the subject of considerable debate since its inception, most notably regarding its emphasis on dissociative symptoms and its ability, relative to other symptom combinations, to predict the development of PTSD (see Bryant, 2000; Bryant & Harvey, 1997).

POSTTRAUMATIC STRESS DISORDER

Derek

Derek was the youngest of four children. His mother committed suicide when he was 7, after suffering severe physical and psychological trauma at the hands of Derek's father for 20 years. While she was alive, Derek's father would physically abuse the children on occasion, though most of the abuse was directed toward Derek's mother. After her death, the children became the prime targets of the father's aggression, and Derek and his siblings experienced years of severe physical and psychological abuse. Derek entered therapy in his early 20s as a college junior. He suffered from severe nightmares several times a week. He also reported occasional flashbacks to abusive situations, particularly when in the presence of strong authority figures. He was unable to maintain relationships due to feeling that he could not "love like other people can." He reported significant problems with anger and faced losing his scholarship, as he was failing several classes due to sleep deprivation and an inability to concentrate on his studies.

Studied and conceptualized under a number of different terms throughout history—including "shell shock," "war neuroses," and "rape trauma syndrome"—common problems reported by individuals following a traumatic event are codified in the third edition of the *DSM* (APA, 1980) as PTSD. After several revisions, the most recent edition of the *DSM* (APA, 2000) considers PTSD to be comprised of three primary categories of symptoms. The first category includes various ways in which someone may reexperience the traumatic event, such as having nightmares about the event, experiencing intrusive thoughts or memories of the event, behaving or feeling as if the event is happening again, experiencing significant distress when exposed to stimuli related to the traumatic event, and having physiological reactions when exposed to stimuli related to the traumatic event. The second category includes both emotional numbing and avoidance criteria, such as avoiding thoughts and feelings about the event; avoiding people, places, and situations that remind the individual of the event; being unable to recall certain parts of the event; decreased interest and participation in activities; feeling detached from others; having a restricted range of emotions; and having a sense of foreshortened future. The third category includes symptoms of arousal, such as problems initiating or maintaining sleep, feeling irritable or having angry outbursts, having trouble concentrating, being hypervigilant, and exhibiting an exaggerated startle response.

Prevalence of PTSD

Prevalence rates of PTSD vary considerably, in part due to the various populations sampled and the differing methods of assessing PTSD and trauma exposure. Overall, population prevalence estimates of past-year PTSD range from 2.3% to 4.2%, and estimates of lifetime PTSD range from 7.8% to 18.3% (Breslau, Davis, Andreski, & Peterson, 1991; Breslau et al., 1998; Kessler et al., 1995; Resnick, Kilpatrick, Dansky, Saunders, & Best, 1993). Breslau et al. (1998) found the risk for lifetime PTSD in trauma-exposed populations to be approximately 9%, and Kessler and colleagues (1995) found lifetime PTSD rates for trauma-exposed individuals to be 8% for men and 20% for women. Results of epidemiological surveys in postconflict areas report higher rates of PTSD (15.8% to 37.4%; de Jong et al., 2001).

Risk Factors for Chronic Problems

As reported above, while many individuals will experience a potentially traumatic event, only a minority will suffer long-term problems. Research studies have identified a number of risk factors that may indicate the potential for heightened negative responses to trauma, including degree of exposure (magnitude or severity of an event, proximity to the event, degree of loss; e.g., Breslau, 1998), female gender (e.g., Breslau et al., 1991; Norris, 1992; Tolin & Foa, 2006), younger age (Norris, 1992), a non-Caucasian ethnicity (Kulka et al., 1990; Norris, 1992), history of personal or familial psychopathology (including neuroticism, major depression, and anxiety disorders) (e.g., Breslau et al., 1991; de Jong et al., 2001; Kessler et al., 1999; Koren, Arnon, & Klein, 1999), negative reactions of others to the victim, avoidance coping (Ullman et al., 2007), previous history of trauma or adversity (e.g., Breslau et al., 1991; Davidson et al., 1991; de Jong et al., 2001), higher initial PTSD symptoms (Koren et al., 1999), and peritraumatic reactions (e.g., Lawyer et al., 2006). The type of traumatic event experienced is also a significant factor. Breslau and colleagues (1998) found that, overall, assaultive violence results in the highest risk of PTSD (20.9%), compared to other injury or shocking experience (6.1%), learning of a trauma occurring to someone else (2.2%), and the sudden unexpected death of a loved one (14.3%). Of the different types of assaultive violence, rape is associated with the greatest risk for developing PTSD (49%), followed by severe physical assault (31.9%) and other sexual assault (23.7%; Breslau et al., 1998; see also Kessler et al., 1995; Norris, 1992).

Although men are more likely to experience traumatic events, women typically report higher rates of PTSD (Breslau et al., 1991; Norris, 1992; Tolin & Foa, 2006). For example, a national study found that 10% of women and 5% of men from the general population met *DSM-III-R* criteria for PTSD (Kessler et al., 1995). Breslau and colleagues (1998) found that 18.3% of women and 10.2% of men met *DSM-IV* criteria for PTSD. In their review, Tolin and Foa (2006) found that women reported greater rates of PTSD for accidents, nonsexual assaults, combat, war or terrorism, disaster or fire, witnessing death or injury, and illness or unspecified injury. When gender differences for PTSD were examined within types of trauma, no differences were found for adult sexual assault. Overall, no gender differences were found for victims of child sexual abuse, although the authors noted some studies found greater PTSD rates for women. Finally, women reported greater rates of PTSD for traumatic events most frequently experienced by men.

THEORIES OF PTSD DEVELOPMENT

Numerous therapists and researchers have attempted to explain the nature and course of typical reactions to traumatic events. These theories draw on research and literature from psychological and biological realms, with varying degrees of supporting evidence. Among the most influential theories to date are those based on the work of behaviorists, cognitive behaviorists, and social-cognitive theorists. Mowrer's (1947) two-factor theory and Lang's (1968) multisystem theory of emotion have been utilized to understand the nature of response to trauma (e.g., Foa & Kozak, 1986; Kilpatrick, Veronen & Resick, 1982; Kilpatrick, Veronen, & Best, 1985). Specifically, the first part of Mowrer's theory suggests that salient stimuli or cues (conditioned stimuli) present during the traumatic event are associated with dangerous stimuli (unconditioned stimuli) and result in the conditioned response of fear and other negative affect through classical conditioning. For example, during combat, the sound of gunshots, shrapnel wounds, and seeing friends killed are unconditioned stimuli that initially elicit feelings of fear and terror. The reaction of fear is considered an automatic reaction to these experiences and is not learned. At the same time, other stimuli that are inherently not dangerous or threatening but are present in the environment during combat experiences (e.g., people, places, time of day, odors, tastes, sounds, and so forth) also become able to elicit the fear response. Therefore, these are conditioned stimuli, and their ability to elicit the fear response may generalize to additional, similar stimuli over time. For example, a soldier who experienced an intense fear response to the sound of gun fire during combat might respond with fear and anxiety to similar sounds (e.g., fireworks) even long after the combat experience is over. Likewise, this response may generalize to other loud, unexpected noises (e.g., door slamming).

The second part of Mowrer's (1947; 1960) theory incorporates the role of operational conditioning in the maintenance of fear and anxious response over time. In order to dampen the negative affect associated with the traumatic event and the related conditioned stimuli, individuals may begin avoiding places, people, or situations that remind them of the trauma and elicit the fear response. Thus, a veteran may not walk through heavily forested areas, watch war movies, or go to fireworks displays; a victim of domestic violence may not become involved in intimate relationships; a motor vehicle accident victim may refuse to drive again or refuse to drive near the particular place at which the accident occurred. A sense of relief and reduction of fear and anxiety often follows the process of escaping a feared situation or avoiding reminders of a trauma. This relief subsequently negatively reinforces avoidance behaviors, does not allow for corrective emotional experiences to occur, and maintains the posttrauma response over time (Foa & Kozak, 1986). The avoidance and numbing responses may also be used to counter the ongoing hyperarousal symptoms (Litz & Keane, 1989).

An information processing approach builds on the work of Mowrer (1947) and Lang (1968). Foa and Kozak (1986) and Foa and Rothbaum (1998) describe a fear structure, a network of associations in the brain that develops following a trauma and includes information about the feared event (and stimuli associated with it), the individual's responses to the event (including behavioral, verbal, and physiological), and the meaning of the event and responses to the event. The information encoded in the fear structure works to aid in the survival of the individual by serving as an alarm system when potential danger exists. The individual typically responds to the activation of the network through escape and avoidance.

For example, Vietnam veterans may experience distress when walking through wooded areas that remind them of Vietnam and subsequently avoid such areas. Unfortunately, as described above, stimuli are encoded in this fear structure that were associated with the event but are not inherently dangerous, including stimuli previously considered safe. The activation of the fear network in response to the myriad emotional, behavioral, physiological, and cognitive stimuli results in many false alarms. Further, if responses to this activation include only escape and avoidance, no corrective information is available or attended to in order to modify the structure, causing problems to continue.

Another information processing approach highlights the impact of trauma exposure on individuals' schemata. Schemata are defined as ways of thinking about one's self, others, and the world (Janoff-Bulman, 1989; McCann, Sakheim, & Abrahamson, 1988; Resick & Schnicke, 1993; Roth & Newman, 1991). Schemata influence the way people think and feel, as well as how they respond to stimuli in their environment. Janoff-Bulman and Frieze (1983) note three assumptions that are affected by experiencing a traumatic event: "1) the belief in personal invulnerability; 2) the perception of the world as meaningful and comprehensible; 3) the view of ourselves in a positive light" (p. 3). Similarly, McCann and colleagues (1988) identify five schemata that are vulnerable to distortion by traumatic events, including safety, trust, intimacy, power, and esteem. Resick and Schnicke (1993) purport that responses to trauma exposure are related to difficulties integrating trauma experiences into existing schemata. Individuals confronted with schema-incongruent events—those that do not fit with previous beliefs—may be overcome by the experience and its accompanying emotions (Resick & Schnicke, 1993), especially if schemata are particularly rigid (Feeny & Foa, 2006). Information processing theory holds that individuals must either alter the information to fit the schema (assimilate) or alter the schema to fit the information (accommodate). For example, if a child's parental schema suggests that parents should love and protect their children, and the child is physically abused by a parent, the child may assimilate, or alter, the information by convincing him- or herself that he or she is to blame for the abuse. Indeed, children will often staunchly defend abusive parents and deny the abuse occurred. If the child were to accommodate the information, he or she may change the parental schema to suggest that sometimes parents may hurt their children. A third possible response is over-accommodation. This process involves an extreme distortion of the belief system. For example, instead of changing the schema to suggest that sometimes parents may hurt their children, the child may believe that all adults want to hurt children, are dangerous, and can never be trusted. Over-accommodation may result in dichotomized thought processes (black and white thinking) and restrict the cognitive flexibility with which individuals interpret and evaluate future information (Feeny & Foa, 2006).

The emotional, cognitive, and behavioral impact of the traumatic event may vary considerably, depending on the information processing method employed. The resultant schema will continue to affect the manner in which the survivor responds to the world. Indeed, research has identified the importance of cognitive appraisals, based on schema, in the role of the development and maintenance of posttrauma problems. For example, studies find differences by trauma status on risk recognition (Wilson, Calhoun, & Bernat, 1999) and appraisal of risky behaviors (Smith, Davis, & Fricker-Elhai, 2004) that may enhance an individual's chance of revictimization and promote risk-taking behaviors (e.g., risky sexual behavior, substance use). These may serve as a means of escaping negative affect, maintaining the chronicity of posttrauma problems.

OTHER POSTTRAUMA PROBLEMS

Of course, not everyone who experiences a trauma will develop PTSD—many have symptoms of PTSD without meeting the full criteria. And the impact of trauma may extend well beyond PTSD to a plethora of other concerns in mental, physical, social, interpersonal, and occupational areas of functioning. Indeed, it is rare that PTSD symptoms are the only complaints reported by clients. Further, much evidence exists to suggest that experiencing multiple traumas has a cumulative negative impact in terms of mental and physical health (Anda et al., 2006). According to the *DSM*, individuals with PTSD may also report difficulties in self-harming behaviors, feelings of guilt and shame, dissociative symptoms, somatic complaints, interpersonal relationship dysfunction, and problems modulating affect, to name a few. PTSD is associated with numerous disorders, including higher rates of panic disorder, agoraphobia, obsessive-compulsive disorder, social phobia, specific phobia, major depressive disorder, somatization disorder, and substance-related disorders (APA, 1994). The National Comorbidity Study (Kessler et al., 1995) found that 88% of men and 79% of women had a comorbid disorder in addition to lifetime PTSD. The most common comorbid disorder was major depression.

The temporal relationship of onset among these disorders is somewhat unclear, however. That is, traumatic events may increase the risk for multiple types of mental health problems, developing PTSD may create a vulnerability to other forms of psychological difficulties, and the presence of other psychopathology may create a vulnerability to PTSD or trauma. The National Comorbidity Study (Kessler et al., 1995) sheds some light on this issue. Specifically, the study found that in more cases, PTSD was the original diagnosis for individuals with comorbid affective and substance use disorders overall, and with conduct disorder in women. In another study, Brady, Dansky, Sonne, and Saladin (1998) examined the order of onset of traumatic events, PTSD, and cocaine dependence in a treatment-seeking sample. They found a fairly even number of individuals who developed cocaine dependence prior to PTSD and those who developed PTSD prior to cocaine dependence, although the developmental pathways appeared to differ by gender. Specifically, the primary PTSD group included more women and was more likely to experience a sexual assault, while the primary cocaine group was more likely to witness a trauma or experience a physical assault. In fact, the investigators noted that most of the traumatic events in the primary cocaine group were related to obtaining and using the drug, while the primary PTSD group's traumatic events were mostly assaults in childhood. More information is needed to better understand the temporal relationships of these conditions, as the findings may have significant implications for treatment and preventative efforts.

The impact of trauma reaches beyond the realm of mental health. Although a full review of the impact of trauma on physical health is beyond the purview of this book, research has increasingly demonstrated that trauma exacts a terrible toll on physical health (for reviews, see Friedman, 1999; Gill & Page, 2006; Resnick, Acierno, & Kilpatrick, 1997; Schnurr & Green, 2003, 2004; Yehuda & McFarlane, 1997). While this may occur in the absence of PTSD, the effect appears worse in its presence. For example, Boscarino (2004) found that chronic PTSD was associated with numerous physical health conditions, including rheumatoid arthritis, psoriasis, diabetes, and thyroid disease, in a sample of Vietnam veterans. Other health and physiological problems associated with PTSD include cardiovascular disease (e.g., Boscarino & Chang, 1999; Felitti et al., 1998), acute physical injury (e.g., Goodman, Koss, & Russo, 1993), sexually transmitted diseases (e.g., Irwin et al., 1995), irritable bowel syndrome (e.g., Irwin et al., 1996), chronic pain (e.g., Walker & Stenchever, 1993), impairment of the hypothalamic-pituitary-adrenocortical axis (e.g., Pfeffer, Altemus, Heo, & Jiang, 2007), and reduced hippocampal volume (e.g., Bremner, 2006; Hedges & Woon, 2007). An exciting new area of research is demonstrating that some physiological impairment (e.g., levels of some stress hormones) may be alleviated following the treatment of trauma-related psychological symptoms (e.g., Lindauer et al., 2005; Olff, de Vries, Guzelcan, Assies, & Gersons, 2007).

Part of the impact of trauma on physical health may result from the increased involvement in risk behaviors (e.g., smoking, poor eating, use of illicit drugs, self-harming behaviors) in individuals exposed to trauma. A copious body of research demonstrates the link between trauma and health-risk behaviors (e.g., Kilpatrick, Acierno, Resnick, Saunders, & Best, 1997), although this relationship is not a simple one. Indeed, some research has found that while victimization may increase the risk of engaging in health-risk behaviors, the involvement in health-risk behaviors may also increase the risk of victimization (e.g., Kilpatrick, Acierno, Resnick, Saunders, & Best, 1997). Regardless of the temporal relationship of trauma exposure and risk involvement, engaging in risk-related behaviors serves as a risk factor for numerous acute and chronic health conditions.

An additional consideration in understanding the impact of trauma on physical health is its association with health-care utilization. Studies find that, in contrast to nonexposed persons, trauma-exposed individuals report greater utilization of medical health-care services and perceive their health status as poorer (e.g., Golding, Stein, Siegel, Burnam, & Sorenson, 1988; Resnick et al., 1997; Stapleton, Asmundson, Woods, Taylor, & Stein, 2006). Mixed findings are reported on comparative use of mental health-care services (e.g., Golding et al., 1988; Kimerling & Calhoun, 1994). In a review of the health impact of interpersonal violence, Resnick and colleagues (1997) suggest that inappropriate health-care utilization may stem in part from the mischaracterization of mental health problems as physical health problems.

SLEEP DISTURBANCES

Sleep disturbances are not uncommon in our society. Sleep disturbances may include disturbances in the quality, timing, or quantity of sleep, or behaviors or physiological events during sleep. They may be primary disorders or be secondary to another mental or physical condition or disorder (APA, 2000). Primary sleep disorders are classified as either dyssomnias (i.e., insomnia, hypersomnia, narcolepsy, breathing-related sleep disorder, circadian rhythm sleep disorder, and dyssomnia not otherwise specified [NOS]) or parasomnias (i.e., nightmare disorder, sleep terror disorder, sleepwalking, and parasomnia NOS; APA, 2000). The most recent edition of the *International Classification of Sleep Disorders* (American Sleep Disorders Association, 2005) recognizes eight categories of sleep disorders, including insomnia, sleep-related breathing disorders, hypersomnias of central origin, circadian rhythm sleep disorders, parasomnias, sleep-related movement disorders, isolated symptoms/apparently normal variants/unresolved issues, and other sleep disorders.

Community surveys of the general population find that 35% to 52% report sleep disturbances (Ford & Kamerow, 1989), and up to one third meet criteria for a sleep disorder, although many are not diagnosed and do not seek treatment (Doghramji, 2004; Hearne, 1991). Women tend to report higher rates of sleep disturbance than men (e.g., Coren, 1994; Hublin, Kaprio, Partinen, & Koskenvuo, 1999; Klink & Quan, 1987). Rates reported in the literature vary considerably, in part due to the nature of the questions asked, the sleep disturbances queried, the population sampled, and the time frame utilized (Ford & Kamerow, 1989). The National Institutes of Health (NIH) estimate that up to 70 million Americans may suffer from sleep loss and sleep disorders, with resulting health-care costs up to $15 billion annually. Further costs result from loss of productivity due to sleep problems (NIH, 2004). Sleep disturbances are commonly associated with a variety of psychiatric and medical conditions (e.g., Ford & Kamerow, 1989; Spoormaker & van den Bout, 2005).

While sleep disturbances are relatively common in the general population, numerous studies find even higher rates of sleep disturbances reported immediately following and long after a traumatic event (Ross, Ball, Sullivan, & Caroff, 1989). In fact, sleep disturbances are the putative "hallmark" of PTSD (Ross et al., 1989) and delayed PTSD (Kramer, 1979), although they may occur with or without PTSD diagnosis (Helzer, Robins, & McEvoy, 1987). Many consider nightmares and sleep problems to be key factors in the development and maintenance of posttrauma problems (e.g., Kramer, Schoen, & Kinney, 1987; Ross et al., 1989). Currently, sleep disturbances are included in two of the three symptom clusters of PTSD. Specifically, "recurrent distressing dreams of the event" is included in the reexperiencing cluster, and "difficulty falling or staying asleep" is included in the heightened arousal cluster (APA, 2000, p. 468).

Normal Sleep

Before reviewing the literature on sleep problems, nonpathological sleep is briefly outlined. Sleep is divided into two primary types: rapid eye movement (REM) and nonrapid eye movement (NREM). REM sleep is often referred to as paradoxical sleep, as electroencephalogram (EEG) recordings during REM resemble those during wake time. Also unique to REM are muscular atonia, eye movement, and muscle twitches. NREM sleep is further divided into four stages. Throughout the night, people typically progress from Stage 1 to Stage 4 NREM sleep, back through stages 3 and 2 and then to REM sleep. The initial REM latency (time until the first REM period starts) is approximately 70 to 110 minutes. The cycle through NREM and REM sleep happens four to six times a night, with REM sleep periods becoming longer as the night progresses and slow-wave sleep becoming shorter. People spend approximately 20% to 25% of sleep in REM sleep. Dreaming occurs in both REM and NREM sleep, although the most vivid dreams are thought to occur in REM (Ross et al., 1989).

Subjective Studies

North and colleagues (1999) surveyed survivors 6 months after the 1995 Oklahoma City bombing and found that nearly 70% of survivors reported insomnia and just over 50% reported nightmares. Roszell, McFall, and Malas (1991) found that sleep disturbances, separate from nightmares, were the most common symptom reported in a group of 116 treatment-seeking Vietnam veterans (91% of veterans with current PTSD). Similarly, Neylan and colleagues (1998) found that 44% of veterans reported difficulty falling asleep and 91% endorsed difficulty staying asleep. In a survey of disaster survivors, Green (1993) also found that "trouble sleeping" was the most commonly endorsed symptom. Overall, survivors of traumatic events, such as combat, natural disasters, and physical and sexual abuse, are most likely to report sleep disturbances (Woodward, 1995). A medical record review of inpatient children revealed that sexually abused children had worse sleep difficulties than physically abused or nonabused children, according to parental reports. However, no differences were noted while the children were in the hospital (Sadeh, Hayden, McGuire, Sachs, & Civita, 1994). In a later study of this group of hospitalized children, researchers using actigraphy, a small sensor used to assess sleep, found that physical abuse was associated with worse sleep problems than sexual abuse and no abuse (Sadeh et al., 1995). The number of traumatic events also appears to impact sleep. In a study of adult members of an HMO, Anda and colleagues (2006) found that the percentage of participants reporting sleep disturbances increased with the number of adverse childhood events reported, from 36% of people reporting no adverse events to 56.1% of people reporting four or more events.

As with many other mental and physical health problems, sleep disturbances appear to be worse in the presence of PTSD. Data from the National Comorbidity Study reveal that 80% of individuals with chronic PTSD also reported insomnia (Leskin, Woodward, Young, & Sheikh, 2002). Ohayon and Shapiro (2000) examined the prevalence of sleep disturbances, PTSD, and psychiatric disorders in a general population sample of 1,832 participants. They found that 70% of those with PTSD reported sleep disturbances, and 76% met criteria for another psychiatric diagnosis. Individuals with PTSD were more likely to report 9 of 10 types of sleep disturbance, including nightmares occurring at least once per month (18.8% of PTSD; 4.2% of non-PTSD). Further, while insomnia and excessive daytime somnolence were more likely to occur prior to the trauma in individuals with PTSD who experienced these problems (in 61% and 71% of participants respectively), parasomnia symptoms, including nightmares, were more likely to occur following a trauma (60%).

Pretrauma Sleep Problems Predict Increased Difficulties

Most studies of sleep difficulties and trauma do not consider sleep problems that may have been present prior to the traumatic event. Mellman, David, Kulick-Bell, Hebding, and Nolan (1995) retrospectively assessed sleep problems before and after 1992's Hurricane Andrew. These authors found that reports of "disturbing dreams" and sleep disturbances in individuals were associated with greater psychiatric problems following the hurricane. They suggest that pretrauma sleep and nightmare problems may be predisposing factors for increased difficulties posttrauma. This vulnerability may be mediated through neurophysiological impairment, a tendency toward heightened arousal, negative emotionality, or difficulties regulating emotion. Individuals who were suffering from sleep problems pretrauma also may be experiencing associated difficulties, including sleep deprivation or other life stressors, that may impede their ability to cope with the traumatic event.

Immediate Posttrauma Sleep Problems Predict Increased Difficulties

Although sleep problems and nightmares will dissipate over time for the majority of trauma-exposed persons, sleep disturbances may become a chronic condition for some, usually in the presence of PTSD. In their five-stage model of the phases of PTSD decompensation, Wang, Wilson, and Mason (1996) suggest that sleep problems typically precede significant decline in other areas, exacerbate symptomatology, and may actually propel the decompensation process. Several investigators have examined sleep disturbances immediately after the event and generally find that they predict future problems. For example, Koren, Arnon, Lavie, and Klein (2002) followed 102 motor accident victims and 19 control participants from 1 week to 12 months after the accident to prospectively assess possible predictors of PTSD. At 1-month posttrauma, significant differences were found in participants, according to their PTSD status; those meeting criteria for PTSD reported higher insomnia and daytime somnolence than those not meeting criteria for PTSD. These differences were maintained at the 12-month follow-up.

SLEEP DISORDERS

The experience of trauma and a diagnosis of PTSD are associated with several sleep disorders (see Table 1.1), including sleep disordered breathing (SDB), periodic limb movement (PLM), sleep onset and sleep maintenance insomnia, sleep terrors, sleep paralysis, and REM sleep behavior disorder. Not only are trauma exposure and various sleep disorders highly associated, their association is related to worse functioning. For example, Krakow and colleagues (2006) compared symptoms of patients of a sleep clinic and crime victims, both meeting criteria for SDB. Subjective measures indicated that the crime victim group reported worse functioning in several areas of sleep. Objective measures found crime victims had more incidents of upper airway resistance syndrome, but less obstructive sleep apnea. Both groups also reported high rates of daytime somnolence, frequent awakenings to urinate, and headaches and dry mouth in the morning. Among trauma victims, those with SDB reported worse sleep quality, PTSD symptoms, depression, and suicidality than those without SDB (e.g., Krakow, Artar, et al., 2000; Krakow, Germain, et al., 2000).

Table 1.1

SLEEP DISORDERS

SLEEP DISORDER	CHARACTERISTICS*	REFERENCES FOR STUDIES THAT INDICATE ASSOCIATION WITH TRAUMA
Sleep disordered breathing	Cessation of or reduction in airflow and subsequent reductions in oxygen saturation; frequent arousals during the night to restore airflow; daytime fatigue and numerous physical and mental difficulties	Krakow, Melendrez, Johnston, Warner, et al., 2002; Krakow, Melendrez, et al., 2001
Periodic limb movement	Stereotyped and repetitive involuntary movements, typically of the legs and feet, which cause brief arousals	Brown & Boudewyns, 1996; Krakow, Germain, et al., 2000; Mellman, Kulick-Bell, et al., 1995; Ross et al., 1994a
Insomnia	Difficulty initiating or maintaining sleep; having nonrestorative sleep	Krakow, Melendrez, Pedersen et al., 2001; Krakow, Melendrez, et al., 2001; Mellman, Kulick-Bell, et al., 1995; Neylan et al., 1998; Ohayon & Shapiro, 2000
Sleep terrors	Abrupt awakening from sleep, usually with a vocalization; difficulty awakening; little recall of event upon waking	Mellman, Kulick-Bell, et al., 1995
Sleep paralysis	Inability to engage in voluntary movement while falling asleep or waking up	Mellman, Kulick-Bell, et al., 1995; Ohayon & Shapiro, 2000
REM sleep behavior disorder	Violent motor activity during REM sleep	Mellman, Kulick-Bell, et al., 1995

* Characteristics taken from APA (2000), Mehra & Strohl (2006), Khassawneh (2006)

The nature of the relationships among sleep disorders and psychological disorders requires more investigation (see Harvey, Jones, & Schmidt, 2003). However, evidence suggests that some conditions, including insomnia, SDB, and PTSD, may have related neurophysiological impairment via the hypothalamic-pituitary adrenal axis and the amygdala-hippocampal complex (Krakow, Melendrez, Johnston, Warner, et al., 2002; Krakow et al., 2006; Maher, Rego, & Asnis, 2006). Krakow, Melendrez, Johnston, Warner et al. (2002) also suggest that residual sleep problems following PTSD treatment may be related to SDB. Recently, intriguing studies assessed the impact on nightmares of treating sleep-disordered breathing and overall found improvements in nightmares, sleep, PTSD symptoms, and indices of daytime functioning (Krakow, Lowry, et al., 2000). However, a case report by Youakim, Doghramji, and Schutte (1998) in which a Vietnam veteran was successfully treated with continuous positive airway pressure (CPAP) reveals that the nature of the sleep problems and nightmares changed, although they did not resolve. Further, in instances in which the CPAP machine dislodged, the nightmares came back as before. This finding suggests that such patients may still benefit from direct treatment of the nightmares. It remains to be empirically determined, however, whether nightmares treated directly would return with the recurrence of SDB or whether improvements would be noted in SDB upon treatment of PTSD.

Objective Studies

While there appears to be a plethora of evidence demonstrating a link between trauma exposure and self-reported sleep disturbances, objective assessments (e.g., polysomnography and actigraphy) find equivocal results, with some studies finding objective indicators of disturbed sleep (e.g., Calhoun et al., 2007; Germain & Nielsen, 2003a; Mellman, Kumar, Kulick-Bell, Kumar, & Nolan, 1995), while others did not find any indicators or found only minor problems (e.g., Breslau et al., 2004; Klein, Koren, Arnon, & Lavie, 2002). Further, results of objective assessments frequently do not match self-reported sleep problems (e.g., Breslau et al., 2004), a finding demonstrated with other populations as well (e.g., Carskadon et al., 1976). Overall, Krakow, Melendrez, and colleagues (2001) suggest that objective studies find four primary patterns of sleep: stereotypic insomnia, REM deficient sleep, REM surplus sleep, and normal sleep. The authors note, however, that objective studies typically do not take SDB into account. It is unclear if SDB influences the identified patterns above or represents a separate category. Further, while not all areas of positive findings reported above are found consistently across studies, a body of evidence is accumulating that suggests that disrupted REM sleep may play an important role in chronic PTSD (Mellman, 2006; although see Wittmann, Schredl, & Kramer, 2007). The most recent meta-analysis of 20 studies using polysomnography found that individuals with PTSD spend more time in Stage 1 sleep, less time in slow-wave sleep, and show evidence of more REM density (a measure of rapid eye movement activity during REM sleep) than individuals without PTSD (Kobayashi, Boarts, & Delahanty, 2007). Further, the authors found that gender and comorbidity moderated results. Specifically, studies that included more men and fewer individuals with depression found greater sleep problems in individuals with PTSD. Harvey, Jones, and Schmidt (2003) conclude that those studies that do find differences in objective assessment of sleep attribute the problems to heightened arousal. These authors also suggest that individuals may misperceive the amount of sleep they are getting, similar to insomniacs. A comprehensive description of the results and potential explanations for findings are beyond the scope of this work. However, a number of excellent reviews addressing these are available (e.g., Harvey, et al., 2003; Kobayashi et al., 2007; Lavie, 2001; Maher et al., 2006; Mellman, 2000; Pillar, Malhotra, & Lavie, 2000).

TRAUMA ASSOCIATED WITH BETTER SLEEP?

Further complicating our understanding of sleep and trauma are the perplexing findings suggesting that although trauma-exposed persons report worse sleep, they may actually achieve deeper sleep than non-trauma-exposed persons (although see Klein et al., 2002). For example, Lavie, Katz, Pillar, and Zinger (1998) found evidence of higher awaking thresholds in PTSD patients compared to non-PTSD controls, but they failed to find any other statistically significant differences in sleep measures. The higher thresholds were positively related to anxiety and depression scores. The authors (see also Dagan, Lavie, & Bleich, 1991; Kramer & Kinney, 2003) note the discrepancy between significant complaints of disturbed sleep and higher awaking thresholds and speculate that this higher threshold may be a compensatory measure that develops over time to counter the hyperaroused state during the day and to obstruct intrusion of trauma stimuli during sleep. The authors suggest that this may also help explain some differences in objective findings, in that sleep proximate to the traumatic event may be characterized more by frequent arousals due to nightmares and night terrors. As the condition continues, the sleep dynamics change to include attempts to deepen sleep, to increase the arousal threshold, and to lengthen time before REM and shorten time in REM, all to allow the individual some respite from memories and nightmares of the traumatic event. Numerous studies also report lower dream recall in individuals with chronic PTSD (e.g., Dagan et al., 1991; Kaminer & Lavie, 1991; see chapter 2), with similar notions that this dynamic develops over time to block nightmares or the recall of nightmares and to enhance sleep. Lower dream recall may also be related to alexithymia, which has been associated with PTSD (Nielsen, 2005).

NIGHTMARES

Although nightmares are typically conceptualized as a ubiquitous post-trauma phenomenon that is often part of PTSD, they may also occur in its absence and often occur in the absence of a traumatic event (although most prevalence studies do not distinguish idiopathic and post-trauma nightmares). Whether or not nightmares occur in the presence of another disorder, they are associated with distress. The presence of nightmares and sleep disturbances in the immediate aftermath of a traumatic event are associated with current and ensuing symptom severity (e.g., Mellman, David, Bustamante, Torres, & Fins, 2001). Specifically, studies find that the presence and severity of nightmares after a trauma are associated with overall levels of reported distress and overall severity of reexperiencing symptoms (e.g., Erman, 1987; Esposito, Benitez, Barza, & Mellman, 1999; Schreuder, Kleijn, & Rooijmans, 2000). Distress tends to be more severe in the presence of PTSD (e.g., Davis, Byrd, Rhudy, & Wright, 2007) and when the content of the nightmare is reflective of the traumatic event itself (e.g., Davis et al., 2007; Mellman et al., 2001).

All post-trauma nightmares are not the same for everyone, and they may not be the same for any individual over time. Nightmares may initially be just like the traumatic event, almost a reenactment of the trauma. Over time, however, the nightmares may begin to include other aspects of life and more recent stressors. They may include people who were not involved in the original trauma. For example, a combat veteran suffered for many years from nightmares about feeling in constant danger and being killed in combat. He reported that after having children, his nightmares evolved to include his children—specifically, that they were also in danger. Nightmares also may change to reflect potent, unresolved issues related to trauma (e.g., powerlessness, esteem, safety, intimacy, trust).

While nightmares and sleep problems are pervasive for some individuals, lasting years and even decades, their manifestation may change over time. Sleep problems may look quite different immediately following the trauma versus those 10 years out from the trauma. Chronicity, or time since the trauma occurred, is not often taken into consideration in studies examining sleep problems, potentially accounting for some of the differences reported above. Indeed, given that not all individuals continue to suffer sleep problems long term, one might expect differences early on in the manifestation of sleep disorders between those who will continue to suffer and those who recover. For example, Tracy was a 20-year-old college student when she was raped by a friend after a party on campus. She suffered from severe nightmares and sleep problems for months after the rape. Her nightmares occurred early in the sleep cycle, leaving her unable to return to sleep. She began drinking alcohol more frequently; when she presented for treatment, she was consuming two bottles of wine per night. She also reported significant depression, daytime panic attacks, and recent onset of severe panic symptoms upon waking from nightmares. Her alcohol use allowed her to fall asleep easier, but she was still frequently awakened from nightmares later in the sleep cycle.

The impact of nightmares extends far beyond the reach of the bedroom. It is well known that sleep disturbances may have long-term negative effects on mental and physical health. The impact of reduced quality and quantity of sleep is pervasive, and problems with sleep and nightmares are increasingly conceptualized as key components of the development and maintenance of posttrauma problems. Given nightmares' theorized pernicious effects, efforts to develop interventions designed to decrease nightmares and enhance sleep quality may be of the utmost importance.

The remainder of this book is dedicated to understanding the nature and characteristics of post-trauma nightmares, including their development, assessment, and treatment. The study of nightmares and, specifically, post-trauma nightmares has made considerable strides over the past 30 years. In many ways, however, the work in this area has just begun. Numerous methodological and definitional issues remain.

There is no clear unifying theoretical understanding of how idiopathic or post-trauma nightmares develop or are maintained over time. It remains unclear why some people experience transient nightmare problems and others suffer for decades. One of the most exciting areas of inquiry relates to the treatment of chronic nightmares. Although much is left to understand about nightmares' nature, characteristics, and developmental progress, treatments have been developed that significantly reduce the frequency and intensity of nightmares and related distress. One such treatment—Exposure, Relaxation, and Rescripting Therapy (ERRT)—is outlined and its efficacy reviewed. First, however, we take a closer look at the nature and characteristics of nightmares.

2 Characterizing Nightmares

Although the lay public would probably chuckle at the notion that scientists struggle with issues as "obvious" as what a nightmare is, there is yet to be an agreed upon standard definition of a nightmare, a struggle reflected in the oft-confused state of the empirical literature (Levin & Nielsen, 2007; Weiss, 2007). Confusions arise clinically as well when assessing nightmares and related distress and determining appropriate diagnoses. This chapter attempts to outline and disentangle the various methodological and definitional issues, outline the differences in various disturbing sleep events, and review the literature on the nature of post-trauma nightmares.

DEFINING NIGHTMARES

We begin by examining the diagnostic criteria for nightmare disorder from the three nosological sources that include criteria for sleep disorders: the *Diagnostic and Statistical Manual of Mental Disorders (DSM-IV-TR)* (APA, 2000), the *International Classification of Sleep Disorders* 2nd edition *(ICSD)* (American Sleep Disorders Association, 2005) and the *International Classification of Diseases (ICD)* (World Health Organization, 2007). The full criteria for each of the diagnostic systems are listed

Table 2.1

NIGHTMARE DISORDER DIAGNOSTIC CRITERIA

DSM-IV-TR (2000, p. 634)

A. Repeated awakenings from the major sleep period or naps with detailed recall of extended and extremely frightening dreams, usually involving threats to survival, security, or self-esteem. The awakenings generally occur during the second half of the sleep period.
B. On awakening from the frightening dreams, the person rapidly becomes oriented and alert (in contrast to the confusion and disorientation seen in Sleep Terror Disorder and some forms of epilepsy).
C. The dream experience, or the sleep disturbance resulting from the awakening, causes clinically significant distress or impairment in social, occupational, or other important areas of functioning.
D. The nightmares do not occur exclusively during the course of another mental disorder (e.g., delirium, Posttraumatic Stress Disorder) and are not due to the direct physiological effects of a substance (e.g., a drug of abuse, a medication) or a general medical condition.

ICSD 2ND EDITION (2005, p. 156)

A. Recurrent episodes of awakenings from sleep with recall of intensely disturbing dream mentation, usually involving fear or anxiety, but also anger, sadness, disgust, and other dysphoric emotions.
B. Full alertness on awakening, with little confusion or disorientation; recall of sleep mentation is immediate and clear.
C. At least one of the following associated features is present:
    1. Delayed return to sleep after the episodes
    2. Occurrence of episodes in the latter half of the habitual sleep period

ICD-10 (2007)

A. Awakening from nocturnal sleep or naps with detailed and vivid recall of intensely frightening dreams, usually involving threats to survival, security, or self-esteem; the awakening may occur at any time during the sleep period, but typically during the second half;
B. Upon awakening from the frightening dreams, the individual rapidly becomes oriented and alert;
C. The dream experience itself, and the resulting disturbance of sleep, cause marked distress to the individual.

in Table 2.1. In the criteria for a nightmare disorder, the *DSM-IV-TR* defines nightmares as "extended and extremely frightening dreams, usually involving threats to survival, security or self-esteem" that cause a person to awaken (APA, 2000, p. 634). The latest revision of the *ICSD* (2005) defines nightmares as "recurrent episodes of awakenings from sleep with recall of intensely disturbing dream mentation, usually involving fear or anxiety, but also anger, sadness, disgust, and other dysphoric emotions" (p. 156). The *ICD* defines nightmares as "Awakening from nocturnal sleep or naps with detailed and vivid recall of intensely frightening dreams, usually involving threats to survival, security, or self-esteem;" (*ICD-10*, 2007). Additional criteria included in some form in each of the nosological classifications include: waking up fully oriented, recalling the nightmare in detail, having nightmares with content that typically includes various themes (e.g., being chased), and occurring during the second half of the night. The *DSM* and *ICD* also require that the nightmare or resultant sleep impairment cause distress, while the *ICSD* does not.

The definition of nightmares and rules guiding appropriate diagnosis vary somewhat among the three nosological systems. These differences include the ability to provide a separate diagnosis of nightmare disorder when another mental disorder is diagnosed, the emotions incorporated in the nightmares, and whether significant clinical distress and impairment is required. Other definitional and methodological issues to consider in the study of nightmares include: (1) determining a problematic frequency, (2) utilizing frequency or severity criteria, (3) the awakening criteria, (4) retrospective versus prospective assessment, (5) distinguishing nightmares from other disturbing nighttime events, and (6) distinguishing between idiopathic and post-trauma nightmares. Each of these issues is outlined briefly in the subsequent text.

Nightmares as Symptom or Primary Diagnosis?

Recently, there has been much discussion in sleep and trauma literature regarding whether nightmares should be considered only a symptom of posttraumatic stress disorder (PTSD) and acute stress disorder (ASD) or whether they may constitute a separate disorder for some trauma-exposed people. Krakow (2006) states that "failing to view nightmares as a comorbid or independent complaint diverts attention from the problem and steers patients away from evidence-based therapies just like insomnia patients who do not receive evidence-based treatments" (pp. 1313–1314). Krakow and colleagues (2007) have long argued for a broader perspective of insomnia and nightmares reported by people with PTSD and state that these sleep disturbances often require "independent clinical attention" (p. 13). Some of the questions raised by researchers and clinicians include: Should nightmares be considered only a symptom of or secondary to PTSD if, when PTSD is treated, nightmares persist? Is there a difference between people whose nightmares are eliminated by broader

PTSD treatments and those who are not? Is there a proportion of individuals suffering from PTSD and nightmares for whom nightmares and sleep disturbances are primary and PTSD is secondary? Are nightmares and sleep problems primary from the start, or do they develop into a primary disorder over time? Researchers are just beginning to address these questions. There is evidence, however, as described in chapters 5 and 10, that treating nightmares in people with PTSD is effective in reducing nightmares, PTSD symptoms, and associated pathology (e.g., Davis & Wright, 2007). This finding suggests that, for some, nightmares may not just be a symptom of a broader problem, but rather a significant problem that requires direct intervention.

Currently, however, it remains to be determined whether nightmares may be the underlying, hence primary, diagnosis for some individuals. Two classification systems currently allow for coding of nightmare disorder and either PTSD or ASD simultaneously. The *ICD-10* suggests the following for making determinations of primary versus secondary classifications:

> In many cases, a disturbance of sleep is one of the symptoms of another disorder, either mental or physical. Whether a sleep disorder in a given patient is an independent condition or simply one of the features of another disorder classified elsewhere . . . should be determined on the basis of its clinical presentation and course as well as on the therapeutic considerations and priorities at the time of the consultation. Generally, if the sleep disorder is one of the major complaints and is perceived as a condition in itself, the present code should be used along with other pertinent diagnoses describing the psychopathology and pathophysiology involved in a given case. (*ICD-10*, 2007)

The *ICSD* also provides for a primary classification of nightmares in the presence of PTSD or ASD:

> Nightmares that occur intermittently during the course of ASD or PTSD are an expected symptom of those mental disorders and do not require independent coding as nightmare disorder. However, when the frequency or severity of posttraumatic nightmares is such that they require independent clinical attention, then a diagnosis of nightmare disorder should be applied. In some cases, other symptoms of PTSD may have largely resolved while the nightmares persist. Nightmare disorder should be coded in these cases as well (pp. 157–158).

While the *DSM-IV-TR* does allow for a diagnosis of sleep disorder related to another mental disorder (only for insomnia and hypersomnia), the assumption remains that the underlying pathophysiological processes of the mental disorder affect the sleep-wake cycle instead of the alternative, that disruptions in the sleep-wake cycle affect the pathophysiological processes of the mental disorder (p. 597). More research is needed to determine whether this is a valid assumption.

Emotional Content Criterion

Emotions included in nightmare definitions vary, not only across the nosological systems, but across research studies as well. The primary point of debate appears to be whether the emotional content of a nightmare should be restricted to fear or anxiety. Studies find that while individuals most frequently experience fear (Nielsen, Deslauriers, & Baylor, 1991), nightmares may also involve other negative emotions, including grief, disgust, confusion, frustration, sadness, anxiety, guilt, and anger (e.g., Cason, 1935; Dunn & Barrett, 1988; Hall & Van de Castle, 1966; Spoormaker, Schredl, & van den Bout, 2006; Zadra & Donderi, 1993, 2000).

In a recent evaluation of the waking and emotion criteria for nightmares, Zadra, Pilon, and Donderi (2006) asked 90 participants to record the frequency, emotion involved, and intensity of bad dreams (defined as "very disturbing dreams which, though being unpleasant, do not cause you to awaken"; p. 250) and nightmares (defined as "very disturbing dreams in which the unpleasant visual imagery and/or emotions wake you up"; p. 250) over a 4-week period. Participants recorded dreams and nightmares each morning or upon waking during the night. Based on self-report, participants were categorized into one of two groups: those who reported nightmares and bad dreams and those who reported only bad dreams. Emotional content was classified into one of eight emotion categories that were included based on previous research. Results indicated that while a large percentage of nightmares (70%) and bad dreams (49% for the nightmare and bad dream group and 56% for the bad dream group) included fear, numerous nightmares and bad dreams incorporated other negative emotions including anger, sadness, frustration, disgust, confusion, guilt, and "other." The authors suggest that the *DSM* emotion criterion be expanded to include other types of negative affect, as in the *ICSD* criteria.

Distress Criterion

As previously mentioned, although the *DSM* and *ICD* require that the nightmares or resultant sleep impairment cause distress, the latest revision of the *ICSD* does not. As this change was not specific to night-mares, it will not be addressed further (for discussion, however, see Levin & Nielsen, 2007; Weiss, 2007).

How Frequent Is Too Frequent?

Another difficulty in empirical studies of nightmares is determining how frequently nightmares need to occur for them to be considered problematic. None of the three classification systems identifies a minimum frequency to designate whether nightmares are problematic. The operationalized frequency of nightmare occurrence is variably defined across studies with some studies simply asking about "frequent nightmares" without specifying what is meant by "frequent," making it difficult to compare nightmare experiences across samples. Several studies have identified a frequency of at least once per week (e.g., Bixler et al., 1979; Hersen, 1971; Levin & Fireman, 2002b) as high, frequent, or an indication of a problem, but currently, there is little information to support this classification.

Frequency vs. Severity

The utility of using the frequency or intensity/severity (or both) of the nightmare to determine whether nightmares are problematic or clinically significant is debated, as nightmare frequency and severity are increasingly seen as different constructs. Frequency and severity ratings of nightmares are typically found to be low to moderately correlated (e.g., Belicki, 1992; Roberts & Lennings, 2006; Wood & Bootzin, 1990), suggesting that different mechanisms or processes may be responsible for frequency and intensity. An empirical question to be determined is whether frequency, severity, or some combination of both is most appropriate in determining clinically significant impairment. For example, is there a difference in impairment of functioning between someone who has nightmares at least once a week and rates them as moderately disturbing and someone who has nightmares about once a month and rates them as severely disturbing?

To examine the differences in nightmare frequency and severity, Levin and Fireman (2002b) compared undergraduates with high (three or more over 21 days), moderate (one to two), or low (zero) nightmare frequency (Levin & Fireman, 2002b). Results indicate that the high frequency nightmare group scored significantly higher than the other groups on some, but not all, measures of psychological disturbance. The low and moderate frequency groups did not differ on any measure. Nightmare frequency and distress were not significantly correlated with each other. Both nightmare frequency and distress were associated with numerous indices of psychological disturbance, although the relationships were stronger for distress. Nightmare distress also accounted for more unique variance in predicting anxiety and depression.

Belicki (1992) examined the relationships among past-year frequency of nightmares, nightmare-related distress, psychological adjustment, and personality in a sample of 85 undergraduates. Results indicated only a slight relationship between nightmare distress and frequency. Nightmare distress was related to several indices of psychopathology, whereas frequency was not. The author suggests that frequency and distress are separate constructs and that distress may be more related to reflection on the nightmares after waking. The findings are limited, however, as it is unclear how reliable memories are for estimating the frequency and distress of nightmares over a 1-year period of time. Similar findings were reported by Blagrove, Farmer, and Williams (2004) in that distress was related to pathology, while frequency was less so. In a study of trauma-exposed individuals seeking treatment for nightmares, Davis, Byrd, Rhudy, and Wright (2007) evaluated whether past-week nightmare frequency and severity contributed to any sleep problems or related distress when controlling for non-sleep-related PTSD symptoms. Results indicated that nightmare *frequency* was a unique predictor of poor global sleep quality and fear of going to sleep. The *severity* of the nightmare approached, but did not reach, significance in predicting panic symptoms upon waking from a nightmare. This study was limited, however, as a treatment-seeking sample is likely to have more severe problems with nightmares, thus the results may not generalize.

It appears that in college samples, nightmare distress may be more strongly associated with pathology. More research is needed to determine if this finding holds true across more diverse samples, including clinical and community samples.

The Awakening Criterion

Many researchers adapted the definition of the nightmare as a long frightening dream, awakening the sleeper out of REM sleep (Hartmann et al., 1981; Hersen, 1971). Researchers, however, disagree about whether a person needs to wake up in order for the experience to be considered a nightmare. As mentioned previously, the basic notion is that a person awakens from a nightmare because of the intensity of emotions involved (Zadra, Pilon, & Donderi, 2006). However, some researchers have suggested that waking may not be an indicator of the intensity of the nightmare, so it may not be meaningful to separate experiences in that way. For example, Kellner, Neidhardt, Krakow, and Pathak (1992; reported in Krakow, Kellner, Pathak, & Lambert, 1995) found that more than three quarters of their chronic nightmare patients reported not always waking from nightmares. Further, the patients suggested that their "disturbing dreams"—from which they did not awaken—were as emotionally intense as the nightmares. Zadra and Donderi (2000), however, found that nightmare frequency was more associated with low well-being (well-being was assessed via six measures of psychological well-being) than bad dream frequency, suggesting that disturbing dream experiences that result in awakening may be more severe events. More recently, the study by Zadra and colleagues (2006) (described previously) revealed that nightmares were rated as more intense than bad dreams by people who experienced both. This was found as a trend for all emotions except fear, which was significantly more intense in nightmares, and guilt, which was significantly more intense in bad dreams. No difference was found between intensity ratings of bad dreams by those reporting both bad dreams and nightmares and those reporting only bad dreams, supporting the notion that nightmares involve a greater intensity of emotion. Based on these findings, the authors concluded that the awakening criterion appears appropriate to signify the increased intensity of nightmares.

Prospective vs. Retrospective Assessment

The method used to assess nightmare experiences also varies (see chapter 4). Most studies have utilized retrospective measures of varying time frames (1 week to 1 year). Recent studies suggest that the use of retrospective measures may substantially underestimate nightmare frequency compared to the use of daily prospective logs (Chivers & Blagrove, 1999; Wood & Bootzin, 1990; Zadra & Donderi, 2000). As most research has utilized retrospective measures, nightmare frequency may actually be higher than previously suggested. Zadra and Donderi (2000) used a 4-week log as well as 1-year and 1-month retrospective questions to assess nightmare frequency. They found that the prorated nightmare log yielded 162% greater 1-year and 92% greater 1-month frequencies than the retrospective measures. Schreuder, van Egmond, Kleijn, and Visser

(1998), however, found good correspondence between past-month ratings of post-trauma nightmare frequency on the Clinician Administered PTSD Scale (CAPS; Blake et al., 1990) and their 4-week prospective logs (completed 6 to 11 months later). It is also suggested, however, that completing daily accounts of nightmares may actually increase nightmare experiences (Levin & Nielsen, 2007), although this remains to be empirically determined.

DISTINGUISHING DISTURBING SLEEP EVENTS

Nightmares are often confused with other disturbing nighttime events, including bad dreams and night terrors. The confusion surrounding the nature of various nighttime disturbances has complicated the study of nightmares. However, research has determined several characteristics that differentiate these events.

Bad Dreams

Bad dreams, or anxiety dreams, are relatively common dream experiences that include negative affect but do not awaken the dreamer. In general, it is presumed that if the dream event is of sufficient intensity, the dreamer would awaken. Thus, waking is purported to be an indicator of intensity and is the primary distinguishing factor between bad dreams and nightmares (Zadra, Pilon, & Donderi, 2006). The use of the waking criterion to distinguish bad dreams from nightmares has been questioned, as discussed earlier, and the research addressing this issue is described below.

Night Terrors

The *DSM-IV-TR* defines night terrors as "abrupt awakenings from sleep usually beginning with a panicky scream or cry . . . accompanied by autonomic arousal and behavioral manifestations of intense fear" (APA, 2000, p. 634). Night terrors are considered a disorder of arousal and occur in the relatively early stages of the sleep period during NREM slow-wave sleep (Stage 3 or 4). The individual is difficult to awaken, is disoriented or confused upon awakening, and has partial or complete lack of recall of a dream or the occurrence of a night terror. Individuals are also inconsolable upon waking. While there is no known etiology of night terrors, they may be more frequent following significant stressors and may be associated with physical illness and certain medications. Night terrors occur more often in childhood and tend to diminish in frequency through adolescence and adulthood (Mahowald & Bornemann, 2005; Pagel, 2000).

In addition to differentiating among nightmares, night terrors, and bad dreams, researchers and clinicians also need to distinguish idiopathic and post-trauma nightmares.

Idiopathic Nightmares

Idiopathic nightmares occur primarily during REM sleep and tend to occur later in the sleep cycle (5 to 7 a.m.). There is rarely body movement associated with idiopathic nightmares, in part because of the atonia associated with REM sleep. Individuals awaken from an idiopathic nightmare nearly fully oriented and have vivid recall of the nightmare. Individuals may experience significant distress upon waking and find it difficult at times to return to sleep. There is often no identifiable trigger for nightmares, although various precipitating factors may be involved (e.g., medications, illness, and stressors).

The vast majority of people have had a nightmare at some point in their lives (Nielsen & Zadra, 2005). Most people report experiencing occasional nightmares, although only approximately 5% to 8% report having a nightmare problem (Bixler, Kales, Soldatos, Kales, & Healey, 1979; Klink & Quan, 1987). According to the ICSD (2005), 10% to 50% of children will experience nightmares between the ages of 3 and 5 disturbing enough to awaken parents. The frequency of nightmare occurrence peaks at around 7 to 9 years of age and then declines with age (although a recent Internet study found that nightmare frequency increased between the age strata of 10 to 19 and 20 to 29 in women; Nielsen, Stenstrom, & Levin, 2006). Elderly individuals typically report significantly fewer nightmares than college students (Salvio, Wood, Schwartz, & Eichling, 1992). A minority of individuals continues to experience nightmares throughout their lives.

Nightmares are associated with certain personality characteristics (see chapter 3) and are commonly reported by individuals suffering other psychiatric difficulties (see chapter 4). Occasional nightmares are not pathological; however, frequent distressing nightmares may indicate other difficulties (e.g., starting or stopping certain medications, anxiety, or stressful life events; Nielsen & Zadra, 2005; Pagel, 2000). Hartmann

(1984) suggests that many frequent nightmare sufferers have no trauma history; while others have questioned whether these individuals may have very early trauma and no conscious memory of the event(s). There is currently little evidence to support this notion, however.

Post-Trauma Nightmares

Post-trauma nightmares have an obvious precipitating event. They tend to occur early in the sleep cycle (1 to 3 a.m.) and may occur in REM sleep or in NREM sleep (most often Stage 2). People awaken from post-trauma nightmares fully oriented and often terrified. They may experience panic symptoms upon waking and find it difficult or undesirable to return to sleep. Recall for the nightmare content is usually vivid. They are more likely to be replicative of an actual event than idiopathic nightmares. Post-trauma nightmares are also often accompanied by gross body movements (including some individuals who reported physical attacks on partners; Pagel, 2000).

Research Comparing Idiopathic and Trauma-Related Nightmares

Several research studies have examined differences between idiopathic nightmares and post-trauma nightmares. Van der Kolk, Blitz, Burr, Sherry, and Hartmann (1984) evaluated 15 combat veterans with post-trauma nightmares and 10 noncombat veterans with lifelong nightmares. The researchers found that those with post-trauma nightmares reported more frequent nightmares, replicative nightmares, repetitive nightmares; nightmares that occurred earlier in the night; and nightmares that were more likely to be accompanied by body movement. The lifelong nightmare group had more pathology and had poorer social functioning.

In Germain and Nielsen's (2003a) sleep lab study comparing individuals with PTSD and nightmares ($n = 9$), idiopathic nightmares ($n = 11$), and healthy controls ($n = 13$), subjective measures reveal that the PTSD group reported worse depression and PTSD severity than the other groups and greater anxiety and nightmare distress than the control group. The idiopathic nightmare group reported greater nightmare distress than the control group. On objective measures, the PTSD group demonstrated more problems related to wake time after sleep onset, number of awakenings, and sleep efficiency than both the idiopathic and control groups. Further, both nightmare groups had higher periodic leg movement indices than the control group.

The distinction between post-trauma nightmares and idiopathic nightmares with regard to nightmare content is less clear. The PTSD reexperiencing criterion for nightmares, set forth in *DSM-IV-TR* (APA, 2000), requires that the dreams are "distressing dreams *of the event*" (italics added; p. 468) and states that individuals with PTSD experience recurrent dreams "during which the event is replayed" (p. 464). In contrast, for children "there may be frightening dreams without recognizable content" (p. 468). According to our clinical experience, and to that of other researchers (e.g., Mellman, David, Kulick-Bell, Ashlock, & Nolan, 1995), the content of nightmares occurring after a trauma may or may not be clearly related to the trauma experienced. For example, one of our research participants reported a recurring nightmare of being in a jungle with wild animals attacking and killing his friends, but not him. While he did not conceptualize this nightmare as being related to his experience of being in combat in Vietnam and losing most of his comrades to the war, his therapist did. While his therapist may have been mistaken in her interpretation of the nightmare content, it is also feasible that failing to make this connection may be part of avoiding trauma-related stimuli.

Individuals who have experienced trauma report a wide variety of content, and the content of nightmares often changes and morphs over time (Hartmann, 1998a). An individual may experience nightmares that replicate the trauma soon after the event, but the content may later change to the extent that it is unclear if the nightmare is related to the trauma or not. Moreover, even content that is dissimilar to the event may include a similar theme, such as danger or powerlessness, and still reflect problems related to the traumatic event. Other complications in distinguishing post-trauma and idiopathic nightmares are that (1) it is possible that individuals who are lifelong nightmare sufferers may experience an increase in the frequency or severity of their nightmares after a traumatic event without the actual event being incorporated into the nightmare. At what point would we then consider the nightmares to be related to the trauma? (2) The content of idiopathic nightmares may include similar themes (e.g., danger, feeling unsafe) as post-trauma nightmares, making it difficult to distinguish them based on content alone. More research is needed to determine whether it is empirically or clinically meaningful to require nightmares to be of the event in order to reflect their association with trauma or serve as a criterion for PTSD. As Phelps, Forbes, and Creamer (2008) put it, "How distressing, and how trauma-related do the dreams need to be to meet criterion?" (p. 339). Perhaps diagnosis should be based on distress and impairment rather than content. This issue is discussed further below.

NATURE AND CHARACTERISTICS OF POST-TRAUMA NIGHTMARES

Interest in chronic post-trauma nightmares has increased significantly since the early 1980s. Numerous studies have investigated the characteristics of these nightmares, although the vast majority of the studies were conducted with veterans, so much less is currently known about nightmares of civilians who experienced trauma.

Prevalence of Post-Trauma Nightmares

Stressful or traumatic experiences may initiate or exacerbate the occurrence of nightmares. Most individuals who experience a traumatic event report at least transient nightmares posttrauma, and persons exposed to traumatic events report significantly higher rates of frequent nightmares than those not exposed to trauma. Reported prevalence rates of nightmares range from 19% to 94% in trauma-exposed individuals (e.g., DeFazio, Rustin, & Diamond, 1975; Forbes, Creamer, & Biddle, 2001; Goldstein, van Kammen, Shelly, Miller, & van Kammen, 1987; Ohayon & Shapiro, 2000). These figures range widely for a number of reasons. Some studies ask about nightmares only in PTSD samples, whereas others assess nightmares in trauma-exposed samples regardless of PTSD status. Some studies utilize treatment-seeking samples, while others use general-population samples. The time since the trauma occurred varies considerably across studies, as do the type, number, and magnitude of the trauma involved. As described above, the operational definition of nightmares also varies considerably. Despite these methodological issues, it is clear that a large proportion of trauma-exposed individuals report a problem with nightmares in the immediate aftermath of a traumatic event, with a significant minority reporting long-term problems.

Duration

While most post-trauma nightmares dissipate within weeks of the traumatic event, for some people the nightmares may last months, years, or even decades. In our most recent treatment study, participants reported an average duration of 15 years of experiencing nightmares (Davis & Rhudy, unpublished data). Nader and colleagues (1990) conducted a 14-month follow-up of 100 children who had been fired on in a sniper attack at a playground. They found that 42% of the children who were on the playground at the time still had "bad dreams" 1 year later. Similarly, Schreuder and colleagues (2001), who studied over 400 individuals in Mozambique affected by war 5 years after the war had ended, found that 63% suffered from "bad dreams." Strikingly, nearly half of these individuals reported that the bad dreams were replicative of their war experiences. They also reported experiencing significant hyperarousal and paniclike symptoms upon waking and greater psychiatric symptoms (measured by the Self-Reporting Questionnaire; Harding et al., 1980) than those without. In addition, Archibald, Long, Miller, and Tuddenham (1962) found that 15 years after combat exposure, nearly 80% of combat veterans reported continued combat dreams, although such dreams were 1 of 3 symptoms (of 24 evaluated) that had decreased since participants returned from the war.

A number of studies have examined nightmares in individuals several decades after they experienced a traumatic event. Guerrero and Crocq (1994) surveyed 817 individuals forced to serve in the German military during World War II and imprisoned in Russian prisoner of war (POW) camps. The investigators found that 4 decades later, sleep problems were the most frequently reported symptom. Specifically, 81% of those held captive for 2 to 6 months and 85% held captive for 7 or more months reported distressing dreams, and 87% held captive 2 to 6 months and 89% held captive 7 or more months reported difficulty falling or staying asleep. Schreuder, Kleijn, and Rooijmans (2000) evaluated nightmares in a sample of Dutch combat veterans and World War II victims. They found that 56% reported posttraumatic anxiety dreams (individuals did not wake up from the dream), posttraumatic nightmares (individuals woke up from the dream), or both at least once per month during the past 6 months and that the nightmares were often replicative of the trauma.

Similarly, in a sample of 124 Holocaust survivors, Kuch and Cox (1992) found that sleep disturbances and nightmares were the most frequently reported PTSD symptoms (96% and 83%, respectively). Rosen and colleagues (1991) evaluated sleep problems in 42 Holocaust survivors, 37 depressed individuals, and 54 healthy controls. Results indicated that 45 years after the Holocaust, the survivors continued to report significant problems with sleep and nightmares. The survivors reported more impairment than healthy controls on all indices. The depressed sample had higher impairment than survivors on all but three indices. The two groups did not differ on sleep disturbances and daytime dysfunction, and the survivors scored higher on awakenings due to bad dreams. Sleep and nightmare problems were positively correlated with time spent in concentration camps.

These studies demonstrate that for a substantial number of trauma-exposed people, nightmares and sleep problems are chronic conditions. Future research should identify characteristics that may distinguish between those who do and do not continue to experience nightmares long term.

Nightmares Associated With Distress

Nightmares are considered both a symptom of pathology (e.g., PTSD) and pathology in and of itself (e.g., nightmare disorder). Research has found that numerous psychological difficulties are related to the experience of idiopathic and post-trauma nightmares, although the causal nature of the relationship is unclear. Nightmares may reflect, precipitate, or exacerbate the distress experienced during the day and likely does all three to some degree. Many believe that this association is likely due to the distress engendered by the nightmares themselves and the loss of sleep due to the fear of going to sleep, frequent awakenings, and difficulty returning to sleep. Sleep disturbances and nightmares and their resultant sleep deprivation increase one's vulnerability to impaired mental and physical health, reduction of coping skills, confusion, irritability, memory loss, emotional lability, and performance impairment (e.g., Dorrian & Dinges, 2006; Horne & Pettitt, 1985), to name a few. Rothbaum and Mellman (2001) suggest that poor sleep quality may heighten reactivity to trauma cues, subsequently increasing efforts to avoid such cues. Achieving good quality and quantity of sleep, however, may boost resources needed to cope with the traumatic event. Similarly, Mellman (1997) suggests that the disruption of sleep denies the individual the benefits of sleep's restorative function and role in the emotional processing of the trauma memories (Mellman et al., 2001), increasing the likelihood of developing long-term problems.

While nightmares and sleep problems are increasingly conceptualized as primary factors in the maintenance of post-trauma problems, few studies have prospectively evaluated nightmares immediately following a traumatic event and their impact on other indices of distress. Mellman and colleagues (2001) evaluated 60 individuals presenting to a trauma center following a life-threatening trauma. PTSD symptoms and the individuals' dreams were assessed via morning dream diaries during their stay in the hospital and approximately 2 months later. Dreams characterized as "trauma dreams" were those rated moderately to exactly similar to the trauma and moderately to severely disturbing. Individuals who reported trauma dreams at the initial assessment were more likely to report greater severity of PTSD at the follow-up assessment. Riggs, Rothbaum, and Foa (1995) prospectively assessed PTSD symptoms in a sample of 60 male and female victims of nonsexual assault. Participants were assessed within 30 days of the assault and then weekly for 12 weeks. At the initial assessment, 71% of the women and 50% of the men met criteria for PTSD, while 21% of the women and 0% of the men met criteria at the 12-week assessment. Initial assessment results revealed that 75% of PTSD-positive women, 52% of PTSD-negative women, and 52% of men reported nightmares. At the final assessment, 50% of PTSD-positive and 7% of PTSD-negative women and 4.5% of men reported nightmares. Harvey and Bryant (1998) investigated symptoms of ASD in survivors of motor vehicle accidents within 1 month of the accident. They reassessed participants after 6 months for PTSD. Although not a statistically significant difference, results indicated that 33.3% of individuals with PTSD and 9.4% of individuals without PTSD at the 6-month assessment reported nightmares at the initial assessment.

Most studies examining the association of nightmares and distress have been retrospective. As described previously, Schreuder and colleagues (2000) examined a sample of combat veterans and civilian war victims. The researchers found that individuals reporting replicative or mostly replicative post-trauma nightmares also reported more frequent nightmares and more symptoms of intrusion; however, they reported fewer psychological symptoms as measured by the Symptom Checklist-90 (SCL-90; Derogatis, 1992). The researchers suggested this may be due to the type of trauma experienced, as combat veterans made up a larger portion of the replicative posttraumatic nightmare group, and they scored lower overall on the SCL-90. When independent contributions to SCL-90 scores were examined, nightmare cases reported higher symptom levels than PTSD cases. Post-trauma nightmares were also related to decreased psychological and physical functioning and increased sleep problems compared to those without such nightmares.

Evidence also suggests that in the presence of psychiatric disorders comorbid with PTSD, participants may report even higher rates of nightmare problems. For example, Leskin, Woodward, Young, and Sheikh (2002) reanalyzed data from the National Comorbidity Study (Kessler et al., 1995) and found that 71% of participants diagnosed *only* with PTSD reported problems with nightmares, compared to 96% of individuals with PTSD and panic disorder.

Although most research investigating the relationship between nightmares and sleep problems has focused on idiopathic or unspecified nightmares, several studies have found an association among post-trauma nightmares and various types of sleep disturbance (Brown & Boudewyns, 1996; Cuddy & Belicki, 1992; Germain & Nielsen, 2003a; Hartmann, 1996; Inman, Silver, & Doghramji, 1990; Koren, Arnon, Lavie & Klein, 2002; Lavie & Hertz, 1979; Mellman, David et al., 1995; Mellman, Kulick-Bell, et al., 1995; Ohayon & Shapiro, 2000). For example, Krakow, Melendrez, et al. (2001) reported that nightmares were associated with sleep-disordered breathing in a sample of sexual assault victims. In Krakow's (2006) large sample of sleep clinic patients, those with (16%) and without (84%) salient complaints of nightmares were compared on 25 indices of sleep problems, physical problems, and psychiatric problems. Results indicated that those with nightmares reported worse functioning on 24 of 25 problems (only sleep efficiency was worse for the non-nightmare group). No patients reported only experiencing nightmares. The most common comorbid sleep complaints included poor sleep quality, sleep breathing problems, insomnia, and sleep movements. Clum, Nishith, and Resick (2001) examined the association of PTSD, depression, sleep disturbance (insomnia and nightmares), and physical health symptoms in a sample of female sexual assault victims. The authors found that PTSD-related sleep disturbance contributed 2% unique variance to physical health symptoms after controlling for PTSD and depression symptoms.

The National Veterans Readjustment Study surveyed Vietnam theater veterans (active duty forces serving in Vietnam, Laos, or Cambodia), Vietnam-era veterans (served in active forces at that time, but not in Vietnam), and a control group of civilians (matched to veterans on age and gender) in the late 1980s. This study found that 52% of combat veterans with PTSD, 5% of combat veterans without PTSD, 6% of Vietnam-era veterans, and 3% of civilians reported nightmares "sometimes" to "very frequently" (Neylan et al., 1998). The authors state that "the nightmare appears to be the primary domain of sleep disturbance related to exposure to war zone traumatic stress" (p. 932). In a model predicting nightmare frequency, Neylan and colleagues found that non-sleep-related PTSD symptoms contributed 48% of the variance. After controlling for physical health problems, comorbid psychiatric and substance problems, the level of combat exposure contributed an additional 9% of the variance. Furthermore, combat exposure was highly correlated with nightmares, moderately with sleep-onset insomnia, and weakly with sleep-maintenance insomnia.

There are few objective studies of nightmares. Similar to sleep disturbances, nightmares occur infrequently in the sleep lab, perhaps due to the increased sense of safety associated with having a lab technician present (Schreuder et al., 2001; Sheikh, Woodward, & Leskin, 2003). Kramer and Kinney (1988) evaluated sleep between Vietnam combat veterans with and without "disturbed dreaming" (labeled a bad dream or nightmare and rated 3 or 4 on a 4-point scale of fear or anxiety) at least once per week. Results indicated that both groups had worse sleep disturbance than norm indices; however, only the disturbed dream group had greater REM latency and more arousals per hour than either the nondisturbed dream group or norm indices. The nondisturbed dream group had greater sleep onset latency than the norm. Finally, while all members of the disturbed dream group met criteria for PTSD, none of the nondisturbed dream group did. A closer examination of the disturbed dreams indicated that 84% of such dreams occurred during NREM sleep, and 50% of the disturbed dream group only had such dreams in Stage 2 sleep. The authors distinguish sleep patterns in the dream disturbed groups from previous findings of depressed and anxious individuals primarily in terms of time of night that awakenings happen (first half for disturbed dreaming, second half for depressed individuals) and REM latency (increased for disturbed dreaming and decreased for anxious and depressed individuals). They conclude that this delay to REM may indicate a defense mechanism to avoid experiencing disturbed dreams.

Content of Post-Trauma Nightmares

Historically, post-trauma nightmares have been considered those that exactly or almost exactly replay a trauma. As noted by Hartmann (1996), although post-trauma nightmares may be described as replicative, there is usually some variation of content from the actual event. The variation may be related to stuck points or hot spots—aspects of the trauma that are difficult for the individual to process. In addition to replicative nightmares, trauma-exposed individuals may also report trauma-similar nightmares (i.e., nightmares that have some components similar to their traumatic event, but such significant features as place, time, and people involved are different) or trauma-dissimilar nightmares (i.e., nightmares with no distinguishable relationship to the trauma). Even those nightmares that appear to have little to do with the traumatic event may still be associated with it. As Halliday (1995) states, "(1) other, more symbolic nightmares may nevertheless be *trauma driven*, and (2) elements of traumatic nightmares may still be symbolic and amenable to interpretation even when the nightmare as a whole appears to be based on an historical memory" (p. 152).

Research on the prevalence of the content categories of post-trauma nightmares is equivocal. Wittmann, Schredl, and Kramer (2007) reviewed several studies and found that approximately 50% of participants reported replicative post-trauma nightmares, while a recent study of treatment seeking individuals found that only 20% of trauma-exposed individuals reported replicative nightmares (Davis et al., 2007). Part of the discrepancy in prevalence rates of various types of post-trauma nightmares is that some researchers have combined nightmares that are exact replays of the trauma and those that are similar to the trauma, making it difficult to ascertain differential impact of each.

Studies with combat veterans generally find that many report nightmares of specific events or that have combat themes, particularly those veterans with PTSD. Wilmer (1996) conducted a study in which he interviewed 316 Vietnam veterans, of whom 304 described a combat nightmare. Fifty-three percent of the reported nightmares were repetitive and replicative of actual war experiences. Twenty-one percent were of combat-related events that could have happened but did not, and 26% were implausible. Wilmer notes that while "veterans were exposed to multiple war traumata, usually one event was so deeply ingrained in their memory that it alone constituted the basis of their characteristic dream, expressing how it had actually happened with attendant feelings" (p. 87). Ziarnowski and Broida (1984) evaluated the nightmares of 23 Vietnam veterans with high-level combat exposure and PTSD. The researchers found that almost equal numbers of veterans reported the types of nightmares described by Wilmer (1996). Very few reported combat nightmares that were not true of their experience and probably could not have occurred in Vietnam. The authors also noted an extensive portrayal of helplessness and powerlessness across the reported nightmares, regardless of their similarity to the combat experience.

Schreuder and colleagues (1998) prospectively examined the dreams of 39 outpatients 40 years following various wars in the 1940s. Both combat veterans and civilian victims of war participated and completed daily reports of nightmare and anxiety-dream experiences over a 4-week period. Nightmares were reported in 20% of the daily reports, and anxiety dreams were reported in 5% of the daily reports. Nightmares were more likely to include war-related content than anxiety dreams. The nightmares of combat veterans were closer to actual events than those of civilian victims. Anxiety dreams for both groups and nightmares for the civilians were often symbolic representations of war experiences. Post-trauma nightmares were more likely to be repetitive than anxiety dreams, particularly replicative nightmares. In a later study, Schreuder and colleagues (2000) assessed both civilian victims ($n = 167$) and veterans ($n = 56$) and found that of the 124 participants who met full criteria for PTSD, 82% reported post-trauma nightmares. Of these, 42% reported mostly or completely replicative nightmares, 28% reported mostly or completely nonreplicative nightmares, and 35% reported mixed replicative and non-replicative nightmares.

The limited research that has been conducted with individuals exposed to civilian traumas finds similar results, although David and Mellman (1997) suggest that while post-trauma nightmares are frequent in noncombat populations, civilian traumas may be less likely to result in replicative nightmares. These investigators assessed 20 PTSD-positive and 12 PTSD-negative victims of Hurricane Andrew who recalled a dream within the last month. Assessments were conducted 6 to 12 months after the hurricane. Overall, 16% reported hurricane-related dreams, 31% reported non-hurricane-related threatening dreams, and 53% reported neutral or pleasant dreams. Although not a statistically significant difference, the only five people reporting hurricane-related dreams all had PTSD. Similarly, Mellman, David, Bustamante, Torres, and Fins (2001) assessed dream content and PTSD in 60 patients after admission to a hospital following a life-threatening event (e.g., motor vehicle accident, industrial accident, and interpersonal assault) and followed up with 39 of these patients 6 weeks later. Using a morning dream diary, a total of 21 dreams were reported, 10 of which included trauma content (4 similar, 6 replicative). Results indicated that "trauma dreams" were associated with greater initial PTSD severity than non-post-trauma nightmares.

Individuals reporting "trauma dreams" also reported greater PTSD severity at both assessment points than individuals who were unable to recall a dream.

Hartmann, Zborowski, Rosen, and Grace (2001) investigated dreams in 306 students with and without childhood or recent physical or sexual abuse and found that while dreams with negative emotions were common in both abused and nonabused students, the abused students reported fewer dreams with positive emotions. Cuddy and Belicki (1992) examined nightmares and sleep problems in 539 female undergraduates. After controlling for depression, the investigators found that women sexually and physically abused in childhood or adulthood reported significantly more frequent past-year posttraumatic nightmares (replicative), repetitive nightmares, and difficulty falling asleep following a nightmare than the nonabused group. The sexual abuse group reported more sleep terrors, idiopathic nightmares, and less sleep per night than the nonabused group.

There is growing evidence that while nightmares may have started out replicating or nearly replicating the trauma soon after the event, many change and distort over time (Hartmann, Russ, Oldfield, Sivan, & Cooper, 1987). Terr (1979) surveyed children who were kidnapped in Chowchilla, California in 1976 and buried underground for approximately 16 hours. She reported that the children were more likely to have replicative dreams or "terror dreams" immediately following the event. After several months, however, the children had more "disguised" or modified dreams. At the 4-year follow-up (Terr, 1983), the children reported repetitive, but not replicative, dreams. Thirty percent had modified kidnapping dreams, 52% had disguised dreams, and 57% had night terrors (some had more than one type). Hartmann (1998a) presents a dream series, following trauma-exposed persons from immediately after the traumatic event up to 2 years posttrauma. This dream series demonstrates that many nightmares initially include numerous aspects of the actual traumatic event. However, he also reports that "exact replays seem to be rare" (p. 224). Hartmann's study (1998a) reports that for many individuals, the nightmares expeditiously change to reflect a different story line; however, they usually centered on a "dominant emotion" or theme. He suggests that nightmares will often "contextualize" the person's primary emotion—usually fear and terror—with story lines involving tidal waves, whirlwinds, and other overwhelming forces. As the person recovers from the trauma, the dominant emotion and story line are altered, more closely approximating "normal" dreams over time. Similarly, Wilmer (1996) suggests that this change in content away from the exact replication of the traumatic event represents healing for the individual.

Relationship of Nightmare Content to Distress

As suggested above, content of dreams following trauma appears related to the severity of the distress. Nightmares may elicit PTSD (Schreuder et al., 2001) and appear to be more frequent and more severe among those suffering from PTSD. In general, studies indicate that replicative or trauma-similar nightmares are associated with PTSD diagnosis and the severity of PTSD symptoms (e.g., Esposito, Benitez, Barza, & Mellman, 1999; Mellman et al., 2001; Mellman et al., 1995; Ross, Ball, Sullivan, & Caroff, 1989; Schreuder et al., 2000; van der Kolk, Blitz, Burr, Sherry, & Hartmann, 1984).

For example, Mellman and colleagues (1995) sampled 58 combat veterans (37 PTSD positive) and found that PTSD-positive individuals were more likely to report having nightmares with and without combat content. Similarly, van der Kolk and colleagues (1984) assessed 15 PTSD-positive combat veterans and 10 PTSD-negative noncombat veterans with lifelong nightmares. None of those without PTSD reported having nightmares that replicated an actual event, compared to 11 of those with PTSD. Moreover, all 15 of the veterans with PTSD reported having recurring nightmares, compared to 3 individuals in the non-PTSD veteran group. Esposito and colleagues (1999) evaluated the dreams of 18 Vietnam combat veterans with chronic PTSD. Veterans completed dream diaries 1 week prior to their assessment. Dream ratings revealed that most were threatening in some way, but only 21% were an exact replication of a traumatic event. Nearly half of the dreams were similar to the trauma in that they contained characters, settings, or objects related to the trauma. The dream ratings, while not correlated with the total CAPS score, were associated with the reexperiencing score.

Kramer, Schoen, and Kinney (1984) examined differences in Vietnam veterans with and without disturbed dreaming. The investigators found that all eight participants with disturbed dreaming met the criteria for PTSD, while only one of eight without disturbed dreaming met the criteria for PTSD. Individuals with disturbed dreaming reported more dreams with military content (44%) than did the control group (4%). Dreams with military content were reported with similar frequency during REM and non-REM sleep. The authors conclude that "disturbed dreaming may well turn out to be at the core of PTSD" (p. 93). Similarly, Lavie, Katz, Pillar, and Zinger (1998) conducted a study to examine sleep character-istics in 12 veterans with PTSD and 12 veterans without PTSD. While few differences were found on sleep characteristics, the investigators reported substantial differences in dream content. Specifically, 50% of those with PTSD and none of those without PTSD reported "dreams containing explicit combat content" (p. 1062). PTSD patients' dreams also were rated as significantly higher in hostility-aggression.

As part of two larger studies, our research group has examined char-acteristics of post-trauma nightmares in 94 treatment-seeking individuals (Davis, Byrd, Rhudy, & Wright, 2007). The majority of the participants were women, Caucasian, had at least some college education, and had a mean age of 39.9 ($SD = 11.99$). Participants reported a mean night-mare frequency of four nightmares per week and an average severity of 3.0 (on a scale of 0 to 4). Participants reported a mean of 5.65 ($SD = 1.77$) hours of sleep per night, and 37% of the sample reported sleep initiation taking, on average, 1 or more hours each night. Participants were asked to indicate to what extent their nightmares were associated with a traumatic event (*exactly or almost exactly like the trauma, similar to the trauma,* or *unrelated to the trauma*). Fifty percent reported a nightmare "simi-lar" to their trauma, 29.5% reported the nightmares were unrelated, and 20.5% reported they were replicative. We then examined the possible associations among the type of nightmares and distress. In general, we found that replicative nightmares were associated with greater problems than either the trauma-similar or unrelated nightmare groups and that the trauma-similar group reported greater problems than the unrelated group. Interestingly, the three groups did not differ on fear of sleep, rest-ful feelings upon waking, the number of nightmares per week (although they did differ on the number of nights with nightmares per week), the disturbance level of the nightmares, and the number of panic symptoms experienced upon waking (Davis et al., 2007).

These studies suggest that nightmares in the presence of PTSD may be particularly problematic and that the closer in content the nightmares are to a traumatic event, the greater the distress. However, they also indicate that even nightmares in which the content appears unrelated to a trauma are associated with difficulties and may have implications for mental and physical well-being, independent of PTSD status.

The literature reviewed above makes a strong case for the pernicious impact of post-trauma nightmares. They are simultaneously symptoms of a broader trauma response (ASD and PTSD) and pathology themselves.

Post-trauma nightmares are associated with a host of other psychological and sleep problems. Some, however, believe that post-trauma nightmares may be adaptive, at least initially. We briefly turn now to a consideration of the possible adaptive function of nightmares.

ARE POST-TRAUMA NIGHTMARES ADAPTIVE?

The question of the possible adaptive nature of nightmares draws in part from the presumed (by some) adaptive nature of dreams. Dreams are thought to play a role in diffusing strong emotion (Cartwright, 1991) and processing memories, particularly emotion-laden memories (Maquet et al., 1996). Some of the information regarding the possible adaptive role of dreams comes from studies of recurrent dreams (dreams that a person has repeatedly, in which some or all of the content remains the same).

Brown and Donderi (1986) compared 67 recurrent, past-recurrent (had a recurring dream for at least 6 months as an adult, but not within the past year), and nonrecurrent dreamers (never had one). Recurrent dreamers evidenced lower "psychological well-being" and had more negative dream content than the other groups. Individuals with past-recurrent dreams scored higher on "psychological well-being," and their dreams contained more positive content than those of nonrecurrent dreamers. The authors suggest an adaptive function of dreams in that problems are repeatedly represented in dreams until the issue is resolved.

Cartwright (1979; 1991) reports some support for this notion of recurrent dreams ending when problems are resolved. Cartwright (1991) assessed depression and dreaming in 49 individuals going through a divorce. Depressed participants had more negative affect in dreams than the nondepressed participants. In addition, depressed individuals whose dreams included their ex-spouse early on fared better at the 1-year follow-up. These dreams also were rated as including stronger negative affect than the dreams of those who did not incorporate the spouse. The author concluded that these findings may point to the fact that depressed incorporators are "working through" the divorce during sleep. As stated above, however, it remains unclear whether dreams reflect, precipitate, or exacerbate waking affect.

Another way that scientists have attempted to determine the possible adaptive function of dreams is through exploring possible relationships among presleep affect, dream affect and content, and postsleep affect. Many researchers have long conceived of REM and its associated dreams as serving to incorporate emotional information into memory systems (e.g., Breger, 1967). In her theory of dreams as mood regulators, Cartwright (2005) argues that the content and structure of dreams are influenced by presleep affect. Starting with the trauma nightmare (whether the content is replicative, similar, or dissimilar to the actual event), the negative emotion related to the event seems to clearly be represented in nightmares. While this connection between presleep and sleep mentation may be less pronounced when presleep affect arousal is low, it is increasingly evident when affect arousal is heightened. Low arousal may be associated with varied themes and content throughout the night, while high arousal narrows the scope of the dreams to focus on the source of the arousal. Thus, dreams may only play an adaptive role when the level of distress is not able to be processed by waking mechanisms. When negative dreams repeat over time, however, this may indicate that the dream mood-regulating processes are overwhelmed (Cartwright, 1979; 2005).

The notion of an adaptive function of dreams is far from being an accepted notion in the field. However, if dreams have such a function, could the nightmare as well? Is there a purpose to the nightmare? Is it simply an oneiric manifestation of waking stress or might it be a signal, an alarm system warning the dreamer of deeper psychic troubles? Is it adaptive initially after a trauma to dream about it? Does it fail to be adaptive when it becomes a chronic condition? Finally, if nightmares have an adaptive function, it is unclear how it works if people wake from nightmares—the act of waking would seem to interrupt any processing that may be occurring (Levin & Nielsen, 2007). These issues are discussed more fully in chapter 3.

IS DREAM RECALL OR A LACK OF RECALL ADAPTIVE?

While post-trauma nightmares may initially play an adaptive role in terms of processing the traumatic event, for many individuals this function fails, and the nightmares continue unabated for years. It appears, however, that our sleep structure may change in response to this failure of processing. As described in chapter 1, an interesting phenomenon is observed in some individuals with chronic PTSD. Despite overwhelming subjective reports of poor sleep, many individuals appear to actually achieve deeper sleep (assessed via awakening thresholds) than those without PTSD. It appears that some people may handle the chronicity of trauma response through decreased dream recall.

Several studies have found reduced dream recall in trauma-exposed samples years after the traumatic event. Dagan, Lavie, and Bleich (1991) found lower than expected dream recall from REM (54.8%) in a sample of 24 individuals with war-related PTSD. The study took place 4 to 6 years after the 1982 Lebanon War. Hefez, Metz, and Lavie (1987) also found lower than expected dream recall in a sample of 11 survivors of various traumatic events. Four participants suffered nightmares during the laboratory study (3 of whom were within 18 months of their trauma), but the remaining participants reported only 4 dream reports out of 21 awakenings from REM sleep and no dream reports from NREM sleep. In a small sample of Vietnam veterans, Kramer and colleagues (1984) found that those with disturbed dreaming had higher dream recall from REM sleep. The disturbed dreaming group had dream recall from 77% of awakenings from REM, versus 50% in those without disturbed dreaming, which is lower than normal rates.

Kaminer and Lavie (1991) found that dream recall was associated with symptomatology. The investigators examined 12 "well-adjusted" and 11 "less-adjusted" survivors of the Holocaust and 10 control participants on indices of sleep structure and dreams 40 years following their trauma. Well-adjusted participants had significantly lower dream recall than either of the other two groups and often did not remember dreaming at all. The less-adjusted and control groups had higher dream recall and knew they had been dreaming even if they could not recall specific content of their dreams. The authors suggest that lower dream recall is an adaptive mechanism, although they note it is unclear if dream recall was always low and this served a prophylactic function or if dream recall decreased following the trauma, serving as a coping strategy. If dream recall decreased immediately following trauma, however, this appears to call into question the notion that dreams serve an adaptive function.

Mellman, David, et al. (1995) gathered dream reports and assessed for PTSD in 60 individuals following a life-threatening incident. At the initial evaluation, 18 of the 60 participants remembered a dream and provided 21 dream reports, of which 46% were considered "trauma dreams." Individuals who initially reported trauma dreams also reported greater distress at the 2-month follow-up than those without dream recall. Participants who initially met criteria for PTSD provided additional dream reports between the assessment points. Two individuals originally had trauma dreams, but at the 2-month assessment, they no longer had PTSD and had dreams that were low in similarity to the trauma. Two other individuals who originally met criteria for PTSD and had trauma dreams at the initial assessment continued to meet criteria and to have trauma dreams at the 2-month follow-up. Unfortunately, it is unclear whether dream recall in general changed from the initial to the follow-up assessment.

The findings of these studies seem to suggest several patterns of dream responding. First, little dream recall initially following a trauma is associated with better functioning. Second, high distressing dream recall initially is associated with worse functioning, but over time, functioning improves and dreams become less reflective of the traumatic event. Third, high distressing dream recall initially is associated with worse functioning, and both the trauma dream recall and distress continue over time. Perhaps initial increases in dream recall do occur for those with more difficulties and represent attempts to cope with the traumatic event. If it is successful, then dream recall could decline to pretrauma levels. Over time, however, the ongoing hyperarousal and intrusions may increase defensive efforts to block these symptoms, increasing emotional numbing and the intensity of dreams (Levin & Nielsen, 2007). This may explain the findings by Kaminer and Lavie (1991) and does not preclude their suggestion that lower dream recall may serve a prophylactic function. Perhaps those with low pretrauma dream recall respond better overall to the event. As suggested by Kramer et al. (1984), the lower dream recall may reflect a healthy adaptation or avoidance of dream experiences. Many questions remain to be answered, however, and it will be important to parse out dream recall in general and content of the dreams in future research.

The past several decades have provided a tremendous body of work regarding the nature of disturbing sleep events, including post-trauma nightmares. Of course, this is just the beginning. We are still at the incipient stage of understanding post-trauma nightmares, how they are associated with distress, what functions they may serve, and how best to treat them. Now that we know a bit more about their nature, we next turn to how they develop and what maintains them over time.

3

Theoretical Formulation of Post-Trauma Nightmares

Davis, Fernandez, Pennington, and Langston

Our understanding of nightmare development following the experience of a traumatic event remains unclear. In fact, theorists and researchers vary considerably regarding if, and to what degree, post-trauma nightmares share the same underlying mechanisms as idiopathic nightmares, night terrors, or dreams (Krystal & Davidson, 2007; Schreuder, Igreja, van Dijk, & Kleijn, 2001). Chapter 2 illustrates several ways in which post-trauma nightmares appear to differ from idiopathic nightmares and night terrors, suggesting the need for alternative theories to understand their development and maintenance. Intuitively, disturbances in sleep may be adaptive immediately following a traumatic event. The intrusions that occur during the day may increase avoidance and hypervigilance, which could initially serve as adaptive responses. It makes sense to be more aware of your surroundings and avoid potentially dangerous situations, places, or people in the early aftermath of a traumatic event. Sleep disturbances may be a side effect of this daytime arousal or may be adaptive in themselves, as we may be more vulnerable to potential threats when asleep.

It is uncertain, however, how nightmares fit in adaptively with this initial reaction. Are they part of the alarm system, reminding people that danger may still be present and trying to wake them? Are nightmares initially a function of the mind attempting to assimilate and make sense of the event? Or are they simply a reflection of the difficult emotions people experience in waking hours? If most posttrauma nightmares are transient, what happens that promotes chronicity?

Numerous scientists and therapists have sought to answer these questions and have put forth theories to explain the development of nightmares following trauma. Most theories across various orientations and theorists, however, share common elements. First, the traumatic event was not properly processed emotionally or cognitively. In this view, nightmares reflect the mind's attempt to process the traumatic event—perhaps similar to intrusive thoughts and flashbacks. Second, when nightmares continue over long periods of time, something within the natural system has failed. Third, avoidance of trauma-related stimuli will maintain nightmares over time. Fourth, the nightmares are likely to continue until they are emotionally processed, perhaps involving a sense of mastery over the process or content. In this chapter, we present first a brief review of several theoretical conceptualizations put forth by leaders in the field, followed by our three-factor model of the development and maintenance of post-trauma nightmares.

WISH FULFILLMENT

One of the earliest modern conceptualizations of dreams came from Sigmund Freud (1900/1955). Freud's theory of dreams, including bad dreams, was that they represented a form of wish fulfillment. Typically the desires represented by the dreams were of a nature (e.g., violent or sexual) that was discomforting to the individual having the dream. By masking the desire in bizarre content, the individual obtained some relief through its expression and sleep was protected. Increasingly, however, evidence was found suggesting that some bad dreams were direct replications of traumatic events, a phenomenon that did not appear to fit well with Freud's theory of wish fulfillment (although see Lidz, 1946). Freud (1920/1955) later came to theorize that post-trauma nightmares were the individual's attempt to achieve mastery over the experience.

COGNITIVE-PROCESSING PERSPECTIVES

Based on a series of studies, Horowitz (1975; see also Horowitz & Wilner, 1976) concluded that the phenomenon of intrusion and repetition was not limited to the experience of traumatic events but also occurred following less severe stressful events, even positive stressors. He also found that the effect was not exclusive to psychiatric populations but was evidenced broadly across various populations. From a social-cognitive framework, Horowitz suggests that information in active memory systems continues to be repeated or experienced until the information is assimilated or accommodated and stored away in long-term or "inactive" memory. This repetition may take the form of intrusive thoughts, nightmares, memories, emotions, or cognitions associated with the event. When faced with significant stressors or traumatic experiences, this need to process and store information rivals the strong desire to escape the emotional pain associated with the memories. For some, this struggle results in ongoing oscillation between attempts to process and make sense of the memories and efforts to avoid reminders of the event (Horowitz, 1975).

The ebb and flow of intrusion and avoidance seems to be a natural process in the early stages of recovery following an unexpected negative event or, in the case of recurrent dreams, struggling with an ongoing problem. Most people are able to gradually integrate the material, and the nightmares cease. However, if the information or event is not processed—if escape and avoidance behaviors dominate an individual's response—the oscillation and struggle will continue. Perhaps the process is especially prohibitive when the event—and, subsequently, the nightmare—is overwhelming emotionally and well beyond an individual's existing view of self, others, and the world. This would suggest a strong avoid and escape reaction to the nightmare, perhaps in the form of waking up and attempting to avoid further thoughts of the nightmare or the original event. Due to subsequent distress related to loss of sleep and increased arousal, the person may feel helpless to control the seemingly unending battle. At this point, natural processes designed to integrate, master, or make meaning of the event fail. The individual may then need to learn a new way of handling the experience.

Nadar (1996) also suggests a relationship between avoidance and reexperiencing of traumatic material. She states that trauma-exposed children who avoid attending to trauma material during the day may be more likely to experience it at night, through dreams or nightmares. She also suggests that children may have an increase in nightmares or reenactment playing over time, with an associated decrease in waking cognitive or imaginal reexperiencing symptoms.

Nightmares as a Component of the Fear Network

Nightmares may be conceptualized as part of a fear network that incorporates aspects of the traumatic event, reactions to the event, and the meaning of the event, as described in chapter 1 (Foa, Steketee, & Rothbaum, 1989; Lang, 1968; Lang, Cuthbert, & Bradley, 1998). In individuals with PTSD, the network is activated by people, places, and situations that remind the individual of the event. More fear stimuli are added to the network through generalization processes. The system is maintained over time through attempts to avoid trauma-related stimuli so that new, non-fear-related information is not incorporated into the network. In order to correct the pathological fear structures, the fear network must be engaged, and corrective information needs to be presented and incorporated into the network (Foa & Kozak, 1986).

Rothbaum and Mellman (2001) extend this theory to explain why "exposure" in the form of chronic post-trauma nightmares is not therapeutic. While idiopathic nightmares and bad dreams may not awaken the sleeper (allowing the story line and accompanying images to transmogrify, thereby making nonfearful or less fearful related connections), post-trauma nightmares are thought to be so emotionally intense or physiologically arousing that the individual awakens. The individual wakes up from a trauma-related nightmare frightened, only experiencing brief exposure. This does not allow for habituation, as therapeutic exposure is thought to require fairly long, sustained exposure and may only serve to heighten the level of fear. Indeed, Esposito, Benitz, Barza, and Mellman (1999) purport that in some combat veterans, the fear response is further generalized in part because of the nightmares. Waking up and realizing it was "only a nightmare" may be akin to escape/avoidance behaviors during waking hours in that the person escaped the terrifying situation, further negatively reinforcing the cycle (Rothbaum & Mellman, 2001).

Rothbaum and Mellman (2001) also note that during a dream we are unable to distinguish dream content from reality. Therapeutic imaginal exposure involves experiencing the trauma memory imaginally but also realizing that it is just a memory, and that no actual danger exists. However, during a nightmare, we do not have the benefit of realizing that what is taking place is not real; therefore, no corrective information is able to be integrated. It is not clear, however, if similar processes are at work when the nightmares are not replicative of the traumatic event. As described in chapter 2, sufficient evidence exists to suggest that, although recurrent nightmares may be similar or dissimilar to the traumatic event, they often have threatening and dangerous themes. It is possible that these themes are generalized aspects of the fear network, and the underlying mechanisms maintaining the nightmares are comparable.

Nightmares as Recontextualizing Emotion

Hartmann (1995; 1998b) believes that the function of dreaming is to help integrate memories by making new connections with related information stored in memory. He perceives the same adaptive function to be true of nightmares. With typical post-trauma nightmares, the primary emotion (e.g., fear, guilt) is reflected in varying story lines and images. As described by Hobson, Stickgold, and Pace-Schott, we can conceive of "dream emotion as a primary shaper of plots rather than as a reaction to them" (1998, p. R1). As Empson (1989) states, "[t]here are no screen credits at the beginnings of dreams to tell you what sort of film you are going to see, but there might as well have been in these nightmares, because the terror, horror or guilt is excruciatingly present before the first scenes have even been played" (p. 90).

Typically, the information related to the nightmare cues information in related networks, and new connections are made. As Greenberg, Pillard, and Pearlman (1972) state, "the past and present become woven together and the traumatic event is gradually mastered" (p. 261). For example, if a patient's nightmare involves fear related to a motor vehicle accident, associated networks may include information about a previous accident or other situation in which the patient was afraid but successfully coped with the emotions. Breger, Hunter, and Lane (1971) suggest that wake-time stressful thoughts and feelings trigger memories of related emotional content during sleep and may provide information on how previous experiences were dealt with. The notion of nightmares as metaphors may help explain the terrible nightmares that are similar to or seemingly unrelated to the trauma in that the primary emotion of the trauma (e.g., fear, terror, guilt, sadness) is dominant, and the mind creates a story line for it through nightmares, often incorporating specific contextualizing images (e.g., tidal wave), although specific trauma-related images are not included (Hartmann, Zborowski, Rosen, & Grace, 2001). This exposure to trauma-related memories and emotions that occur in a relaxed sleep state is similar to exposure-based techniques in which the threat is presented while the person is in a relaxed state or in the safety of the therapist's office (Hartmann, 1995; Mellman, 1997). The incompatible states of relaxation and anxiety may assist in modifying the nature of the trauma memory for many people.

Thus, it appears that post-trauma nightmares may have some adaptive function early on, as opposed to being a sign of pathology. If this is indeed a possibility, where and how does the process go wrong with chronic post-trauma nightmares? Nightmares cease to be functional when sleep is disrupted, various connections are not made, trauma-related information is not integrated, and content or painful emotions and memories are continually replayed. Is the problem related to the emotional system's being overwhelmed? Perhaps the traumatic event is so shocking and powerful that we do not have related memory networks in which to incorporate the experience and its emotions (Cartwright, 1991). Hartmann (1984; 1991) suggests that part of the reason chronic nightmares may develop following traumatic experiences is due to the cognitive, emotional, and behavioral avoidance that trauma-exposed people may engage in. By avoiding trauma-related stimuli, the memories and painful emotions are "walled off" (1984, p. 216). The individual may make such extraordinary attempts to avoid these reminders that there is little opportunity for integration to occur, even during sleep. Hartmann (1984) further suggests that those individuals with " thin boundaries" may be better able to connect and integrate trauma material, while those with "thick boundaries" may be more likely to avoid or wall off trauma stimuli, leaving them disconnected and unprocessed.

REM SLEEP DISRUPTION

Substantial variability exists in findings among studies examining the role of REM sleep activity in post-trauma nightmares. Ross, Ball, Sullivan, and Caroff (1989) theorize that dysfunctional REM sleep mechanisms may play an important role in the development and maintenance of chronic nightmares. As reported in chapter 1, numerous studies have found disrupted or altered REM sleep (e.g., REM density, REM latency, REM sleep phasic activity) in trauma-exposed individuals, although the results have been contradictory. The contradictions may stem from differential reporting and inclusion of a variety of factors, including medications and comorbid conditions. Also, much of the work was conducted with individuals with chronic PTSD. It is likely that the particular manifestation of REM disruption may change between the acute phase and the chronic phase of the condition (Mellman & Hipolito, 2006). In support of the idea that REM plays a key role, Ross and colleagues (1989) also note that the nightmares described by trauma-exposed persons are similar to those reported during REM sleep by non-trauma-exposed persons in that they are easily recalled, vivid, and bizarre. The key role of REM sleep seems contradictory, however, to findings that nightmares may occur during all stages of sleep. But Mellman (1997) suggests that, while post-trauma nightmares occur in both REM and non-REM sleep, studies generally find that waking from a nightmare is preceded by REM in the majority of cases.

Similarly to Horowitz and others, Mellman (1997) suggests an adaptive function of REM sleep. The disruption of REM posttrauma is thought to play a significant role in maintaining sleep and nightmare problems and may also impact the role of REM in memory processing. For example, the depression literature finds some support for an association of REM sleep and emotional adaptation. Shorter REM latencies are not uncommon in individuals with depression (Giles, Kupfer, Rush, & Roffwarg, 1998) and have been found to increase upon treatment with antidepressants (e.g., Shen et al., 2006). In a study of depressed individuals going through a divorce, Cartwright, Kravitz, Eastman, and Wood (1991) found that those with shorter REM latency at the initial assessment were functioning better than individuals with normal REM latency at a 1-year follow-up. The authors speculate that this shortened REM latency may play an adaptive role in helping to accelerate the alleviation of negative mood states. Greenberg and colleagues (1972) assessed adaptation to anxiety-provoking stimuli in three groups of participants: REM deprived, non-REM deprived, and undisturbed sleep. They found that of those participants who reported anxiety related to an autopsy film, those who were REM deprived were still anxious during the second viewing, compared to the other two groups.

Although much more work is needed to determine how REM sleep, dreams and nightmares, or other mechanisms related to REM sleep may serve an adaptive function, it would appear that this function breaks down for some people suffering from chronic post-trauma nightmares, particularly those that replay the traumatic event. In trauma-exposed individuals, the purported adaptive function of dreaming may be interrupted by awakenings resulting from disturbances of the physiological mechanisms underlying REM sleep. Indeed, Mellman and Hipolito (2006) suggest that the disruption of REM through awakenings and arousals, plus the heightened activity of the noradrenergic system, maintaining increased arousal, do not allow for the natural adaptive processes involved in REM sleep and dreaming to function properly. Hartmann (1984) also suggests that trauma memories may be provoked by physiological activity corresponding to change in sleep stage, setting off a trauma-related nightmare.

The physiological impact of SDB, including numerous microarousals, may likewise interfere with adaptive processes (Krakow, Lowry, et al., 2000). Krakow and colleagues suggest that reduced airflow resulting from SDB may increase nocturnal anxiety and subsequently increase nightmares. The sleep fragmentation from SDB could also result in higher recall of nightmares. Upper airway resistance may be associated with nightmares via increased microarousals. Trauma may also increase the risk of SDB via weight gain posttrauma. Physiological changes associated with PTSD may disrupt REM sleep, interfere with normal breathing, and increase vulnerability to developing a sleep breathing disorder, which could exacerbate the disruption of REM. Alternatively, a sleep breathing problem may be present first and exacerbated by these other mechanisms. Either way the problems temporally develop, the result is likely to be chronic PTSD and nightmares via REM disruption.

The investigation of the roles of REM sleep and dreaming as adaptive functions and the disrupted processes that may or may not reflect the disturbances of such functions is in its infancy. Hartmann (1998a) states, "I believe dreaming does have a function which can be related to, but is not the same as, the function of REM sleep" (p. 235). Exciting and innovative research that will enhance our understanding of the nature of the relationship between REM sleep and dreaming continues.

LEARNED SLEEP DISORDER

Several investigators have conceptualized nightmares as learned behaviors. Specifically, it is posited that the negative emotions resultant from nightmares serve as conditioned stimuli, causing a conditioned reaction of waking to avoid further negative emotion (Krakow & Zadra, 2006; Spoormaker, Schredl, & van den Bout, 2006). The relief experienced upon waking from a nightmare may negatively reinforce the response and promote fears of sleep and the sleep environment and poor sleep habits designed to avoid sleep. Thus, while trauma may initiate nightmares, it is suggested that a separate, learned sleep disorder develops over time (Krakow, Hollifield, et al., 2001; see also Inman, Silver, & Doghramji, 1990). Evidence for this perspective comes from objective studies that find decreased frequency of nightmares when participants sleep in the laboratory. Maher, Rego, and Asnis (2006) suggest that some individuals with PTSD may actually sleep better in a sleep lab. These individuals may feel less anxious away from their home sleeping environment, which, if they have long suffered sleep problems, may be conditioned stimuli for poor sleep. This change in nightmare experience suggests that the nightmare may be more controllable than nightmare sufferers believe (Spoormaker et al., 2006).

IMAGERY DISTURBANCE

Similarly to Horowitz (1983), Krakow and Zadra (2006) also propose that individuals suffering from post-trauma nightmares have a dysregulated imagery system or, in other words, an imbalance between thoughts, feelings, and images. This is evident in the inability to control the intrusions of unwanted trauma imagery and their accompanying negative emotions. In an effort to defend against intrusive images, it is suggested that trauma survivors may focus more on their thoughts rather than their feelings and images because they are easier to manage. This avoidance of imagery and subsequent primary focus on thoughts, however, interferes with a person's natural ability to work with his or her imagery system. The avoidance of imagery may also contribute to individuals' becoming increasingly numb emotionally.

As discussed in chapter 2, nightmares have a natural capacity and inclination to change; most people who experience a trauma may have nightmares initially, then the nightmares change and fade over time. However, if a person is avoiding imagery by waking from nightmares at night and avoiding imagery during the day, he or she does not have the opportunity for self-correction and change. Avoidance of imagery, while initially an attempt to adapt to the disrupted imagery system, may play a role in the chronicity of nightmares of some trauma-exposed persons.

A few studies have investigated the role of imagery in trauma-exposed persons. Stutman and Bliss (1985) found that veterans with high PTSD scores also had high non-trauma-related imagery vividness and hypnotizability scores compared to veterans with low PTSD scores. Laor and colleagues (1998) did not find differences in vividness by PTSD status but did not separate PTSD positive individuals into "low" and "high" PTSD as did Stutman and Bliss. Bryant and Harvey (1996) examined the ability of a group of motor vehicle accident victims to engage in non-trauma-related visual imagery. Comparisons were made among individuals with PTSD, phobia, and low anxiety. Results indicated that those with low anxiety had significantly more vivid visual imagery than those with PTSD or phobia. While individuals with PTSD and phobia had lower vivid imagery scores, vividness of imagery was significantly related to nightmares and flashbacks in those with PTSD and to flashbacks in the phobia group. The authors speculate whether anxiety might hamper the cognitive processes necessary for imagery. They suggest that high imagery vividness may serve as a risk factor for experiencing trauma imagery, so those individuals with high vividness prior to the trauma may be vulnerable to experiencing flashbacks and nightmares. Another possibility is that after a traumatic event, individuals may focus on and subsequently heighten the vividness of nontrauma imagery in an effort to avoid trauma imagery.

To examine this issue further, our research group examined nontrauma-related imaginal vividness ability in a treatment-seeking group of chronic nightmare sufferers (Pennington, Davis, & Rhudy, unpublished data). Imagery was measured using the *Betts Questionnaire Upon Mental Imagery-Shortened Form* (Sheehan, 1967). At baseline, greater vividness of imagery was associated with higher past-month frequency of post-trauma nightmares on the CAPS (Blake et al., 1990). Although not statistically significant, vividness was also related to higher intensity of past-month post-trauma nightmares. Interestingly, imagery vividness was unrelated to a separate question that assessed frequency and intensity of nightmares generally (not specified as trauma-related or idiopathic) and did not change following treatment of chronic nightmares. On the Impact of Events Scale II, better vivid imagery ability was associated with more intrusive thoughts, flashbacks, and emotional reexperiencing and with less avoidance of talking about the trauma. Finally, while vividness did not significantly change following treatment, greater vividness of imagery at baseline was associated with greater reduction in past-month trauma-related nightmare frequency, with a trend for reduction in past-month intensity of post-trauma nightmares at the 1-week posttreatment assessment. Thus, imagery vividness was specific to post-trauma nightmares and was not associated with idiopathic nightmares. These results are consistent with previous studies, suggesting a link between imagery vividness and posttraumatic functioning. The finding that better imagery skills were associated with greater reduction in nightmare frequency suggests that imagery-based treatments may be especially suited to these individuals.

Rauch, Foa, Furr, and Filip (2004) examined vividness of the traumatic event in 69 women with PTSD. The women were involved in one of two treatments: prolonged exposure or prolonged exposure plus restructuring. The authors found that vividness of the imagery for the traumatic event was associated with anxiety in early sessions and decreased over the course of treatment but was not related to treatment outcome. Imagery vividness to nontraumatic events was not assessed. Finally, Belicki and Belicki (1986) examined nightmares in 841 college students (the authors do not indicate whether participants experienced a traumatic event). They found that frequent nightmares (at least one per month) were associated with higher non-trauma-related imagery vividness.

While not examining nightmares, Laor and colleagues (1998) did find interesting relationships among image control, image vividness, PTSD status, and physiological responding to script driven imagery. Individuals did not differ for either image measure by PTSD status. However, in individuals with PTSD, image control and physiological responding were inversely related. Individuals with PTSD and low image control had significantly greater physiological response to trauma stimuli. Those with high image control did not differ from participants without PTSD. The authors suggest that high image control may be a safeguard for individuals with PTSD. To determine if this might hold true for symptomatology, Laor and colleagues then examined the relationship of PTSD status, PTSD and related symptoms, and image control. The researchers found that image control plays a different role depending on PTSD status. For individuals with PTSD, high image control was related to lower anger and intrusive symptoms and greater ability to control anger. In individuals without PTSD, high image control was associated with greater anger expression and lower control of anger. These relationships suggest that future research should examine the specific relationship between nightmares and image control.

Growing evidence suggests that non-trauma-related imagery vividness and control may play a role in the development or maintenance of the imagery symptoms of PTSD (flashbacks, nightmares, intrusive images), and imagery ability in general may also be associated with positive response to treatment. If people are focused on avoiding trauma images due to flashbacks and nightmares and focusing on nontrauma imagery instead, helping them refocus their imagery skills on the nightmare may help the brain's natural capacity to engage with associated networks, allowing the nightmare images to change and morph as non-post-trauma nightmares do.

THREE-FACTOR MODEL OF NIGHTMARE DEVELOPMENT AND MAINTENANCE

Although the various theories discussed thus far have some empirical support, many do not account for individual differences in terms of response to trauma experiences, allow for multiple factors to contribute to the development of posttrauma nightmares, or capture the cyclical nature of interaction among these factors. The three-factor model we propose suggests the consideration of predisposing, precipitating, and perpetuating factors in understanding chronic post-trauma nightmares (see Figure 3.1). Predisposing factors may include pretrauma psychological disorders, personality traits, and lifestyle characteristics that may increase the individual's vulnerability to developing nightmares. Precipitating factors include the traumatic event, aspects of the trauma, or the individual's peritraumatic or posttraumatic cognitive, behavioral, emotional, and physiological responses to the trauma that increase the risk of nightmares. Perpetuating factors include those physiological, behavioral, and cognitive conditions posttrauma that serve to maintain nightmares over time. Our conceptualization incorporates many of the ideas described above and is based on models of insomnia (e.g., Drake, Roehrs, & Roth, 2003; Morin, 1993; Spielman, Caruso, & Glovinsky, 1987). This approach represents an interdisciplinary perspective, drawing upon the trauma, anxiety, dream, and sleep literature. This perspective also incorporates various systems to understand chronic nightmares, including emotional, cognitive, behavioral, and physiological systems.

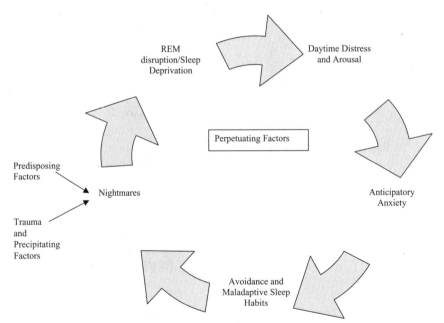

Figure 3.1 Three-Factor Model of Nightmare Development and Maintenance.

Predisposing Factors

Early research on nightmares explored factors that may be associated with a greater susceptibility to nightmares in general. Although many of these factors await empirical evaluation or replication, they may also inform a predisposition to the development of post-trauma nightmares. Predisposing factors may include psychological disorders, personality traits, genetic factors, and lifestyle characteristics that may increase an individual's vulnerability to developing nightmares.

Epidemiologic studies have found evidence for a genetic link for nightmare experiences. Hublin, Kaprio, Partinen, and Koskenvuo (2001) conducted a national twin cohort study in Finland, examining the role of genetic factors in parasomnias. Results indicated that nightmares frequently occurred with sleep talking in childhood ($r = .50$) and adulthood ($r = .43$). The estimated shared genetic effects were 26% for sleep talking and nightmares. Further, the authors found significant stability in the presence of parasomnias from childhood to adulthood ($r = 0.71$). At this time, it is unclear if someone who has a genetic predisposition to idiopathic nightmares is also more likely to develop post-trauma nightmares.

No demographic variables have been linked to a heightened risk of experiencing nightmares, with the exception of gender. As with PTSD, it appears that women are more likely to report dreams with negative emotions (e.g., Opalic, 2000) and to have problems with nightmares (e.g., Nguyen, Madrid, Marquez, & Hicks, 2002; although see Chivers & Blagrove, 1999). This may not be the case in childhood. Nielsen and colleagues (2000) found that, while no differences exist between boys and girls in their childhood nightmare experiences, a gender difference emerges between ages 13 and 16. In the epidemiologic study conducted by Hublin and colleagues (1999), they found that women had 10% higher rates of nightmares in childhood and 25% higher rates in adulthood. They also found a slightly higher stability rate of nightmares in women from childhood to adulthood (Hublin, Kaprio, Partinen, and Koskenvuo, 1999). These findings suggest that women may be more vulnerable to developing these difficulties posttrauma.

Numerous studies have investigated the association between nightmares and various personality traits and psychopathology. While this relationship remains unclear, there is some evidence that for some people, frequent nightmares may be related to particular personality traits. Hartmann, Russ, van der Kolk, Falke, and Oldfield (1981) investigated the personality characteristics of 38 individuals reporting nightmares at least once per week. All participants reported that the nightmares be-gan in childhood or adolescence. Overall, the authors found significant psychopathology as well as creativity in their sample. Specifically, 4 met criteria for schizophrenia, 9 for borderline personality disorder, and 6 for schizotypal personality. Further, 4 participants reported mental-health-related hospitalizations, 29 reported seeking psychotherapy, and 7 at-tempted suicide while 15 "seriously considered suicide" (p. 795). The authors note that most of the participants described themselves as "un-usually sensitive since childhood" (p. 795) and reported considerable familial mental illness. Finally, most participants had what the authors describe as "somewhat unusual occupations and lifestyles" (p. 795) typi-cally associated with the arts.

The above findings related to the personality characteristics, height-ened sensitivity, and lifestyles constitute Hartmann's notion of "thin boundaries" (i.e., open-mindedness, sensitivity, vulnerability, creativity, and artistic ability). This concept was evaluated and supported in sev-eral studies (e.g., Levin, Galin, & Zywiak, 1991; Pietrowsky & Köthe, 2003; although see Hartmann, 1989; Spadafora & Hunt, 1990). Having a type-A personality was also linked to the experience of idiopathic and post-trauma nightmares and disturbing dreams in college undergraduates (Tan & Hicks, 1995). Tan and Hicks suggest that type-A individuals are less capable of handling stress in waking life, and the disturbing dreams may indicate an attempt to cope with the stress. Other personality char-acteristics associated with nightmares include creativity (e.g., Hartmann, Russ, Oldfield, Sivan, & Cooper, 1987; although see Chivers & Blagrove, 1999; Levin et al., 1991), neuroticism (Berquier & Ashton, 1992; Kales et al., 1980; Zadra & Donderi, 2000; although see Chivers & Blagrove, 1999; Hartmann et al., 1981; Hartmann et al., 1987), lower ego strength (Hersen, 1971), and trait anxiety (e.g., Zadra & Donderi, 2000; Levin & Fireman, 2002b; although see Wood & Bootzin, 1990; Belicki, 1992). Nielsen and Zadra (2005) suggest that these associations may reflect other mediating factors including chronicity, distress, and coping style. Most of the studies discussed above were conducted primarily with people suffer-ing idiopathic nightmares, or unspecified nightmares. It is unclear to what extent personality factors may be associated with post-trauma nightmares.

Another predisposing condition for nightmares, similar to insomnia, may be arousability (Coren, 1988; Morin, 1993). Arousability may mani-fest through cognitive, behavioral, or physiological channels, any of which may interfere with sleep (Coren, 1988). Arousability may be related to other predisposing conditions noted in the literature. For example, as

Morin (1993) notes, arousability characterizes a number of other disorders, including mood disorders and anxiety disorders. Higher levels of anxiety are often reported by nightmare sufferers (Dunn & Barrett, 1988; Haynes & Mooney, 1975; Levin & Fireman, 2002b; Nguyen et al., 2002; Nielsen et al., 2000; Zadra & Donderi, 2000), although the temporal relationship of anxiety and nightmares is not clearly understood. Higher arousability and anxiety may increase an individual's vulnerability to difficulty falling asleep, nighttime awakenings, difficulty returning to sleep, being a light sleeper, and experiencing negative imagery in sleep. In support of this association, research finds that pretrauma nightmares and sleep disturbances are associated with greater problems in these areas posttrauma (e.g., Mellman, David, Kulick-Bell, Hebding, & Nolan, 1995). If arousability was a contributor to pretrauma sleep and nightmare problems, it may serve as a vulnerability factor for sleep and nightmare problems posttrauma.

Arousability may also be related to particular personality traits found to be associated with frequent nightmares. For example, Hartmann's notion of thin boundaries (1998b) suggests that certain individuals may be especially sensitive, such that circumstances more easily affect them, perhaps in both positive and negative ways. These individuals tend to be less guarded and more vulnerable to the daily stressors that individuals with thicker boundaries may not notice or pay much heed to. Disorders that are associated with thin boundaries and nightmares include schizotypal, borderline, schizoid, and schizophrenia (e.g., Hartmann et al., 1987; van der Kolk & Goldberg, 1983; van der Kolk, Blitz, Burr, Sherry, & Hartmann, 1984). Again, the temporal nature of these associations is unclear. Studies have found that these disorders are associated with nightmare experiences, and there is some evidence to suggest that frequent nightmares may predate the onset of the disorders (Hartmann, Mitchell, Brune, & Greenwald, 1984). Studies have also found that nightmare distress may be a better predictor of pathology than nightmare frequency (e.g., Levin & Fireman, 2002a; Schredl, 2003). Research is needed to determine whether such disorders in the presence of a traumatic event are associated with an increased risk of post-trauma nightmares.

Pretrauma coping styles may influence the manner in which one handles a traumatic event. The role of avoidance in maintaining posttrauma difficulties over time is well documented. Preexisting avoidant coping styles may be associated with heightened avoidance following a traumatic event, subsequently maintaining problems (including nightmares) over time. To date, few studies have examined the relationship between coping styles and idiopathic nightmares, and no studies were found that examined pretrauma coping styles and post-trauma nightmares.

The factors identified above were, for the most part, identified as salient for frequent nightmare sufferers. Currently there is little prospective data to draw on, so issues of causality cannot be ascertained. Indeed, it may be that having frequent nightmares may increase an individual's arousability and vulnerability to the associated factors. There may also be a third variable we have not considered. Further, most of this work was conducted with persons suffering from lifelong idiopathic nightmares. More research is needed to determine whether persons with these predisposing conditions may also be more vulnerable to experiencing post-trauma nightmares. Evidence from trauma literature outlined in chapter 1 also identifies variables that may predispose individuals to a vulnerability to PTSD; it is unclear if these variables also predispose individuals specifically to nightmares.

Precipitating Factors

Experiencing a stressful or traumatic event is often associated with the initiation or exacerbation of nightmares and is the obvious precipitant for post-trauma nightmares. However, nightmares do not materialize for everyone who experiences a traumatic event, and some individuals may experience nightmares without necessarily experiencing a trauma or high levels of stress. In addition to predisposing factors, there may be factors associated with the trauma itself, peritraumatic reactions, or immediate posttrauma reactions that heighten the risk for experiencing nightmares. To date, little empirical work has been done in this area.

A heightened risk for development of nightmares may be related to the nature of the traumatic event. Future research efforts may draw on the broader PTSD literature and determine whether identified risk factors for PTSD are also risk factors specifically for post-trauma nightmares. One area in which there is some preliminary evidence specific to nightmares is the type of traumatic event. In a general population study, Ohayon and Shapiro (2000) examined the relationship between type of trauma and sleep disturbances, including nightmares. Results indicated that being a victim of aggression increased the risk of having nightmares (OR = 2.4). As reported in chapter 1, assaultive victimization was also found to increase risk for PTSD (Breslau et al., 1998). Some have theorized that traumas that are in some way related to night, sleep, or the bedroom environment may be more likely to result in sleep and nightmare problems due to conditioning. Zayfert and DeViva (2004) found that individuals who continued to experience insomnia following successful treatment of their PTSD symptoms were more likely to have experienced a trauma that was in some way related to sleep (e.g., it happened in a bed or at night). This needs to be further examined to determine possible relationships to the experience of nightmares. One study found that combat exposure was strongly correlated with frequency of nightmares, but less so for problems falling asleep, and even less so for staying asleep (Neylan et al., 1998). Van der Kolk, Blitz, Burr, Sherry, and Hartmann (1981) examined self-reported nightmare experiences from 816 combat veterans and 716 noncombat veterans. Overall, 30% of the sample reported nightmares at least once per month. Compared to the noncombat veterans, combat veterans reported more frequent nightmares, and the content was more likely to include combat experiences. They also reported an older age of onset of nightmares and fewer family members with nightmare experiences.

Associated aspects of the trauma may also be related to increased risk for nightmares. For example, Hartmann and colleagues (1984) evaluated Vietnam veterans and found that those reporting post-trauma nightmares were younger, less educated, and more likely to be emotionally involved with a close buddy who was killed or injured, compared to those who did not have nightmares. The authors suggest that those individuals without nightmares had purposely decided not to get emotionally involved with fellow soldiers, which may have served to make them less vulnerable. Younger age at the time of a traumatic event was also found to be a risk factor for PTSD (e.g., Norris, 1992).

Physical health problems (e.g., fever) and certain medications and substances have been related to the experience of nightmares. For example, nightmares may be induced by substances (e.g., stimulants, such as cocaine or amphetamines), or certain medications (e.g., dopaminergic agonists, beta-adrenergic antagonists, alpha agonists, and other antihypertensive medications). Additionally, withdrawal from antidepressants or alcohol can be associated with experience of nightmares (APA, 2000). If these occur following a traumatic event, they could potentially spur nightmares and start a spiral of decompensation. Research will need to determine if certain health problems and medications in the face of traumatic events increase the risk for nightmares.

Research does find that acute sleep and nightmare problems in the immediate aftermath of a traumatic event heighten risk for long-term problems (see Koren, Arnon, Lavie, & Klein, 2002). While more research is needed to determine the exact nature of this association, it may speak to the importance of implementing treatments directed at nightmares and sleep problems early on following the traumatic event for those who report such difficulties. Research should also determine whether a brief treatment directed at nightmares is sufficient to stem the tide of long-term problems or if nightmare-specific interventions should be combined with other early interventions that target PTSD more broadly.

Perpetuating Factors

While many people report nightmares and sleep disturbance in the acute period following a traumatic event, this is a transient response for the majority of these individuals. For a significant minority of individuals, however, these problems continue. A variety of cognitive, behavioral, and physiological factors likely contributes to the perpetuation of nightmares and sleep problems over time. As suggested by Krakow and Zadra (2006), what initiates nightmares may not be what maintains them. What starts off as a transient response to a traumatic event may continue to evolve via different mechanisms, becoming a learned condition. These mechanisms may prove to be the necessary targets of treatments for chronic nightmare problems. We next outline possible perpetuating factors through physiological, cognitive, and behavioral channels.

Physiological Channel

The "mind-body" problem has been debated since before Aristotle. Are the mind and body separate? If so, how do they impact each other? If not, where does one end and the other begin? This issue has manifested in the study of dreams and nightmares. How do the mechanisms active in the brain during sleep impact the cognitive, behavioral, and affective components we are aware of? How do our thoughts, feelings, and behaviors during the day impact our dreams/nightmares at night? Biological studies in this area have come to fruition in the past 15 years, but most studies have focused on PTSD broadly, and few have targeted post-trauma nightmares in particular; as such, many of the issues are not specific to nightmares, but are extrapolated.

The sympathetic nervous system responds to stressors and traumatic events with a flight or fight response, which at one time was very adaptive. It helped increase the chance for survival of our ancestors, who faced real life-threatening situations to a far greater extent than we do today. In today's world, these responses are not appropriate for the kinds of stressors that are most troublesome and prevalent—psychological and psychosocial stressors. The physiological changes that accompany stressors—particularly chronic stressors—have significant impact on the body and are responsible for many life-threatening conditions. Hyperarousal or hypervigilance may be expressed through difficulty going to sleep and carry over into sleep time through increased awakenings and increased body movement. Although asleep, individuals may still experience the sense that they are in danger and need to be alert. In fact, several of our participants reported doing "checks" of the locks on doors and windows several times before going to bed and upon awakening from hearing any small noise in the house.

Panic symptoms upon waking from a nightmare are common. The increased arousal evident in these symptoms makes it difficult to return to sleep. The physiological symptoms may also serve as cues for physiological effects of the trauma itself, further perpetuating the arousal and anxiety (Falsetti, Resnick, & Davis, 2005). Movements during sleep are likely to stem from hyperarousal and the experience of nightmares and lead to increased awakenings.

Sleep deprivation, resulting from significant disruptions in sleep related to nightmares, can have significant and sometimes debilitating effects, including confusion, memory loss, irritability, excessive daytime somnolence, performance impairment, difficulties engaging in creative thinking, lowered response inhibition, and emotional highs and lows (e.g., Ford & Kamerow, 1989; Morin, 1993). So, much of the impairment observed in people suffering with PTSD—irritability, confusion, decreased ability to concentrate, anxiety—may be in part attributable to the impact of reduced quality and quantity of sleep (Mellman, 1997). The combination of insomnia and nightmares is likely to amplify the problems in sleep structure, including enhancing the likelihood of developing sleep disordered breathing and significantly increasing negative daytime effects (Krakow, 2004).

Epidemiological studies also find that sleep disturbances, particularly insomnia, are associated with mental health disorders, including depression and anxiety disorders, and their remission may reduce the risk for such disorders (Ford & Kamerow, 1989). A recent study using functional magnetic resonance imaging has found that sleep deprivation negatively impacts systems that modulate brain response (i.e., greater extent of amygdala response and greater amygdala volume activated) to negative aversive stimuli (Yoo, Gujar, Hu, Jolesz, & Walker, 2007). Further, sleep deprivation resulted in weaker connectivity between the amygdala and the medial-prefrontal cortex, indicating a disruption in affective processing that is related to depressive symptoms.

The arousability that may serve as a predisposing condition may also exacerbate and extend difficulties following a traumatic event. Increased daytime arousal, memories of the nightmare's content, and possible memories of the trauma likely lead to increased distress. Increased physiological arousal close to bedtime may be a continuation of daytime arousal and may be heightened by anticipatory anxiety. Anticipatory anxiety is outlined below, under "Cognitive Channel."

Dysfunction of other physiological systems, including the hypothalamic-pituitary-adrenal axis, may play a role. Specifically, norepinephrine levels, which typically decline at night, have been found to remain at high levels in people with sleep disturbances posttrauma (e.g., Mellman, Kumar, Kulick-Bell, Kumar, & Nolan, 1995). REM sleep disruption (discussed in detail above) is associated with heightened arousal and is also a likely contributor to maintaining sleep problems over time. For more information on the neurobiological dysfunction of sleep following trauma, readers are referred to Woodward (1995) and Mellman (2000).

Cognitive Channel

There are several ways in which disruptions in cognitions or cognitive processes may enhance the likelihood of experiencing nightmares. Chronic nightmare sufferers may develop maladaptive schema (e.g., sleep is dangerous) in response to the nightmares that persist long after the initial trauma has passed, and these schema may play a role in maintaining nightmares over time through subsequent attempts to avoid sleep. Other distorted cognitions (inaccurate, maladaptive ways of thinking) may also fuel negative emotions. For example, instead of telling themselves, "I'm having some difficulty dealing with this," individuals suffering chronic sleep problems may think, "I'm such a loser!" or "I'll never get to sleep—why can't I just get over this?" Such thoughts likely represent various "stuck points" associated with trauma, as described in chapter 1 (e.g., powerlessness/control, trust, intimacy, esteem, and safety). These schema and negative self-talk may increase the negative emotionality an individual experiences prior to falling asleep, extending the time to fall asleep and increasing the chance of experiencing a nightmare.

Broomfield, Gumley, and Espie (2005) describe the role of various cognitive processes in insomnia that may also inform our understanding of nightmares, including attentional bias. Sleep is an essential component of living; thus, insomnia may be perceived as a threat to an individual's survival. Sleep cues and the associated conditioned arousal may be perceived as threat cues, further increasing an individual's arousal, therein making sleep less likely. The same processes may also be evident for chronic nightmare sufferers in that sleep-related cues may be conditioned threat cues due to fears of having nightmares. These cues may increase the level of arousal and anticipatory anxiety, subsequently increasing the chance for a nightmare to occur.

Harvey (2002) also suggests that worry related to the loss of sleep may increase an individual's selective attention to these threat cues, thereby maintaining the problem. Harvey (2000) evaluated cognitions prior to sleep in a sample of individuals with insomnia and "good sleepers." She found that cognitions in individuals with insomnia focused more on various worries and problem-solving and attended to external cues (e.g., listening to noises in the house). Good sleepers reported not focusing on anything in particular. Few studies have explored specific presleep cognitions in chronic trauma-related nightmare sufferers, so it is unknown if this might be part of the structure maintaining nightmares over time. Harvey, Jones, and Schmidt (2003) conjecture, however, that "it is possible that for PTSD patients, the presleep period constitutes a specific inactive time when it is more difficult to adopt avoidance strategies, resulting in free-flowing intrusions. Intrusions are often accompanied by a sense of current threat as well as symptoms of arousal, anxiety, and other emotional responses (Ehlers & Clark, 2000), all of which are likely to prolong sleep-onset latency and promote fear of sleep" (p. 400). Indeed, Horowitz et al. (1980) found that 51% of veterans studied reported having presleep intrusive thoughts.

Others have also suggested that sleep-onset insomnia may be driven by the fear associated with anticipating nightmares (e.g., Neylan et al., 1998) and that anxiety experienced around sleep time may serve as a defense against falling asleep and possibly having a nightmare (Krakow, Melendrez, Pedersen, et al., 2001). Neylan and colleagues (1998) found that fear of going to sleep was significantly correlated with experiencing nightmares. The authors suggest that "sleep onset insomnia in PTSD subjects is driven predominantly by sleep phobia resulting from the experience of frequent nightmares" (p. 932). Presleep fear may also represent a fear of vulnerability that naturally occurs during sleep (e.g., Freed, Craske, & Greher, 1999). Numerous studies have found that people who suffer from nightmares experience increased fear about going to sleep in anticipation of having a nightmare. In a previous study (Davis, Byrd, Rhudy, & Wright, 2007), we found that nightmare frequency, but not severity, was predictive of fear of going to sleep after controlling for non-sleep-related PTSD symptoms.

An intriguing question that has not been studied extensively is the possible relationship of fear of sleep and specific trauma-related stimuli (e.g., sexual abuse occurring in a bed), distinct from the fear of having a nightmare (Freed et al., 1999). In an inpatient sample of women, Allen et al. (2000) found correlations between sexual abuse and phobic sleep disturbances and between physical abuse and intrusive sleep disturbances, suggesting more nuanced relationships between particular types of trauma and types of sleep disturbance.

Racing thoughts (cognitive arousal) may lead to, be a consequence of, or interact with physiological arousal. At this point, the extent to which physiological arousal is related to nightmares is unclear. The physiological arousal that stems from feeling the need to always be on guard and alert may increase the level of cognitive activity and may increase the degree of negativity of the content and affect associated with the cognitions. In studies of insomnia and sleep disturbances, cognitive arousal (worry, intrusive thoughts) shows greater association with sleep complaints than physiological arousal (Coren, 1988; Nicassio, Mendlowitz, Fussell, & Petras, 1985). A study by Lichstein and Rosenthal (1980) asked insomniacs whether they attributed their poor sleep to cognitive arousal, somatic arousal, both, or neither. Participants were also asked to rate the disturbance of both cognitive and somatic arousal. The results indicated that over half of insomniacs attributed their sleep difficulties primarily to cognitive arousal, while only 5% attributed their problem primarily to somatic arousal, 35% reported both, and 5% reported neither. In terms of disturbance, cognitive arousal was rated as more troubling than somatic arousal. Additionally, there is some evidence (see chapter 10) that cognitive strategies are more efficacious than somatic strategies in reducing sleep-onset latency. To what degree these factors may hold true for chronic post-trauma nightmares is currently unknown.

As suggested by Harvey, Jones, and Schmidt (2003), chronic nightmare sufferers may also misperceive the quality and quantity of sleep they achieve, and their distorted cognitions may be reflected in this misperception. This misperception is commonly seen in insomniacs and is thought to play a significant role in maintaining insomnia over time. Morin, Blais, and Savard (2002) evaluated change of dysfunctional attitudes and beliefs about sleep after treatment for insomnia. The treatments that were compared included cognitive behavioral therapy (CBT), pharmacotherapy, combined CBT and pharmacotherapy, and a pill placebo condition. Results indicated that although all active treatments resulted in increased sleep efficiency, dysfunctional attitudes and beliefs decreased from pre- to posttreatment only for CBT and the combined treatment. Further, posttreatment levels of dysfunctional attitudes and beliefs were associated with maintenance of treatment gains at follow-up, suggesting the importance of addressing cognitive distortions in treatment for insomnia. It remains to be seen what role addressing cognitive distortions may play in treating chronic post-trauma nightmares, although many of the more successful treatments outlined in chapter 5 incorporate cognitive restructuring components.

Finally, many victims of trauma perceive that they had little or no control over what happened to them during the trauma—and rightly so. The problem is that this line of thinking continues, and clinically we observe that people eventually begin to believe that they do not have control over much in their lives. Often, their emotions will be somewhat dysregulated, and they are not sure how to control or modulate them. The fear of loss of control may be a central component of posttrauma difficulties for many people. This fear and the sense of vulnerability may intensify when the time to sleep approaches. Most of us believe that we have little control over what happens when we are sleeping. For someone who needs to be vigilant and on guard, this increased sense of vulnerability through being unaware during sleep may be overwhelming (Craske & Rowe, 1997). Indeed, fear of lack of control during sleep combined with a general notion of not having much power or control in other areas of life, plus the strong desire to avoid, may result in people who kind of "give up" in terms of their nightmares (Krakow & Zadra, 2006). They may not mention the nightmares to professionals or seek treatment for them, because they truly believe that nothing can be done. They may also believe that the nightmares are not going to go away until they are able to process the trauma as a whole (Krakow & Zadra, 2006). Indeed, the notion that nightmares may be controlled was almost uniformly surprising to participants in our studies. Thus, mastery via the process of rescription, or successfully exposing themselves to the nightmare, may be a primary impetus to change in treatments of nightmares (see chapters 5 and 10).

Behavioral Channel

The behavioral reactions to trauma in general primarily involve avoidance mechanisms. Avoidance is part of posttraumatic stress disorder and may be initially adaptive. If a woman were raped by an acquaintance, it would make sense for her to then stay away from that person. The problem that develops, however, is that fear is often generalized to things/people/situations that are not dangerous (see chapter 1). Avoidance thus serves to maintain problems over time (Schnider, Elhai, & Gray, 2007; Ullman, Townsend, Filipas, & Starzynski, 2007). For example, a rape victim may start to fear and avoid all men, not just the particular man who committed the rape. Generalized avoidance results in restrictions in people's lives, maintains hypervigilance, and does not allow for corrective emotional experiences. Avoidance may also play a role in maintaining nightmares. During the day, people may be distressed because of a nightmare the night before and may avoid thinking about the nightmare's content. This prohibits the opportunity to think through the nightmare, to face it, and to try to really understand what it means or to reframe it.

Ziarnowski and Broida (1984) found that "some veterans even report conscious and explicit avoidance of sleep, solely to avoid the nightmares. Particularly distressing, however, is the unpredictability of their occurrence" (p. 63). The manner in which people try to avoid sleep or to avoid the fear and anticipatory anxiety that precedes sleep varies widely. Avoidance may include using substances (e.g., alcohol, sleeping pills) at night to get to sleep; watching television in bed to try to forget about the nightmares; and avoiding situations, places, or people that serve as reminders of the nightmares and traumatic event. In the extreme, avoidance may involve attempts to avoid sleep to the point of utter exhaustion. One client in our study reported that she would work and clean her house every night until she was totally exhausted and could lie down and fall asleep immediately. These tactics may be perceived as safety behaviors, behaviors that are designed to decrease the likelihood of having a nightmare through restricting the amount of sleep or trying to achieve a rapid entry to sleep, thereby restricting dream sleep.

The ways in which people avoid sleep or try to enhance sleep may work initially but are unlikely to continue working long-term. One of the most common means of avoidance we find in our own studies is drinking alcohol to fall asleep faster. Part of our psychoeducation is informing participants that, while alcohol may initially assist them in falling asleep faster, it actually may increase the chance of sleep disturbance and nightmares later in the sleep cycle. People who drink alcohol prior to going to sleep will have greater slow-wave sleep in the initial part of the night and a rebound of REM exceeding the normal lengthening of REM during the later half of the night. Also, the combined effects of alcohol and sleep deprivation are likely to increase poor function and sleepiness the following day. In addition, tolerance develops to the soporific effects of alcohol, requiring more use over time and thus further exacerbating the effects (for a review, see Roehrs & Roth, 2001).

Avoidance techniques may eventually become a regular part of an individual's sleep hygiene, more a habit than a symptom (e.g., Krakow, Johnston, et al., 2001). So, it is likely that instead of diminishing nightmares, avoidance may play a key role in maintaining nightmares over time. For example, although not specific to nightmares, Lawrence, Fauerbach, and Munster (1996) evaluated a sample of burn injury patients and found that avoidance at discharge predicted intrusive thoughts at the 4-month follow-up, after initial intrusive symptoms were controlled. When controlling for avoidance at discharge, intrusive thoughts at discharge were not associated with intrusive thoughts at the 4-month follow-up.

The Vicious Cycle. Thus, it appears that, regardless of how the initial impetus for the development of the nightmare is conceptualized, it is a vicious cycle that maintains the problem over time. Nightmares are characterized as terrifying, and people often awake experiencing high distress, fear, and panic symptoms (e.g., racing heart, sweating, trembling). These physiological responses, along with the dream content, may serve as trauma cues that further heighten the level of arousal and distress, perhaps especially for those individuals with PTSD. Due to the nightmares, survivors do not get the quality or quantity of sleep that they need. After waking from a nightmare, they may fear returning to sleep and will stay awake or will require some length of time for the cognitive and physiological arousal to decrease, decreasing quantity of sleep and perhaps resulting in sleep deprivation. The confusion, lack of concentration, and emotional lability associated with sleep deprivation, in addition to thoughts of the nightmare (and perhaps the trauma itself), lead to increased daytime distress and arousal. Avoidance coping may be employed to handle the distress. Avoiding thinking about the nightmare's content does not allow for the opportunity to process it and attempt to understand what it means; without the opportunity to assimilate the nightmare, it is likely to be maintained. By the time evening approaches, individuals may experience anticipatory anxiety—fearful that they will have another nightmare—feel unsafe, and believe they have no control over the nightmares. This may be exacerbated by distorted cognitions and negative self-talk, such as, "Why can't I get over this?" or "I'm never going to be able to sleep peacefully," or "Why am I powerless to stop this?" The cognitive arousal increases physiological arousal. Individuals may engage in various learned safety behaviors or maladaptive sleep habits to avoid sleep or to try to ensure a deep sleep without nightmares. Unfortunately, the increased arousal, distress, and safety behaviors, while sometimes effective in the short term, may actually increase the chance of having another nightmare.

The sense of loss of control and mental defeat associated with trauma may also impact seeking help for the nightmares and sleep problems. Most people think that they have little control over what happens during sleep. They may not mention them or seek treatment for them because they truly believe that nothing can be done. Alternatively they may believe that the nightmares are not going to go away until they are able to process the trauma as a whole—in other words, "once I deal with what happened to me, the nightmares will go away." And without treatment, the vicious cycle continues.

SUMMARY

The conceptualization outlined above is largely speculative in nature. Much research is needed to determine the legitimacy of factors within each component of the model specific to post-trauma nightmares. It is inevitable that, as research continues, the model will change; we hope, however, that this may be a launching point for future research efforts.

4

Assessment of Trauma, Nightmares, and Sleep Problems

Pruiksma and Davis

The focus of this chapter is methods of assessing trauma, PTSD, sleep, and nightmares. Here we highlight the importance of assessment in treating nightmares; considerations for assessment; methods of assessment and their application to assessing sleep problems; and specific assessments for trauma, PTSD, sleep, and nightmares.

As with any pathology, individuals reporting nightmares are likely to be vastly different across numerous variables, including associated symptoms, coping skills, social support, resources, previous trauma history, and previous and current psychopathology, to name a few. For example, nightmares may constitute a disorder in and of themselves, be an associated symptom of an anxiety or mood disorder, or be related to the initiation of or withdrawal from medications or illicit drugs. While we know that brief cognitive behavioral treatments are effective for individuals with chronic nightmares, it remains unclear who is most and least likely to benefit, although it is safe to say that a "one size fits all" approach is unwarranted and may result in more harm than good. Thus, a comprehensive assessment is a crucial first step in determining the appropriate treatment plan.

SCREENING CONSIDERATIONS

In clinical practice, unless sleep disorders are a specialty, chances are that therapists would already be seeing clients for another reason and would elect to administer ERRT if complaints of nightmares were identified as a prominent problem. Therefore, screening considerations may vary considerably, depending on whether the client is new or ongoing. For the purposes of our research studies, and to increase the generalizability of our findings, we used only a few exclusionary criteria. These included apparent psychosis or mental retardation, being under the age of 18, active suicidality or recent parasuicidal behaviors, or current drug/alcohol dependence. These criteria were based on practical aspects of the research setting and sound clinical practice (see chapter 9 for additional information on the exclusion criteria). While ERRT may have utility with clients who meet some of these criteria, it has not yet been evaluated as such.

Despite centuries of interest and research, investigators continue to detangle questions regarding the processes and functions of sleep (Harvey, Jones, & Schmidt, 2003; Vgontzas & Kales, 1999). Subsequently, the assessment of sleep and related disorders, such as chronic nightmares, is still an area of growth and refinement. The *DSM-IV-TR* (APA, 2000) differentiates between primary sleep disorders and sleep disorders associated with other issues, such as sleep disorders related to another mental disorder, sleep disorders due to a general medical condition, and substance-induced sleep disorders. Furthermore, the *International Classification of Sleep Disorders, Revised: Diagnostic and Coding Manual* (American Sleep Disorders Association [ASDA], 2001) includes a major category for sleep disorders associated with medical or psychiatric disorders in addition to the categories of dyssomnias and parasomnias. According to *DSM-IV-TR*, the mental disorders most frequently associated with sleep disorders are mood disorders and anxiety disorders (APA, 2000), and it is presumed that "the pathophysiological mechanisms responsible for the mental disorder also affect sleep-wake regulation" (p. 597).

Nightmares are associated with PTSD and other anxiety disorders (e.g., generalized anxiety disorder), delirium, schizophrenia, mood disorders (e.g., depression, mania, and seasonal affective disorder), adjustment disorders, and personality disorders (APA, 2000; Bootzin, Manber, Loewy, Kuo, & Franzen, 2004). The *DSM-IV-TR* (APA, 2000) includes the diagnoses of nightmare disorder and sleep terror disorder within the parasomnia category. Nightmares and sleep terrors (also referred to as "night terrors") are often confused and the terms often used interchangeably. However, there are important differences, as described in chapter 2, and these parasomnias should be distinguished during the assessment to establish an appropriate treatment plan.

ASSESSMENT METHODS

There are several approaches to assessing sleep and related problems. Objective assessment of sleep includes sleep lab assessments (i.e., polysomnography) and actigraphy, and subjective assessment includes retrospective self-report questionnaires, prospective sleep diaries or logs, and semistructured interviews. Other methods (not included in this review) involve regular observations by nurses in hospitals and assessments completed by bed partners. In this section, we discuss various methods for assessing sleep and nightmares and evaluate the advantages and disadvantages of each. In subsequent sections, we describe specific instruments for assessing trauma, PTSD, sleep, and nightmares.

Sleep Lab Assessments

Polysomnography is considered to be the "gold standard" for assessing sleep (Harvey et al., 2003) and certain sleep disorders, such as sleep apnea (Bastien, Vallières, & Morin, 2001). Polysomnography (PSG) involves the placement of electrodes on the scalp, muscles, and eyes to monitor "electrical brain activity (electroencephalogram, EEG), eye movement (electro-oculogram, EOG), and muscle tone (electromyogram, EMG)" (Harvey et al., 2003, p. 379). Patterns in electrical activity differentiate the stages of sleep, and the output is utilized in studying sleep patterns of various sleep disorders (Bear, Connors, & Paradiso, 2006). Smith, Nowakowski, Soeffing, Orff, and Perlis (2003) provide a detailed description of PSG, and the American Academy of Sleep Medicine maintains detailed practice parameters for appropriate usage of PSG (Kushida et al., 2005).

PSG is painless and provides accurate data regarding brain wave activity and other physiological changes during the night. These measurements have established objective, physiological definitions of sleep onset and the stages of sleep (Harvey et al., 2003) and are often utilized to provide evidence for psychometric validation of other sleep measures, such as the Pittsburgh Sleep Quality Index (Buysee, Reynolds, Monk, Berman, & Kupfer, 1989), discussed below.

However, there are limitations associated with sleep lab assessments (Spoormaker, Schredl, & van den Bout, 2006). PSG is not routinely indicated for all sleep disorders, including "cases of typical, uncomplicated, and noninjurious parasomnias when the diagnosis is clearly delineated" (Kushida et al., 2005, p. 499). Also, PSG occurs in a very different environment from the examinee's normal sleep situation. The effects of this difference are not completely understood in trauma-exposed persons. The term *first-night effects* refers to the situation in which sleep is more disturbed on the first night of an assessment relative to subsequent nights (Woodward, Bliwise, Friedman, & Gusman, 1996). Often times, results from the first night are discarded to reduce the effects of the sleep lab situation. However, individuals in inpatient settings, specifically individuals with PTSD or depression, may not exhibit first-night effects as they are already removed from their typical sleep environment. Further, trauma-exposed persons may actually obtain better sleep in a laboratory setting, away from the conditioned cues of poor sleep in their own bedroom environment (Woodward et al., 1996). Additionally, nightmares may not be observed over the span of a few nights in the sleep lab (Bootzin et al., 2004; Germain & Nielsen, 2003a; Woodward et al., 1996). Spoormaker and colleagues (2006) suggest that, when utilizing sleep labs for assessing nightmares, it may be best to conduct recordings for a longer period of time to allow for adjustment to the setting. However, sleep lab assessments are relatively expensive and require a substantial amount of time and overnight monitoring. Due to these complications, data cannot typically be gathered over an extended period, limiting the practicality of PSG for nightmare assessment. In-home polysomnography is a developing area that could potentially prove useful in overcoming these limitations (Germain, Hall, Shear, Nofzinger & Buysse, 2006).

Actigraphy

As an alternative to sleep lab assessments, actigraph devices are increasingly utilized for sleep assessment (Littner et al., 2003). These devices are most appropriate when the goal of the assessment is to monitor the distribution of sleep and wakefulness throughout the night (e.g., sleep latency, time awake after sleep onset, and total sleep time; Bootzin et al., 2004). Actigraph measurements are taken based on activity and inactivity throughout the night. Sleep is indicated by absence of movement during the night, and wake periods are indicated by the presence of movement during the night. Actigraphs utilize "accelerometers to detect wrist (alternatively ankle and trunk) movement which is sampled several times a second. These data are stored within the actigraph for up to several weeks" (Littner et al., 2003, p. 338) and subsequently transferred to a computer.

Actigraphy devices are inexpensive relative to PSG (Smith, Nowakowski, Soeffing, Orff, & Perlis, 2003) and also provide objective data over an extended period (weeks or months) as opposed to just a few nights (1 to 3 nights) in the sleep lab. Actigraphy can also be used throughout the day to monitor rest-activity patterns. Actigraphy is unobtrusive and does not disturb the examinee's natural environment. Minimal effort is required on the part of examinees, which enhances compliance (Smith et al., 2003).

However, the American Academy of Sleep Medicine Practice Parameters (Littner et al., 2003) suggests "actigraphy is reliable and valid for detecting sleep in normal, healthy adult populations," but it is not yet "indicated for the *routine* diagnosis, assessment of severity, or management of any of the sleep disorders" (p. 338), including nightmares. Research is needed to establish the reliability and validity of actigraphy in detecting and monitoring examinees with sleep disorders, including nightmares.

Retrospective Self-Report

Self-report assessments are the most widely utilized measure in many areas of psychology (Kazdin, 2003), including nightmare characteristics (Spoormaker et al., 2006). Retrospective self-report assessments measure past sleep experiences, whereas prospective measurements, such as sleep diaries (discussed below), are repeatedly administered over a period of time. Retrospective measures are inexpensive, do not require training, and, most often, are not excessively time consuming.

However, self-report measures are vulnerable to several sources of bias. Smith, Nowakowski, Soeffing, Orff, and Perlis (2003) note that examinees likely rely on several heuristics, such as primacy, recency, and saliency, when asked to estimate typical (or average) sleep experiences. Smith and colleagues explain, "subjects may estimate how they have been sleeping based not on their personal average, but rather on the worst case scenario (saliency), how they slept last night (recency), or how they slept on the first night of the time increment in question (primacy)" (p. 32). Researchers have also noted that individuals with sleep disorders may be especially likely to overestimate or underestimate their sleep (McCall & Edinger, 1992; Trajanovic, Radivojevic, Kaushansky, & Shapiro,

2007). In estimating nightmare frequency, Spoormaker and colleagues (2006) note that retrospective assessment of nightmares may underestimate nightmare frequency (see chapter 2).

Overall, the accuracy of retrospective measures may be questionable. However, retrospective measures are also very valuable and practical instruments. The usefulness of retrospective measures may depend on the purpose of the assessment. For example, Smith and colleagues (2003) suggest retrospective self-report measures are most useful in clinical settings and in between-subject research designs, but they are less useful as pre- and postmeasurements.

Prospective Self-Report

Prospective self-reports, such as sleep diaries and sleep logs, are considered to be the gold standard for assessing nightmare frequency (Robert & Zadra, 2008) and are unique in that the examinee makes frequent recording of specific behaviors or experiences in the span of a recent time frame. In the case of sleep and nightmare assessments, respondents are often required to complete sleep diaries each morning, each night, or both. Sleep diaries and logs may be in the form of checklists or narratives (Robert & Zadra, in press).

Sleep diaries and sleep logs reduce the reference time frame to a manageable span. Examinees are not asked to provide an average or overall estimate of their experiences. Completion of the assessment as behaviors/experiences occur or soon thereafter may reduce the chance that biases or memory distortions will interfere with responses (Spoormaker et al., 2006). Prospective sleep measures also allow for contingency analysis (Smith, Nowakowski, Soeffing, Orff, & Perlis, 2003)—that is, the therapist and client can examine if sleep problems at night are related to certain behaviors during that day, suggesting intervention for modification of that behavior. For example, is drinking alcohol in the evening related to poor sleep quality at night for that individual? These assessments are inexpensive and require no or minimal training.

Whereas prospective sleep diaries and logs may reduce the vulnerability of bias as compared to retrospective self-report measures, accuracy is still questionable. The very act of monitoring a certain behavior may influence the occurrence of that behavior. For example, if clients know they must log their sleep behaviors, they may intentionally, or unintentionally, change certain habits (e.g., taking sleep medications, modify bedtime) to make their results appear better or worse. It has also been suggested that keeping a dream log may increase both dream recall and the actual frequency of dream or nightmare occurrence (Spoormaker et al., 2006). Another concern with sleep logs and diaries is obtaining good compliance from clients, as these assessments require frequent completion (Smith, Nowakowski, Soeffing, Orff, & Perlis, 2003). Clients may not follow directions precisely or may simply forget or refuse to complete the assessments on a regular basis (Bootzin et al., 2004). Individuals may be especially resistant to record a noxious event, such as a nightmare, on a daily basis (e.g., Neidhardt, Krakow, Kellner, & Pathak, 1992).

Semistructured Interviews

Semistructured interviews are typically administered by trained interviewers and are composed of specific questions and ratings for each question. Semistructured interviews ensure that a therapist inquires about a range of relevant issues and allows for clarification and follow-up questioning. This may broaden the scope of information gathered in the assessment period, and the interaction with the client may provide important behavioral and interpersonal information. Structured interviews require training on the part of the therapist, additional psychometric evaluation to determine interrater reliability, and more time to administer than self-reports.

ASSESSMENT INSTRUMENTS

In the previous section, we described various methods for assessing problems. Next we briefly review assessments for trauma and PTSD, and then we describe specific assessments for sleep and nightmares.

Trauma

Given the significant proportion of the population that is exposed to trauma in their lifetime, and the resulting adverse impact, a comprehensive trauma assessment should be standard practice in mental and physical health clinics. While a trauma or its consequences may be the problem that brings individuals to seek services, often people do not disclose trauma unless specifically asked. Even if a client presents with a specific traumatic event, it is important to conduct a thorough assessment to determine lifetime experience with various traumatic events. Numerous studies indicate that experiencing multiple traumas may result in a cumulative negative impact on an individual's functioning (e.g., Cohen, Hien, & Batchelder, 2008; McGuigan & Middlemiss, 2005; Mullen et al., 1996; Wind & Silvern, 1992), and the effect of each trauma should be considered. Further, certain trauma characteristics (e.g., threat of death or physical injury, actual physical injury, frequency, duration) are associated with worse effects and are thus relevant areas for assessment (Halligan & Yehuda, 2000; Kilpatrick, Saunders, Amick-McMullen, Best, Veronen, & Resnick, 1989).

Many interview and self-report measures are currently available to assess traumatic experiences. Gray and Slagle (2006) recently reviewed various instruments available to assess the type and nature of traumatic events. The utility of such instruments for a particular professional will largely depend on the resources (e.g., time, support staff, financial) available. The frequency of use of various instruments to assess trauma exposure and PTSD were recently examined (Elhai, Gray, Kashdan, & Franklin, 2005). Results indicated that the most commonly used measures to assess trauma exposure include the Posttraumatic Stress Diagnostic Scale (Foa, Riggs, Dancu, & Rothbaum, 1993), Life Events Checklist (Gray, Litz, Hsu, & Lombardo, 2004), Detailed Assessment of Posttraumatic Stress (Briere, 2001), and Combat Exposure Scale (Keane, Fairbank, Caddell, Zimering, Taylor, & Mora, 1989).

Posttraumatic Stress Disorder

Mental and physical health problems are often more severe in the presence of PTSD. Numerous therapist-administered interviews and self-report measures are available to assess PTSD symptoms and diagnosis. If time and resources permit, a therapist-administered interview may provide the most valid and reliable information. The CAPS (Blake et al., 1990) is among the most commonly used interview (Elhai et al., 2005) and is largely considered to be the "gold standard" for assessing PTSD. A unique feature about the CAPS is that it was designed to yield both continuous (i.e., severity) and dichotomous (i.e., diagnostic) information. The CAPS assesses the presence and severity of the 17 symptoms of PTSD that comprise the *DSM-IV* diagnosis, associated symptoms, and functional impact of symptoms. The measure assesses past week, past month, and lifetime presence of the disorder. The Structured Clinical Interview for *DSM-IV* (SCID; First, Spitzer, Gibbon, & Williams, 1996) PTSD module assesses the presence or absence of each *DSM-IV* PTSD symptom. Respondents are asked to rate symptoms in terms of their "worst" trauma experience, and symptoms are rated on a 3-point scale (absent/false, subthreshold, threshold/true). The principle limitation of the SCID is its restriction to the presence or absence of symptoms without consideration of the frequency and severity of the symptoms, associated features, or impact of the symptoms.

Due to time and resource constraints, many professionals elect to utilize self-report questionnaires. Elhai and colleagues (2005) determined that the most commonly used self-report measures to assess PTSD symptoms include the Trauma Symptom Inventory (Briere, 1995), PTSD checklist (Weathers, Huska, & Keane, 1991), and the Posttraumatic Stress Diagnostic Scale (PDS; Foa, Riggs, et al., 1993). The Trauma Symptom Inventory (TSI) does not yield a PTSD diagnosis or assess the symptoms directly, but it assesses a broad range of posttrauma problems. The TSI includes 3 validity subscales (Atypical Responses, Response Level, and Inconsistent Response) and 10 clinical scales (Anxious Arousal, Depression, Anger/Irritability, Intrusive Experiences, Defensive Avoidance, Dissociation, Sexual Concerns, Dysfunctional Sexual Behavior, Impaired Self-Reference, and Tension Reduction Behavior). The PTSD Checklist (PCL) has both military and civilian versions, as well as a version designed to assess a single stressful experience. The PCL includes 17 items corresponding to the *DSM-IV* criteria, which are rated on a 5-point scale ranging from 1 (*not at all*) to 5 (*extremely*).

The PDS (Foa, Cashman, Jaycox, & Perry, 1997) includes an assessment of all PTSD criteria and the effects of the symptoms on daily functioning. The PDS yields a total severity score, and a diagnosis may be determined based on criteria met. Another self-report measure is the Modified PTSD Symptom Scale Self-Report (MPSS-SR; Resick, Falsetti, Resnick, & Kilpatrick, 1991). The MPSS-SR is a modification of the PTSD Symptom Scale developed by Foa and colleagues (1993). It was modified to include an assessment of the severity of PTSD symptoms. The MPSS-SR may be used to determine a diagnosis of PTSD.

As stated above, rarely are PTSD symptoms the sole complaint reported by clients. Indeed, numerous studies, including epidemiological studies, find significant comorbidity with PTSD. Among the most common comorbid conditions that are important to assess for are substance use (abuse or dependence), depression, other anxiety disorders or symptoms, problems in interpersonal functioning, and sexual dysfunction (e.g., Kessler et al., 1995). Falsetti (1997) also suggests including assessments of social support, cognitions, and causal attributions and describes various assessment tools for use in these areas.

Sleep

There is a plethora of sleep assessments available. Several researchers have set forth general parameters for assessing sleep. Bootzin and colleagues (2004) suggest using multiple measures in evaluating sleep. Rogers (1997) and Elliott (2001) suggest that a proper examination of sleep should include a comprehensive health history (including history of the current problem), medication history, social history, and family history of sleep problems. Due to the large breadth of assessments available, we will review only a select few. Also, although sleep and nightmares are intimately related, assessments of sleep often do not include thorough evaluations of nightmares. Therefore, in the following review, we highlight those sleep assessments that include items regarding parasomnias and discuss the degree to which nightmares are assessed. The subsequent section reviews assessments that are specific to nightmares.

Devine, Hakim, and Green (2005) conducted a systematic review of sleep outcome measures. The authors propose that sleep dysfunction can be classified into four broad domains: sleep initiation, sleep maintenance, sleep adequacy, and somnolence (daytime sleepiness). The authors identify 22 sleep assessments with content in these four areas and examine the reliability, validity, responsiveness (sensitivity to measure changes in a population over time), and interpretability (understandability of results) according to criteria proposed by the Scientific Advisory Committee of the Medical Outcomes Trust (2002). While none of the instruments met every criteria proposed by the authors, the following measures were determined to be adequate in that they included items measuring the four aspects of sleep: Basic Nordic Sleep Questionnaire (Partinen & Gislason, 1995), Leeds Sleep Evaluation Questionnaire (Parrott & Hindmarch, 1978), Medical Outcome Study—Sleep Problems Measure (Hays & Stewart, 1992), Pittsburgh Sleep Diary (Monk, Reynolds, & Kupfer, 1994), Pittsburgh Sleep Quality Index (Buysse, Reynolds, Monk, Berman, & Kupfer, 1989), Self-Rated Sleep Questionnaire (Morriss et al., 1993; Morriss, Wearden, & Battersby, 1997), and the Sleep Dissatisfaction Questionnaire (Coyle & Watts, 1991). We will describe the three most frequently cited self-report measures that assess the four important domains of sleep identified by Devine and colleagues (2005) and three additional measures not included in their review (i.e., the Pittsburgh Sleep

Quality Index-Addendum [PSQI-A; Germain, Hall, Krakow, Shear, & Bussye, 2005], the Global Sleep Assessment Questionnaire [Roth et al., 2002], and the SLEEP-50 Questionnaire [Spoormaker, Verbeek, van den Bout, & Klip, 2005]).

The Basic Nordic Sleep Questionnaire

The Basic Nordic Sleep Questionnaire (BNSQ; Partinen & Gislason, 1995) was developed in 1988 by the Scandinavian Sleep Research Society to provide a standardized measure of sleep apnea and snoring in order to establish valid comparisons across studies. This assessment consists of 27 items that measure the frequency of symptoms related to sleep apnea and snoring. This measure has been widely utilized, primarily in Nordic countries (Partinen & Gislason, 1995); however it has received inadequate psychometric evaluation (Devine et al., 2005).

The Leeds Sleep Evaluation Questionnaire

The Leeds Sleep Evaluation Questionnaire (Parrott & Hindmarch, 1978) was developed primarily for sleep assessment in studies of hypnotic drugs. The measure consists of 10 items that assess ease of getting to sleep, perceived quality of sleep, ease of awakening from sleep, and early morning behavior after awakening. Validation research has been conducted with this measure, and it has been widely utilized. However, reliability coefficients have not been reported (Devine et al., 2005).

Pittsburgh Sleep Quality Index

Buysse, Reynolds, Monk, Berman, and Kupfer (1989) developed the Pittsburgh Sleep Quality Index specifically for use with clinical populations. The measure consists of 19 items rated on a 5-point scale. These items make up seven component scores: subjective sleep quality, sleep latency, sleep duration, habitual sleep efficiency, sleep disturbances, use of sleeping medication, and daytime dysfunction. The authors report simple scoring instructions and have determined that a cut-off score of 5 distinguishes between "good" and "poor" sleepers. The authors report overall internal reliability of .83, test-retest reliability of .85 for the global index, and test-retest reliabilities ranging from .65 to .84 for the component scores over an average of 28.2 days (range: 1 to 265 days). To determine validity, the authors compared PSQI scores across groups with various problems (e.g., depression, disorders of initiating and maintaining sleep, disorders of excessive somnolence) and a control group, and they compared PSQI scores with polysomnography. The authors conclude that "the validity of the index is supported by its ability to discriminate patients from controls, and, to a more limited degree, by concurrent polysomnographic findings" (p. 201); however, the PSQI is not useful for distinguishing between sleep disorders. The PSQI has been widely used in sleep research studies and clinics and is useful for monitoring changes in sleep quality and for alerting professionals to possible sleep disorders (Buysee, Reynolds, Monk, Berman, & Kupfer, 1989).

Pittsburgh Sleep Quality Index—Addendum

The Pittsburgh Sleep Quality Index-Addendum (PSQI-A; Germain et al., 2005) was developed as an addendum to the Pittsburgh Sleep Quality Index (Buysse, Reynolds, Monk, Berman, & Kupfer, 1989), discussed above, to assess the frequency of disruptive nocturnal behaviors specific to PTSD. The authors suggest the PSQI-A could be utilized as a screening tool to determine if individuals with sleep complaints need to be assessed for PTSD. The PSQI-A consists of seven questions formatted similarly to the items in the PSQI that address "frequency of hot flashes; general nervousness; memories or nightmares of traumatic experience; severe anxiety or panic not related to traumatic memories; bad dreams not related to traumatic memories; episodes of terror or screaming during sleep without fully awakening; and episodes or acting out dreams, such as kicking, punching, running, or screaming" (Germain et al., 2005, p. 235). The PSQI and PSQI-A were administered to 168 women with PTSD and disruptive nocturnal behaviors and a control group of 63 healthy women. Germain and colleagues report internal reliability of 0.85 and convergent validities of 0.53 with the global score on the CAPS (Blake et al., 1990) and 0.51 with the CAPS with sleep items removed. They also report convergent validities of 0.56 with the global score on the PTSD Symptom Scale Interview (PSS-I; Foa, Riggs, et al., 1993) and .49 with the PSS-I with sleep items removed. The authors report that a cutoff score of 4 differentiates between PTSD cases and non-PTSD cases with a sensitivity of 94%, a specificity of 82%, and positive predictive power of 93%.

For the purposes of assessing the frequency of nightmares, the PSQI-A has several limitations. First, the question regarding post-trauma nightmares also asks for the frequency of memories of the trauma. Therefore, an examinee's response may reflect the occurrence of nightmares, memories, or both. Second, the psychometric properties of the PSQI-A have only been evaluated with female sexual assault survivors. Research among other populations is needed.

Global Sleep Assessment Questionnaire

Roth and colleagues (2002) developed the Global Sleep Assessment Questionnaire (GSAQ) to improve upon available measures. Specifically, the authors designed the GSAQ to be a reliable and valid screening tool for distinguishing between the following sleep disorders: insomnia, insomnia associated with a mental disorder, obstructive sleep apnea, restless leg syndrome, periodic limb movement disorder, parasomnias, and shift work sleep disorder. Test-retest was conducted over an average of 12.6 days. Results indicate test-retest reliabilities ranging from .51 (parasomnias) to .92 (shift work sleep disorder) and sensitivities and specificities of 79% and 59% for primary insomnia, 83% and 51% for insomnia associated with a mental disorder, 93% and 58% for obstructive sleep apnea, 93% and 52% for periodic limb movement disorder, and 100% and 49% for parasomnias. Several limitations of this measure are worth mentioning. Although the measure has demonstrated valid assessment of various sleep disorders, this measure does not differentiate parasomnias (i.e., post-trauma nightmares, idiopathic nightmares, and sleep terrors), and the parasomnia group had the lowest test-retest reliability. The authors suggest this low correlation is due to limited variability. Additionally, the sample size of the parasomnia diagnostic group was relatively small compared to other diagnostic groups. Only a few healthy participants were included in the study, so the measure has unknown validity among people without sleep disorders, and the measure lacks questions regarding narcolepsy (Spoormaker et al., 2005).

SLEEP-50 Questionnaire

The SLEEP-50 Questionnaire (Spoormaker et al., 2005) was developed to assess the sleep disorders as listed in the *DSM-IV-TR* (APA, 2000), to distinguish sleep disorders from subclinical sleep complaints, and to assess other factors that influence sleep. The Sleep-50 consists of 50 items scored on a 4-point Likert scale according to the severity of the symptom (1 = *not at all*, 2 = *somewhat*, 3 = *rather much*, 4 = *very much*) for the

4 weeks prior to assessment and 2 additional items assessing overall subjective sleep quality and sleep time. The items make up nine subscales: Sleep Apnea, Insomnia, Narcolepsy, Restless Legs/Periodic Limb Movement, Circadian Rhythm Sleep Disorder, Sleepwalking, Nightmares, Factors Influencing Sleep, and Impact of Sleep Complaints on Daily Functioning. This sleep assessment includes items regarding nightmares but does not require enough information to distinguish between post-trauma and idiopathic nightmares. Some of the items (e.g., "I remember the content of these dreams" and "I can orientate quickly after these dreams" [p. 245]) may assist a therapist in differentiating between nightmares and sleep terrors, but the assessment does not directly differentiate the two parasomnias. The authors report an internal consistency of .85 among a sample of undergraduate college students, an overall test-retest reliability of .78, and scale test-retest reliabilities ranging from .65 (Sleepwalking scale) to .89 (Nightmares) over a 3-week time frame among Master's level graduate students. Construct validity was evaluated via principal component analysis and revealed a "factor structure that closely resembled the originally designed structure" (p. 242). Preliminary analyses were also conducted to evaluate predictive validity. The psychometric components of the SLEEP-50 are preliminary, but the SLEEP-50 is a promising tool for differentiating and diagnosing various sleep disorders.

Modified Daily Sleep Activities Log

Davis, Wright, and Borntrager (2001) utilize the Modified Daily Sleep Activities Log (adapted from Thompson, Hamilton, & West, 1995), which consists of seven dichotomous (yes/no) and Likert-scale questions that address sleep and nightmare experience for each night during treatment. This activity log is simple and short, which increases the likelihood of compliance, and is useful for closely monitoring sleep experience. Davis and colleagues also report convergent validities of 0.82 for nights with nightmares and 0.81 for number of nightmares with the Trauma Related Nightmare Survey.

Pittsburgh Sleep Diary

The Pittsburgh Sleep Diary (Monk et al., 1994) is the only sleep diary identified by Devine and colleagues (2005) to have adequate properties, as described above. The Pittsburgh Sleep Diary consists of components to be completed at bedtime (regarding events of the day) and at wake time (regarding the previous night's sleep). The Pittsburgh Sleep Diary is sensitive to sleep patterns due to weekends, age, gender, personality, and circadian type, and the authors report adequate validity with actigraph measures. The Pittsburgh Sleep Diary is useful in quantifying sleep and wake behaviors and may provide important information with regard to treatment.

Sleep Disorder Questionnaire

The Sleep Disorder Questionnaire (SDQ; Douglas et al., 1994) is a therapist-administered interview consisting of 175 items adapted from Stanford University's Sleep Questionnaire and Assessment of Wakefulness (Guilleminault, 1982). Responses are made on a 5-point scale regarding the 4 weeks prior to assessment. The authors modified the SDQ in order to develop four clinical diagnostic scales to assess sleep apnea, narcolepsy, psychiatric sleep disorder, and periodic limb movement disorder. The psychiatric sleep disorder group consisted of participants diagnosed with schizophrenia and depression. It is unclear whether the participants were screened for other diagnoses, such as PTSD. For the clinical diagnostic scales, the authors report test-retest reliabilities of 0.84 for sleep apnea, 0.75 for narcolepsy, 0.85 for psychiatric sleep disorder, and 0.82 for periodic limb movement disorder over a 4-month time frame. The SDQ has some support as a screening tool for four categories of sleep disorders. However, the authors report an administration time of 30 minutes, which may limit the practicality and utility of the assessment (Spoormaker et al., 2005).

Nightmares

Several assessments of nightmares have been developed. Each targets different characteristics of nightmares. Some pertain to the content of nightmares, whereas others focus on the frequency and severity of nightmares.

Dream Rating Scale

Esposito, Benitz, Barza, and Mellman (1999) developed the Dream Rating Scale (DRS) to conduct content analysis on PTSD dreams in order to delineate characteristics of nightmares in combat veterans with PTSD. After listening to a detailed account of the nightmare, trained assessors rate the dream on a scale from 0 to 4 on various domains. Specifically, the assessment evaluates the degree of similarity between the nightmare and traumatic experience with regard to the setting of the nightmare, characters and objects in the nightmare, degree of overt threat to the dreamer, contemporaneity (i.e., past, present, or future), and degree of distortion from actual or plausible events. Although the authors report respectable reliability (ranging from 0.93 to 0.99), validity measures for the DRS are inadequate, and the DRS has limited clinical utility (Donovan, Padin-Rivera, Chapman, Strauss, & Murray, 2004). The DRS requires substantial training, is time consuming, and does not provide information relevant to evaluation of treatment progress.

Nightmare Distress Scale

The Nightmare Distress Scale (Belicki, 1992) assesses the estimated frequency of nightmares for the year prior to assessment and the degree of distress associated with experiencing nightmares. The scale consists of 13 items answered on a 5-point Likert scale, with internal reliabilities ranging from 0.83 to 0.88 in four samples of undergraduate students. The scale was developed to investigate the relationship between nightmare frequency and distress associated with the experience of nightmares. Belicki purports that nightmare frequency is only modestly associated with distress, and research and treatment should evaluate both nightmare frequency and distress as "separate, albeit related, constructs" (p. 146). Donovan and colleagues (2004) suggest the Nightmare Distress Scale may not be appropriate for clinical populations due to the lack of psychometric evaluation. Also, the scale only addresses distress associated with nightmares and interest in therapy but does not include other aspects of sleep disturbance. Donovan and colleagues also suggest the scale is too short to measure nightmare distress adequately. Further, Spoormaker and colleagues (2006) note that the measure is rated on a frequency scale, potentially confounding nightmare distress with nightmare frequency. Finally, the Nightmare Distress Scale assesses nightmare frequency and distress over the past year. This time frame may be too long to obtain accurate reports.

Trauma Related Nightmare Survey

In 2001, Davis and colleagues developed the Trauma Related Nightmare Survey (TRNS) to evaluate outcome in their trials of ERRT. The TRNS is a self-report measure that utilizes open-ended, dichotomous (yes/no), and Likert scale questions to assess frequency and severity of nightmares, similarity between nightmares and the traumatic experience, the number of different nightmares experienced, the content of the nightmares, and the length of time the individual has experienced nightmares. The TRNS also focuses on cognitions, emotions, and behaviors related to nightmares. Two-week test-retest reliabilities for various items ranged from 0.63 to 0.77, and convergent validity with daily behavior logs were 0.82 and 0.81 for nights with nightmares and number of nightmares, respectively. Convergent validity with nightmare frequency and severity measures from the Modified PTSD Symptom Scale-Self Report (MPSS-SR; Resick et al., 1991) was determined to be 0.64 and 0.45, respectively. Although the TRNS provided adequate information for evaluating ERRT, we are in the process of modifying the TRNS to add additional elements to more thoroughly assess chronic nightmares and related sleep problems.

Nightmare Frequency Questionnaire

In 2000, Krakow, Hollifield, and colleagues developed the Nightmare Frequency Questionnaire (NFQ) for use in research trials of imagery rehearsal therapy (IRT) for nightmares. Examinees report nightmare frequency retrospectively on a yearly, monthly, or weekly basis. The authors focused on improving upon previous measures and providing consistency in the literature by including questions about "nights with nightmares" and actual "number of nightmares" (Krakow, Hollifield, et al., 2000, p. 592). The authors report weighted kappa test-retest reliabilities of 0.85 for nights with nightmares and 0.90 for the number of nightmares over a 2-week time period. Krakow and colleagues (2002) retrospectively measured nightmare frequency with the NFQ and prospectively with nightmare dream logs and reported validity correlations of 0.53 for nights with nightmares and 0.63 for number of nightmares. The NFQ has been utilized in numerous studies. However, Donovan and colleagues (2004) point out several limitations of this assessment. The NFQ does not assess the severity of nightmares and asks examinees to remember the number of nightmares experienced over a wide range of time. Recall of nightmares for the past year is not likely to be reliable. The psychometric properties of the NFQ have only been evaluated with a limited trauma population (sexual assault survivors), which may preclude use of the assessment with individuals who experienced different types of trauma. In addition, this measure does not include items for the differentiation between post-trauma nightmares, idiopathic nightmares, and sleep terrors.

Nightmare Intervention and Treatment Evaluation

More recently, Donovan and colleagues (2004) developed the Nightmare Intervention and Treatment Evaluation (NITE) to assess subjective distress related to nightmares among individuals with PTSD. The evaluation consists of 32 items, 6 of which are validity items (to detect unusual response tendencies) and 2 of which are frequency items. Factor analysis was conducted to identify latent constructs, and two factors, labeled Nightmare Mastery and Nightmare Helplessness, were extracted. The Nightmare Mastery scale consists of 11 questions that reflect a sense of control over nightmares, such as "Recently, some parts of the nightmare have changed for the better" and "I don't get so upset about this nightmare anymore" (p. 54). The Nightmare Helplessness scale consists of 10 items that reflect either emotions or sleep disturbances related to the nightmare, such as "I am afraid to go to sleep because I am afraid I will have this nightmare" or "This nightmare keeps me from sleeping well" (p. 54). Among a sample of mostly male veterans, analyses revealed test-retest reliabilities of 0.69 and 0.80 for the Mastery and Helplessness scales, respectively, over a time frame ranging from 1 to 3 months. To date, the utility of this scale in assessing treatment progress is unknown, and psychometric values are only available for a sample of veterans, the majority of whom were male.

CONCLUSION

In conclusion, while there are various methods available for assessing sleep and related disturbances, each of these methods has inherent strengths and limitations. There is yet to be a thorough and comprehensive assessment developed that addresses the multitude of issues related to sleep disturbances. As with most assessment strategies, multiple sources of information are necessary to develop a thorough conceptualization of the issues at hand and, subsequently, guide treatment. For instance, the extent to which the measures reviewed differentiate nightmares from night terrors is unclear. The Sleep-50 includes items to differentiate between the two. For other measures (e.g. Nightmare

Distress Scale, NFQ), researchers provided descriptions of characteristics of nightmares prior to the examinee's completion of the assessment. In clinical practice, the distinction between the two is necessary in developing an appropriate treatment plan. We next turn to an examination of the treatments available for nightmares and the development of ERRT.

5

Introduction to Exposure, Relaxation, and Rescripting Treatment

EVIDENCE-BASED APPROACHES TO TREATING NIGHTMARES

The empirical foundation supporting treatments for posttrauma difficulties has grown substantially over the past 2 decades. At present, there are a number of empirically supported treatments available for relieving symptoms of PTSD (e.g., Falsetti, Resnick, & Davis, 2005; Foa et al., 1999; Foa, Rothbaum, Riggs, & Murdock, 1991; Keane, Fairbank, Caddell, Zimering, 1989; Resick & Schnicke, 1993; for reviews, see Foa, Keane, & Friedman, 2000; Foa & Meadows, 1997). While these treatments are quite successful in the amelioration of PTSD symptoms, a growing literature suggests that sleep disturbances, including nightmares, may be resistant to psychological treatments that broadly target PTSD symptoms (e.g., Davis, DeArellano, Falsetti, & Resnick, 2003; Forbes, Creamer, & Biddle, 2001; Johnson et al., 1996; Keane, Fairbank, Caddell, Zimering, 1989; Schreuder, van Egmond, Kleijn, & Visser, 1998; Scurfield, Kenderdine, & Pollard, 1990; Zayfert & DeViva, 2004). For example, Forbes, Creamer, and colleagues (2001) evaluated 97 male Vietnam veterans at baseline and 9 months following involvement in a 3-month PTSD treatment program. Prior to treatment, 88% of the sample reported experiencing nightmares and 99% reported sleep difficulties compared to 77% and 84%, respectively, at follow-up. The ineradicable nature of posttrauma nightmares has also been found in non-Western cultures using traditional healing methods (Schreuder, Igreja, van Dijk, & Kleijn, 2001).

It is unclear why nightmares and sleep disturbances may not be affected by broad-based treatments; however, such findings suggest a need for a more direct approach in the treatment of nightmares.

PHARMACOLOGICAL STUDIES

Practitioners have tested the efficacy of numerous medications for the amelioration of nightmares, with little success. Studies to date consist largely of case studies or uncontrolled investigations. A recent review suggests that not enough data from methodologically sound, controlled studies exists to establish evidence-based pharmacotherapeutic guidelines (van Liempt, Vermetten, Geuze, & Westenberg, 2006). Studies evaluating the impact of medications specifically for sleep and nightmares find that some medications have been found to have no effect on or to worsen sleep and nightmares (e.g., cyproheptadine; Clark et al., 1999; Jacobs-Rebhun et al., 2000). Other studies find that certain medications may be helpful for the amelioration of other PTSD symptoms but do not affect sleep or nightmares (e.g., sertraline; Davidson et al., 2002).

In their review, van Liempt and colleagues (2006) note two medications with "limited but promising evidence" (p. 504) in the alleviation of post-trauma nightmares and sleep problems: olanzapine as an add-on to an SSRI, and prazosin. Olanzapine with an SSRI reduced nightmares, insomnia, PTSD symptoms, and depression in combat veterans (Stein, Kline, & Matloff, 2002), but olanzapine alone had no impact on sleep or PTSD symptoms in a sample of sexual assault victims (Butterfield et al., 2001).

The most encouraging medication currently is prazosin, an alpha-1 adrenergic antagonist. It has been suggested that this medication may impact noradrenergic activity, thus decreasing the disruption of REM sleep (Mellman & Hipolito, 2006; Raskind et al., 2003), although Krystal and Davidson (2007) report that it is too early to indicate specific actions of prazosin on REM sleep in light of inconsistent findings in animal studies. A number of case studies, uncontrolled studies, and a chart review study (e.g., Peskind, Bonner, Hoff, & Raskind, 2003; Raskind et al., 2002; Taylor & Raskind, 2002) suggest that it is promising in the reduction of post-trauma nightmares. A recent two-period, two-treatment cross-over study (Raskind et al., 2003) was conducted comparing prazosin and placebo in 10 male Vietnam veterans with PTSD. Results indicated a positive effect on nightmare frequency and other PTSD symptoms as measured by the CAPS (Blake et al., 1990) and the Clinical Global Impression of Change (Guy, 1976). Participants who initially responded to prazosin but were then switched to placebo "almost always returned to their pretreatment nightmare intensity 1 or 2 days after prazosin discontinuation (i.e., there was no 'carryover' therapeutic effect)" (p. 372).

A second placebo-controlled study (Raskind et al., 2007) randomly assigned 40 veterans to a prazosin or placebo condition. Medication or placebo were initiated and increased (if needed) for 4 weeks; participants then were maintained on their maximum dosage for 8 weeks (maintenance phase). The assessments occurred at 4 weeks and 8 weeks of the maintenance phase. Thirty-four participants completed the study. No differences were found for distressing dreams or sleep quality by week 4 of the maintenance phase (8 weeks from baseline). Results indicated a statistically significant reduction in post-trauma nightmares and improved sleep quality by week 8 of the maintenance phase (12 weeks from baseline) compared to the placebo group, and mild to moderate improvement on global clinical status. PTSD and depressive symptoms, however, did not improve over placebo. Nonmilitary nightmares and unpleasant dreams did not statistically significantly change over time in either group.

Unfortunately, while prazosin appears to reduce nightmares while in use, its effect may be merely palliative. When discontinued, the nightmares return for many individuals (e.g., Daly, Doyle, Raskind, Raskind, & Daniels, 2005; Raskind et al., 2003). It appears that prazosin may interrupt, but not redress, the underlying mechanisms of post-trauma nightmares. Nightmares may be suppressed with its use but remain ineffaceable. Hartmann (1984) cautions, "[w]hile medication may reduce anxiety and reduce the immediate intensity of the nightmares, it may make the connecting process more difficult, perhaps by reducing REM sleep, thus making the traumatic nightmares more likely to become chronic" (p. 239). The specific impact of medications on REM sleep and the resultant nature of the nightmare experience, however, are yet to be determined.

PSYCHOTHERAPEUTIC APPROACHES

While most of the evidence-based, first-line PTSD psychotherapy treatments include exposure techniques, none currently include direct exposure to nightmare content. Evidence is accumulating that suggests direct psychotherapies for nightmares in trauma-exposed persons are more successful than pharmacotherapy for nightmares and psychotherapy targeting PTSD symptoms generally (Coalson, 1995; Halliday, 1987). Interestingly, people do not often present with a primary complaint of nightmares, even if they are frequent and distressing. Krakow (2006) notes, and we have observed in our own studies, that patients often are quite skeptical that nightmares can be treated.

A number of treatment approaches have been found to be promising for nightmares, such as lucid dreaming (e.g., Brylowski, 1990; Spoormaker, van den Bout, & Meijer, 2003; Zadra & Pihl, 1997), imagery rehearsal therapy (Kellner, Neidhardt, Krakow, Pathak, 1992; Krakow, Kellner, Neidhardt, Pathak, & Lambert, 1993), and numerous exposure techniques (see Marks, 1987). The majority of these studies are case reports and did not assess for or report whether the nightmares were trauma related, idiopathic, or a combination of both. Further, while many approaches were successful in reducing nightmare frequency, other symptomatology, including PTSD symptoms, was often unchanged (e.g., Spoormaker et al., 2003). A cognitive behavioral treatment approach for chronic nightmares, IRT, has garnered increased attention over the past decade and appears quite promising for reducing chronic nightmares. The literature on IRT is briefly reviewed below.

Imagery Rehearsal Therapy

In general, IRT involves some degree of exposure to the nightmare content through script or oration of the nightmare in session, as well as rewriting or rescripting components of a participant's nightmare. An early example of combining repeated rehearsal of the original nightmare and writing modified versions of the nightmare to include triumphant endings is described by Marks (1978). Using this approach, he successfully treated a woman with a recurring nightmare that was not replicative of any event in her life but depicted a story line suggestive of a difficult relationship with her mother. Marks suggested three possibilities for the success of his case and similar cases described by others, including exposure, abreaction, and mastery. These possible mechanisms of change are explored further in chapter 10.

Several research groups have evaluated variants of IRT. Differences in specific procedures exist among the various research groups, however. Some protocols involve repeated rehearsal of the original nightmare (e.g., Marks, 1978), while most others involve repeated rehearsal of the changed version of the nightmare (e.g., Davis & Wright, 2007; Forbes, Phelps, & McHugh, 2001; Krakow, Hollifield, et al., 2001). The degree of exposure to the original nightmare varies considerably as well, with some research groups minimizing the degree of exposure employed (e.g., Krakow, Hollifield, et al., 2001) and others enhancing it (e.g., Davis & Wright, 2005; 2007). Some groups also incorporate additional techniques, including positive imagery (Krakow, Hollifield, et al., 2001), relaxation, and various sleep-enhancing techniques (e.g., Davis & Wright, 2005; 2007). Finally, the number and length of sessions has varied considerably. It is unclear at this point if there is differential efficacy for the various protocols. A review of studies that have compared components is included in chapter 10.

IRT for Acute Post-Trauma Nightmares

The author is aware of only one uncontrolled study that examined the use of IRT for acute nightmares (within 30 days of the traumatic event; Moore & Krakow, 2007). Eleven soldiers were administered four sessions of IRT and were followed for 1 month posttreatment. Results indicated that 7 participants improved in nightmare frequency, PTSD symptoms, and insomnia. The study is obviously limited by the small sample size, lack of control group, and short follow-up period, but the results appear promising.

IRT for Chronic Nightmares

Overall, a number of studies have evaluated the use of variants of IRT with chronic idiopathic or unspecified nightmares and found positive results (Bishay, 1985; Marks, 1978; Kellner et al., 1992; Krakow, Kellner, Neidhardt, Pathak, & Lambert, 1993; Krakow, Kellner, Pathak, & Lambert, 1996); Neidhardt et al., 1992; Germain & Nielsen, 2003b). Thompson, Hamilton, and West (1995) were among the first to describe the use of IRT with combat veterans. Their article is primarily a description of the treatment, not of the treatment study, but the authors do report that one third of the participants were successful in eliminating their nightmares in the 4 weeks following the intervention.

Uncontrolled studies utilizing IRT that targeted individuals with posttraumatic symptoms generally found positive results for nightmare and sleep outcome (e.g., Forbes, Phelps, & McHugh, 2001; Forbes et al., 2003; Germain & Nielsen, 2003b). For example, Forbes, Phelps, and McHugh, (2001) conducted an uncontrolled trial of IRT with 12 Vietnam veterans. Treatment proceeded in a group format for 1.5 hours over 6 weeks. Participants chose a nightmare, wrote it in detail, and read it aloud to the group. Group members discussed potential changes to everyone's nightmares; participants then wrote out their rescripted nightmare and read it aloud to the group. They were instructed to change the nightmares to reflect greater mastery or control. At the 3-month follow-up, statistically significant improvements were found for the frequency and intensity of the target nightmare and intensity of nightmares overall (the mean frequency of nightmares overall was reduced by half, but this difference did not reach significance). Improvements were also reported for PTSD symptoms, depression, and general symptoms. No difference in treatment outcome was found for replicative versus trauma-similar nightmares. The investigators followed the participants for 12 months posttreatment and reported maintenance of treatment gains regarding frequency and severity reductions in the target nightmare, and reductions in symptoms of PTSD, depression, and anxiety. Further, the participants continued to improve in terms of their nightmares in general, even though only one nightmare was addressed in the treatment (Forbes et al., 2003).

A randomized controlled trial was conducted with 58 participants who reported either post-trauma or idiopathic nightmares (Krakow, Kellner, Pathak, & Lambert, 1995). Approximately 68% of participants reported having a traumatic event or significant stressor precede the onset of the nightmares. Participants were randomly assigned to one of two treatment conditions or a wait-list control group. The treatment conditions were the same, with the exception of the instructions given for the rescription. One treatment condition was told to "change the nightmare anyway you wish," and the other was told to "change the ending." The treatment was a one-time, 2.5-hour session. For this study, the treatment protocol consisted of training in positive imagery, writing down a nightmare, changing it according to the instructions for their group, writing a changed version, rehearsing the changed version, and sharing the original and modified nightmare with the group. Participants were encouraged to work on two or three nightmares per week. At the 3-month follow-up, results revealed no differences between the two treatment groups. Significant improvements in the treatment groups were found for frequency of nightmares and sleep quality for both pre- to post- and between group comparisons. Within the group, pre- to post changes on anxiety, depression, and somatization were significant for the treated group, hostility was unchanged, and no significant interaction for the group and change over time was found. While these results are quite promising, participants continued to report a mean of approximately two nightmares per week.

The participants in the study just described were subsequently assessed at the 18-month follow-up. Individuals who had been in the control ·group were then treated with IRT, for a total of 53 treated individuals. Forty-one people participated in the follow-up study. Results indicated maintenance of treatment gains at the 18-month follow-up, with continued improvement in nightmare frequency (Krakow, Kellner, Pathak, & Lambert, 1996). Decreases were reported for all measures of distress (i.e., anxiety, depression, somatization, and hostility), although this was only significant for anxiety.

Krakow, Hollifield, and colleagues (2001) evaluated the efficacy of IRT with 168 adult women who had been sexually assaulted and had PTSD or PTSD symptoms, nightmares at least once per week for more than 6 months, and insomnia. Participants were randomly assigned to treatment or wait-list control groups. IRT was delivered in two 3-hour sessions and one 1-hour session. To minimize the exposure element, participants were asked to choose a less intense nightmare to begin with and to not choose one that replicated the traumatic event. This protocol also involved education about handling unpleasant images while awake. Results indicated that the treatment was effective in improving sleep quality and in reducing the frequency of nightmares per week, nights with nightmares per week, and PTSD symptoms. Symptoms remained in the moderately severe to severe range for approximately 30% to 40% (depending on the measure) of the treated sample, however. Treatment gains were maintained across the 6-month follow-up.

Krakow, Sandoval, and colleagues (2001) evaluated a one-session, 6-hour version of IRT in a nonrandomized study with 19 adjudicated adolescent girls (9 in the treatment group, 10 in the control group). The authors report that all but one participant had a history of sexual assault but do not indicate whether their nightmares were related to the trauma. The protocol was similar to that of Krakow, Hollifield, and colleagues (2001). At 3 months posttreatment, reductions were found for nightmare frequency and distress, but no differences were found for posttraumatic stress symptoms or sleep quality.

Germain and Nielsen (2003b) examined the efficacy of a 3-hour session of IRT with 12 individuals (6 with post-trauma nightmares and 6 with idiopathic nightmares) on subjective and objective assessments of sleep and self-reported psychological difficulties. The protocol included psychoeducation about nightmares, choosing and writing out a nightmare (not the worst or a replicative nightmare), choosing a revised version and writing that down, and rehearsal of the revised dream. Overall, when the nightmare groups were combined, statistically significant results were found for reduction of nightmare frequency assessed retrospectively, but not prospectively, and anxiety scores. When the nightmare groups were assessed separately, no statistically significant differences were found for nightmares, bad dreams, or night terrors (although most effect sizes were moderate to large). Individuals with post-trauma nightmares had statistically significant reductions in anxiety and PTSD severity. Individuals with idiopathic nightmares had statistically significant reductions in depression.

Germain, Shear, Hall, and Buysse (2007) evaluated the efficacy of a one-session, 90-minute variant of IRT in 7 trauma-exposed adult participants who met criteria for PTSD. The protocol consisted of psychoeducation about sleep and nightmares, imagery rescription (pick a nightmare to change any way you want; rehearse one or two new dreams imaginally at least 3 times per week, for at least 5 minutes), stimulus control, and sleep restriction. Participants utilized a workbook, but it is unclear whether they wrote out the nightmare or rescripted dream. Participants were administered the treatment in one session and asked to engage in the techniques for 6 weeks. Results at 6 to 8 weeks' follow-up revealed statistically significant improvements for daytime intrusions and hyperarousal PTSD symptoms. Given the quality results of longer versions of IRT, Germain and colleagues (2007) conclude that one session may not be the best length for this treatment. This contention may also be supported by the findings of Krakow, Sandoval, and colleagues (2001).

Thus, controlled and uncontrolled studies find promising results for the efficacy of IRT on chronic nightmares in people exposed and not exposed to traumatic events. The protocols appear to vary, however, in the specific areas of distress they affect. More research is needed to determine the most appropriate dosage and mode of delivery of this treatment. Another treatment approach utilizing IRT has been to combine it with other techniques to address broader sleep concerns. This literature is reviewed next.

Nightmares and Insomnia

One uncontrolled study combined IRT and techniques for insomnia and assessed the efficacy of this approach in a sample of 62 crime victims with PTSD (Krakow, Johnston, et al., 2001). Sessions were held for 10 hours over 3 weeks. At the 3-month follow-up, findings revealed improvements in nightmare frequency, sleep quality, PTSD symptoms, and anxiety and depression symptoms, although symptoms remained in the borderline-moderate to borderline-severe range for all measures. Participants reported an average of 2.10 nights with nightmares per week and 2.65 nightmares per week at the follow-up. Further, 11% of the sample reported worsening PTSD symptoms and 35% reported unchanged PTSD symptoms. Comparison of outcome for those with primarily post-trauma nightmares ($n = 38$) and those with non-post-trauma nightmares ($n = 24$) revealed that, while those with post-trauma nightmares reported higher symptoms at baseline, there was no difference in treatment outcome between groups. As this was an uncontrolled study, it is unclear if the symptom improvement or worsening was related to the treatment.

A second study examined a combined treatment for insomnia and nightmares with a sample of individuals who evacuated from the Cerro Grande Fire 10 months previously (Krakow, Melendrez, Johnston, Clark et al., 2002). The treatment was administered in a large group ($N = 66$) over six 2-hour sessions. Participants had a 12-week follow-up posttreatment assessment. Approximately 80% of the participants reported improvement in symptoms, including PTSD symptoms, insomnia severity, anxiety, depression, and nightmare severity. All effects sizes were small to medium, with the exception of nightmare severity, which had a large effect size. An additional 17% reported worsening insomnia, and 15% reported worsening PTSD symptoms. As this was an uncontrolled study, it is unclear if symptom worsening was related to the treatment. The authors also do not specify how they determined worsening.

Thus, there are several studies indicating promising results in the use of variants of IRT for reducing nightmare frequency and severity, improving sleep quality, and improving related areas of distress. The clinical significance is less clear, as symptoms often remained in the abnormal range, and some studies reported worsening of symptoms in 11% to 17% of participants (Krakow, Johnston, et al., 2001; Krakow, Melendrez, Johnston, Clark et al., 2002). It is unclear whether increasing the exposure to the nightmare and incorporating other sleep, anxiety, and trauma therapy techniques may enhance treatment effects. The fact that many of the symptoms assessed remained in the moderate range of symptomatology may suggest that, for some, a treatment targeting nightmares may be part of the clinical puzzle but may not be enough to allow trauma-exposed persons to reach optimal functioning. Much more research is needed to determine who benefits most from this brief intervention and under what conditions. Related issues are discussed more fully in chapters 9 and 10.

The studies reviewed above also address in part an issue raised in chapter 2 regarding whether nightmares and sleep disturbances should be considered primary or secondary problems in trauma-exposed persons. As stated by Harvey, Jones, and Schmidt (2003), the findings that interventions targeting nightmares also reduce PTSD symptoms "cannot be taken as evidence that sleep is a primary mechanism in PTSD. They do, however, suggest that the assumption that the sleep symptoms are secondary to PTSD should be revisited" (p. 400). Further calling the primacy of PTSD into question are the findings of continued sleep and nightmare problems while PTSD symptoms overall are reduced after broad-based PTSD treatments are implemented (e.g., Davis, DeArellano, Falsetti, & Resnick, 2003; Forbes, Creamer, et al., 2001; Johnson et al., 1996; Keane, Fairbank, Caddell, & Zimering, 1989; Schreuder et al., 1998; Scurfield et al., 1990; Zayfert & DeViva, 2004).

EXPOSURE, RELAXATION, AND RESCRIPTING THERAPY

Developing Exposure, Relaxation, and Rescripting Therapy

ERRT was developed between 1999 and 2000. The author was working in a clinic that specialized in trauma victims and was seeing a young woman who presented with PTSD, panic disorder, and major depression. The author administered a 3-month treatment of Multiple Channel Exposure Therapy (MCET; Falsetti & Resnick, 1997; Falsetti, Resnick, & Davis, 2005) with this client specifically focused on the PTSD and panic disorder. At the posttreatment assessment, the client no longer met criteria for PTSD, panic disorder, or major depression, but she continued to suffer from nightmares related to an experience of rape. A review of the literature on treating nightmares, while sparse in terms of controlled trials with post-trauma nightmares, led me to IRT. With this particular client, the author capitalized on several of the techniques she had already learned through MCET and added sleep-specific components as well as IRT. At the third session, the client continued to report problems with nightmares, and, while doing a review of how she was implementing each of the components, it became clear that instead of rehearsing the rescripted dream, she had been engaging in pleasant imagery before sleep. As stated in the case report (Davis et al., 2003):

> She reported doing this because she "didn't want to think about him [the perpetrator] at all." The therapist explained the necessity of engaging the fear network for the procedure to work, as with the exposure procedures conducted during MCET. We again reviewed her altered dream, and Anne opted to change it so that she was more active in the dream, felt more powerful, and felt greater support. (p. 290)

The author saw the client again at booster sessions 1 month and 3 months later. Over those months, she no longer had the replicative, recurring nightmare; the client reported that she had dreamt of the perpetrator three times but she was no longer scared when dreaming about him. She also reported her sleep was significantly improved (Davis et al., 2003).

Following this case, the author determined to continue exploring this manner of addressing post-trauma nightmares. Over the next year, the author wrote a client manual, incorporating many of the techniques used in the case study as well as some additional techniques based on factors that possibly maintain nightmares over time. The development of ERRT was influenced by several evidence-based treatments for anxiety and post-trauma difficulties, including Mastery of Your Anxiety and Panic (Barlow & Craske, 1989; 1994), Cognitive Processing Therapy (Resick & Schnicke, 1993), Multiple Channel Exposure Therapy (Falsetti & Resnick, 1997), and Imagery Rehearsal Therapy for nightmares (Krakow, Kellner, Pathak, & Lambert, 1996; Thompson et al., 1995). Additionally, it was informed by cognitive behavioral treatments for insomnia (Morin, 1993).

Post-trauma nightmares were conceptualized as being trauma initiated or exacerbated and perpetuated by numerous complicating factors. ERRT was designed to target three systems in which anxiety may manifest, as proposed in the three-factor model presented in chapter 3: physiological (e.g., increased arousal close to the time an individual typically goes to bed), behavioral (e.g., using substances to aid in falling asleep), and cognitive (e.g., a person's belief that he or she will have a nightmare if he or she falls asleep). As mentioned above, some variants of IRT purposively minimize the amount of exposure to the nightmare, which is curious due to the vast empirical literature supporting its use with trauma-exposed individuals. The author decided to utilize an exposure component to potentially enhance the impact of the treatment by more fully engaging the fear network, of which the author hypothesize the nightmare is a part.

With the treatment manual complete, the author then conducted a case series, treating four individuals with various trauma histories (Davis & Wright, 2005). The treatment appeared to work well for these participants, and my research lab then designed a randomized clinical trial to further evaluate its efficacy. The results of that original RCT and preliminary results of the second RCT are reported in chapter 10. Next is an overview of the treatment protocol.

Setting

The work that my research group has conducted on ERRT has taken place in a university research lab (with the exception of the initial case study). As my background is primarily as a trauma therapist and researcher, not a sleep medicine specialist, the lab is not set up for conducting objective sleep studies, which are not needed to conduct this treatment. Conducting sleep studies as part of determining treatment outcome is expensive, time consuming, and obviously not an option for many therapists. However, as understanding the potential impact of treatment on sleep structure and identifying any additional sleep problems that may continue to interfere with clients' functioning are important next steps in this area, it would be beneficial for therapists to establish a professional relationship with a sleep medicine specialist in their area. Therapists might also consider using actigraphy (see chapter 4) devices in consultation with a sleep medicine specialist.

ERRT will work quite well on an outpatient basis, in private practice, or Veterans Affairs clinics. Although ERRT may be utilized in an inpatient setting, there may be some limiting factors to this approach. First, many individuals who have significant sleep and nightmare problems at home tend to not experience those difficulties or experience them less when receiving inpatient treatment. This may be due to a heightened sense of safety or being away from their bedroom environment that likely serves as a cue for poor sleep. Relatedly, clients may have some difficulties generalizing these techniques outside the hospital due to the cues in their home environments. If this is an issue, however, the therapist may prepare clients for this and include some additional techniques to aid in the generalization (see chapter 8 for additional information). Therapists could also consider having a booster session once the patient is discharged to follow up and problem-solve any remaining issues.

Format

ERRT may be conducted in an individual or group format, depending on the needs and resources of the therapist. My research lab has conducted ERRT both individually and within groups. Largely this has been based on the timing of clients entering into the treatment study and the availability of a therapist. We have not yet conducted comparative analysis by modality. Based on clinical observation, the clients who we have seen in a group format do appear to gain perspective, support, and encouragement from group members. Whether these factors translate to differential treatment outcome, however, remains to be determined. ERRT is typically conducted once per week over 3 weeks, and sessions run approximately 2 hours each. We have not explored whether this structure and timing is optimal; however, the positive findings of our outcome studies suggest that, at least for most people, this format is appropriate.

Although the vast majority of research on ERRT was conducted with adults (e.g., Davis & Wright, 2007), it has been used successfully with an adolescent (see Davis, DeArellano, Falsetti, & Resnick, 2003). IRT was also utilized successfully with adolescents (e.g., Krakow, Sandoval, et al., 2001) and numerous case studies describe using similar techniques with children (see Halliday, 1987). We are currently assessing the efficacy of a modified version of ERRT with school children—Exposure, Relaxation, and Rescription Therapy for Children (ERRT-C)—which also includes a parent component.

Assessment

As discussed in chapter 4, a comprehensive assessment is vital prior to beginning treatment. It is important to develop a case formulation and to determine the specific areas of need. Areas we believe are important to consider fall under four domains: background information, mental health status, nightmares and sleep, and quality of life. An example of various measures to consider is included in Table 5.1.

Background information generally includes demographic information and a trauma history assessment. For mental health status, we

Table 5.1

OUTLINE OF ASSESSMENTS

ASSESSMENT	MEASURE
Baseline	**Domain 1: Background information** Demographic information Trauma Assessment for Adults (Resnick, Best, Kilpatrick, Freedy, & Falsetti, 1993) **Domain 2: Mental health status** Clinician Administered PTSD Scale (Blake et al., 1990) Modified PTSD Symptom Scale (Resick, Falsetti, Resnick, & Kilpatrick, 1991) Beck Depression Inventory II (Beck, Steer, & Brown, 1996) Beck Anxiety Inventory (Beck & Steer, 1993) Drug Abuse Screening Test (Skinner, 1982) Alcohol Use Disorders Identification Test (Babor, Biddle-Higgins, Saunders, & Monteiro, 2001) **Domain 3: Nightmares and sleep** Trauma-Related Nightmare Survey (Davis, Wright, & Borntrager, 2001) The Pittsburgh Sleep Quality Index (Buysse, Reynolds, Monk, Berman, & Kupfer, 1989) Daily Sleep Activities Log (Thompson et al., 1995) Global Sleep Assessment Questionnaire (Roth, et al, 2002) Sleep Hygiene Index (Mastin, Bryson, & Corwyn, 2006) **Domain 4: Quality of Life** Rand 36-Item Health Survey (Ware & Sherbourne, 1992). Work and Social Adjustment Scale (Mundt, Marks, Shear, & Greist, 2002)
Session 1, 2, 3	Modified PTSD Symptom Scale (Resick et al., 1991) Beck Depression Inventory II (Beck, Steer, & Brown, 1996) Beck Anxiety Inventory (Beck & Steer, 1993) Trauma-Related Nightmare Survey (Davis et al., 2001) The Pittsburgh Sleep Quality Index (Buysse, Reynolds, Monk, Berman, & Kupfer, 1989) Daily Sleep Activities Log (Thompson et al., 1995)
Homework	Daily Sleep Activities Log (Thompson et al., 1995) Daily PTSD Symptom Checklist (Falsetti & Resnick, 1997). Monitoring Forms—included in manual (see Appendix)
Post and follow-up	All measures from baseline assessment except the Demographic Information; Trauma Assessment for Adults is only completed if individual affirms a new traumatic event since the last evaluation. Post Treatment Clinical Significance Scale (Davis, Wright, Byrd, & Rhudy, 2006) is given at the last follow-up assessment.

recommend measures assessing PTSD, depression, anxiety, and drug and alcohol use. Nightmare experience should include a measure to distinguish nightmares from other parasomnias, and an assessment of the frequency, severity, and impact of the nightmares. Although it does not appear to impact treatment outcome, it may also be helpful to include questions of whether the nightmares began before or after a traumatic event and whether they are similar to the traumatic event. Sleep assessment should include measures of sleep quality and quantity and sleep disorders. The quality of life can include measures of physical health and general functioning (e.g., work, school, relationships). For research purposes, we give the same measures at posttreatment and follow-up assessments for comparison. The two exceptions are the demographic form and the trauma history (we only ask about any new traumas since the previous evaluation). For clinical purposes, it is also helpful to do this so that both the therapist and the client can see the progress made and any areas that may still need to be addressed. At the last follow-up assessment, we also give the Posttreatment Clinical Significance Scale (see Appendix B) to determine changes in particular areas related to the treatment and to determine the client's perception of the treatment.

In addition to the baseline and posttreatment follow-up assessments, we also ask participants to complete measures at the beginning of every session. This is done for several reasons. First, this allows us to do a quick check to determine if a participant may be evidencing rapid change, either significantly improving or deteriorating. In the case of deterioration in functioning, the therapist will want to do a more thorough assessment to determine the nature and potential cause of the deterioration. If the decrease in functioning is related to the treatment, the therapist may need to consider modifying the protocol or stopping altogether. In our clinical experience, this is a very uncommon occurrence. If the decrease is related to a stressor or crisis apart from the treatment, the therapist may need to temporarily halt treatment of the nightmares to refocus on the current problem until it is resolved. More information is provided on issues that may arise during treatment in chapter 9. Second, the weekly assessments allow us to determine at which point in the protocol particular changes occur.

Finally, we also ask clients to complete monitoring forms in between sessions. These include forms to monitor anxiety levels before and after progressive muscle relaxation and diaphragmatic breathing, a daily PTSD symptom scale, a form to document changes in sleep habits, and a daily sleep log to assess sleep and nightmares. In general, participants have been quite compliant in the completion of these forms, and they provide a good point of departure for the weekly review of progress and potential trouble spots. For example, we often are able to point out patterns related to stress levels or maladaptive sleep habits and poor sleep or nightmares by querying about what was happening on specific nights that they report bad sleep or an increase in nightmares. Although they are completing the forms each morning, many participants do not recognize these patterns until they are pointed out, as they typically have been suffering these problems for so long.

Depending on the nature of your clinical practice, much of the baseline information we are recommending be assessed may have been gathered at some earlier time, if the client presented for another problem. If this is the case, you may still want to ask clients to fill them out again just prior to beginning the nightmare treatment. Also, if you suspect that the client may have a sleep disorder in addition to nightmares, we recommend a referral to a sleep specialist, as this may complicate treatment.

Treatment Components[1]

The majority of the following information on treatment components was initially published in *The Journal of Trauma and Dissociation* (Davis & Wright, 2006). Article copies are available from The Haworth Document Delivery Service (1-800-HAWORTH; e-mail address: docdelivery@ haworthpress.com). Outlines of the treatment sessions are provided in Tables 5.2, 5.3, and 5.4.

Educational Components. Education regarding trauma and nightmares is explained from a generalist perspective, as the type of trauma exposure is not limited for this protocol. Information for this section was derived from current trauma literature (Falsetti & Resnick, 2000; Foa, Davidson, & Frances, 1999; Foa & Rothbaum, 1998; Resick & Schnicke, 1993), sleep literature (Morin, 1993; Perlis & Lichstein, 2003), and anxiety literature (Barlow, 1988; Lang, 1968).

Exposure Components. Exposure exercises are adapted and modified from Falsetti and Resnick (1997), Resick and Schnicke (1993), and Foa and

---

[1] © by The Haworth Press, Inc., Binghamton, NY; Davis, J.L., & Wright, D.C. (2006). Exposure, relaxation, and rescripting therapy for post-trauma-related Nightmares. *Journal of Trauma and Dissociation, 7*, 5–18.

Table 5.2

TREATMENT: SESSION 1

1. Treatment overview
2. Explanation of the manifestation of anxiety specific to nightmares
   a. Physiological
   b. Behavioral
   c. Cognitive
3. Psychoeducation
   a. Trauma
      1. Prevalence
      2. Impact
      3. PTSD symptoms
   b. Nightmares
      1. Prevalence
      2. Theories of development
      3. Impact
   c. Sleep habits
      1. Impact on sleep and wake functioning
      2. Do's and don'ts
      3. Identification of helpful and nonhelpful sleep habits
4. Relaxation
   a. Rationale
   b. Progressive muscle relaxation
5. Homework
   a. Practice progressive muscle relaxation
   b. Sleep habit modification
   c. Monitoring forms

Rothbaum (1998) and involve both written and oral exposure to the nightmare content in an effort to access the cognitive channel of anxiety stemming from the nightmare. In session, participants are exposed to the nightmare's content by writing about the nightmare in present tense, as if the nightmare were occurring right then, and in significant detail, utilizing all their senses. After participants write the nightmare in session, they are given the opportunity to read their nightmare aloud to the group. This exposure helps to identify unresolved cognitive-affective meaning structures and processes (i.e., themes; Lebowitz & Newman, 1996; Resick & Schnike, 1993) that may be manifested in participants' nightmares. Identification and use of traumatic themes has several advantages in the treatment of trauma. According to Lebowitz and Newman, identification of unresolved traumatic themes aids in treatment by increasing a participant's insight into how present schemata are organized

Table 5.3

TREATMENT: SESSION 2

1. Review Homework
   a. Assess completion of and difficulties with:
      1. Progressive muscle relaxation
      2. Sleep habit modification
   b. Monitoring forms
   c. Query about changes in:
      1. Nightmares
      2. Sleep
      3. PTSD symptoms
2. Review relationship between traumatic event and nightmare
3. Exposure to the nightmare
   a. Rationale for exposure
   b. Rules for writing nightmare
   c. Examples of written nightmare
   d. Participant writes nightmare
   e. Participant reads nightmare aloud
4. Identify themes in nightmare
5. Rescription
   a. Rules for rescription
   b. Participant writes rescription
   c. Participant reads rescription aloud
6. Diaphragmatic breathing
7. Assign homework
   a. Practice progressive muscle relaxation
   b. Sleep habit modification
   c. Rehearse rescripted dream
   d. Practice diaphragmatic breathing
   e. Monitoring forms

by past influences (e.g., trauma) and that, by focusing upon themes, work may proceed even if the participant has fragmented memories or is more comfortable addressing these issues indirectly through associated sequelae rather than directly through traumatic triggers or flashbacks. Additionally, the authors state that the construct of themes reside in the larger construct of the self, and through identification and resolution of these broad underlying meaning structures, multiple areas of functioning should be positively affected.

Rescripting. Within ERRT, rescripting the nightmare includes the incorporation of the previously identified traumatic themes. For example, if

Table 5.4

TREATMENT: SESSION 3

---

1. Review homework
   a. Assess completion of and difficulties with:
      1. Progressive muscle relaxation
      2. Sleep habit modification
      3. Monitoring forms
      4. Diaphragmatic breathing
      5. Rehearsal of rescripted dream
   b. Query about changes in:
      1. Nightmares
      2. Sleep
      3. PTSD Symptoms
2. Slow breathing
3. Review treatment gains
4. Maintenance and relapse prevention

---

the participant feels unsafe in the nightmare, he or she is encouraged to change the nightmare to reflect feeling very safe and secure. The rescripting is thought to not only increase participants' sense of power and control over the nightmare content (mastery) but also to foster eventual resolution and decreases in symptom and nightmare frequencies by incorporating themes into the rescripted nightmare. Although participants are rescripting their nightmare, it is necessary to make a clear distinction between the nightmare as an associated feature of experiencing a trauma and the actual trauma itself and to ensure the participants understand that this rescription pertains only to the former. After participants rescript their nightmare and read aloud the altered version, they are given homework in which they are directed to imaginally rehearse the rescripted nightmare each night before they go to sleep.

Relaxation. Three separate relaxation procedures (see Craske, Barlow, & Meadows, 2000; Falsetti & Resnick, 1997) are employed in this brief treatment, with participants learning one type each session. During the first session, participants are taught progressive muscle relaxation (PMR). PMR is explained as a procedure during which participants alternately tense and relax different muscle groups in their body to learn the difference between feelings of tension and relaxation. The effects of improper breathing are explained in relation to the second relaxation technique, diaphragmatic breathing. This technique provides explicit instruction in the mechanics of proper breathing and provides verbal cues to classically condition a state of increased relaxation. The last relaxation procedure taught to participants is slowed breathing to enhance feelings of relaxation.

The next three chapters outline the treatment session by session. The actual treatment manual is provided in Appendix A.

6 Session 1

Session 1 is designed to provide the educational basis for the treatment and to begin addressing components of the vicious cycle maintaining the nightmares. Clients are provided information about potentially traumatic events, PTSD, and nightmares. The theories of nightmare initiation and maintenance are briefly reviewed. Information is then provided about sleep hygiene, and PMR is taught.

INTRODUCTION

Prior to starting the educational component, clients are given a basic overview of the treatment and an introduction to the ways that anxiety may manifest in individuals exposed to potentially traumatic events. This information is based largely on the broader trauma and anxiety literatures (e.g., Barlow & Craske, 1989; Falsetti & Resnick, 1997; Lang, 1968; Resick & Schnike, 1993). Essentially, nightmares are viewed, at least initially, as a manifestation of anxiety, as a part of the posttraumatic stress constellation of symptoms. Nightmares in turn cause additional anxiety. Anxiety is not portrayed as negative but rather as essential to survival; however, for individuals with chronic problems, the anxiety system may be misfiring. There may be problems with the intensity, direction, or timing of the anxiety response, which can lead to problems. We describe the manner in which anxiety may become evident through the physiological, behavioral, and cognitive channels specific to the experience of nightmares (Lang, 1968).

The following is a section from the patient manual specific to the information above. Throughout the psychoeducation sections, clinicians are encouraged to present the information in an interactive manner. For example, in the section below, we typically discuss the first part of the information (physiological channel) and then ask the clients if and how they experience symptoms within the physiological channel. We then do the same for the behavioral and cognitive channels. To make the psychoeducation section less didactic and more personally relevant, we strongly encourage clinicians to do this throughout. In the patient manual we include questions for the clients to consider and for the clinician to ask in bold.

> The treatment targets three systems in which anxiety may manifest: physiological, behavioral, and cognitive. Physiological reactions to nightmares may include increased arousal close to the time you typically go to bed, panic attack symptoms upon awakening from a nightmare (e.g., racing heart, sweating, choking), symptoms of sleep deprivation during daytime hours (e.g., confusion, memory loss, irritability or emotional highs and lows, exacerbation of other emotional difficulties), and increased arousal during the daytime. The behavioral reactions to nightmares may include using substances (e.g., alcohol, sleeping pills) at night to help you get to sleep; watching television in bed to try to forget about the nightmares; and avoiding situations, places, or people that remind you of the nightmares and traumatic event (even avoiding sleep!). The cognitive reactions to nightmares may include telling yourself you will never be able to get to sleep, feeling too afraid to sleep because you fear having another nightmare, or believing that you will never "get over" the trauma because it continues to be disruptive, even while you sleep. This treatment was designed to target each of these systems. [See Appendix A]

The introduction to the treatment also tries to frame the clients' expectations for the treatment. The brevity of the treatment, while attractive to many clients, may also engender doubt in others. A considerable amount of literature supports the notion that clients' expectations of treatment success significantly predicts favorable treatment outcome (e.g., Lambert & Barley, 2001). We attempt to establish realistic goals for the treatment, discuss the importance of doing the homework and exercises outside of treatment, and instill hope in clients to serve as motivation for treatment completion and compliance. Specifically, we inform the clients that, while it is common for other manifestations of distress to improve following treatment, the primary goal is to reduce the frequency and severity of the nightmares. Clients are informed that the treatment was not designed to fit one type of traumatic event or people who have experienced trauma only once. Indeed, participants in our treatment studies reported a wide variety of trauma experiences and averaged approximately five traumatic events in their lifetimes.

> ERRT is a three-session treatment. You may find it difficult to imagine that three sessions would be sufficient to rid you of nightmares. The purpose of the treatment is to try to reduce the frequency and intensity of your nightmares. It may also reduce your level of distress during the day as your sleep improves and you begin to understand the ways in which the trauma and the nightmares are affecting you. The treatment requires that you attend all three sessions of treatment. Homework will be assigned at the end of the first two sessions. Completion of the homework assignments is very important to your success in this treatment. We will review the homework at the beginning of each session. You will also be asked to complete additional measures at the beginning of each session. The treatment sessions and this manual will provide a guide for working through the nightmares, but it is up to you to do the work. The treatment manual is yours to keep so that you can review the material between sessions. [See Appendix A.]

CONFIDENTIALITY

Confidentiality is then reviewed. Although this information is presented in the informed consent forms that all participants sign and receive copies of, we review the information verbally. This is particularly salient when the treatment is conducted with a group.

> As you know, everyone involved in this treatment has had a traumatic event occur in his or her lifetime. In an individual therapy situation, all information would be kept confidential with several exceptions that are outlined in the copy of the informed consent form that you received. In a group situation, the therapist cannot guarantee total confidentiality, as group members will hear about the histories and concerns of the other group members over the course of treatment. It is very important for each group member to protect and respect the information they hear in treatment. No one should discuss

any information brought up in the context of treatment or talk about who is in the group to any person outside of the group. In order for treatment to work, everyone needs to feel free to discuss sensitive matters openly, without fear that their information will be shared outside the group. [See Appendix A.]

EDUCATION

Clients are introduced to basic psychoeducational material about trauma and its effects. The goal for this section of the treatment is to normalize responses to traumatic events. We do this through providing prevalence rates for lifetime experiences of trauma and discussing common responses to trauma. We emphasize the various ways in which people cope with traumatic events to reflect the individual nature of trauma impact and recovery. The symptoms of PTSD are described in detail.

The psychoeducation component is conducted in an interactive style, with the therapist querying clients about whether they experience the symptoms within each cluster and specifically how the symptoms are manifested, as well as their intensity, frequency, and duration. Of course, if the clients are not suffering from PTSD symptoms, this component can be truncated. However, clinicians should not assume that, because the clients do not meet criteria for PTSD, they do not suffer from subclinical symptoms.

Case Example

Therapist: Before we talk about nightmares specifically, I'd like to talk about how people respond to trauma more generally.

Client: Okay.

T: People respond to traumatic events in a number of ways. Some individuals feel intense distress almost immediately; for some this will dissipate over time, while others will continue to experience significant distress. Others may feel little distress at first or be in a state of shock, then experience more difficulties later on, even years after the event. Still others report experiencing few difficulties at all. The manner in which a traumatic event may impact a person's life is quite varied. How did you respond to the trauma?

C: I barely remember the few days following the rape—I was so out of it. It was only after I got out of the hospital that it started to hit me.

T: It sounds like you may have been in a bit of shock immediately after—that while you were in the hospital you may have felt somewhat safe.

C: Yeah, it was okay not to think about it because I was focused on being physically okay.

T: How did things change when you left the hospital?

C: Everything changed—it seemed like I was in danger no matter where I went. And I couldn't stay away from the place where it happened—that's where I work. So it was in my face all the time.

T: Did the experience of having to be near the place where the rape occurred change over time?

C: Yeah, it got worse—much worse. I started parking a few blocks away and walking a different route to get to the office.

T: It sounds like you have experienced some of the common reactions people have to a traumatic event. You may have heard of a group of symptoms that are known as posttraumatic stress disorder.

C: That's what soldiers get.

T: Yes, soldiers may develop posttraumatic stress disorder—or PTSD for short. Actually people who have been through any type of traumatic event may develop PTSD—including natural disasters, car accidents, physical assaults, and sexual assaults. In fact, approximately one third of individuals who experience trauma may develop PTSD.

The therapist then explains each of the three categories of PTSD and elicits specific examples from the clients of how they might experience each category, if at all. The following is an excerpt of the text, including the questions posed to the clients throughout. Specific questions are included in bold, and clients are encouraged to expand on those areas.

PTSD includes three different categories of symptoms. The first category includes symptoms that involve reexperiencing the traumatic event in some way, such as feeling as if the event were occurring again, having nightmares about the event, and thinking about the event when you don't want to. (**Do your nightmares tend to be about the trauma? Do you experience any other reexperiencing symptoms?**) The second category includes the ways that people attempt to avoid people, places, situations, and things that remind them of the traumatic event. Common ways in which people try to avoid include pushing thoughts of the event out of their minds, not interacting with someone who reminds them of a perpetrator, and using substances to try and forget what happened. (**Have you found yourself trying to avoid thoughts or reminders of the trauma?**) The second category also includes numbing responses, such as feeling detached from other people or unable to have loving feelings. (**Have you experienced emotions as strongly as you used to?**) The third category of symptoms involves a heightened state of arousal. Individuals might experience physical sensations when reminded of the trauma, including increased heart rate, breathing faster, and sweating. People may also feel as if they are always on guard, trying to be aware of possible dangers in their environment, and have difficulty falling and staying asleep. (**Do you feel increased arousal if something reminds you of the trauma?**) [See Appendix A.]

Before moving on to a specific discussion of nightmares, it is helpful to provide clients with a contextual understanding of the development of PTSD symptoms. This can be personalized with reference to the clients' particular experiences, or it can be explained independent of their experiences. Zayfert and Becker (2007) discuss several potential obstacles related to discussion of personal trauma information at this early stage. These include eliciting memories, increasing arousal, and decreasing concentration—all of which may increase the chance that clients may not remember much of the psychoeducation component. For these reasons, as well as to enhance the education component, it is helpful to provide clients with written information, either as part of a manual or as a handout to take home. Foa and Rothbaum (1998) and Zayfert and Becker (2007) include examples of handouts in their works. Handouts are also available online (e.g., http://academicdepartments.musc. edu/ncvc/resources_public/victim_reactions_general_trauma.pdf). In general, therapists can conceptualize symptoms of PTSD as a normal response to an unexpected and terrifying situation.

If you think about these symptoms, they really do make sense and may be helpful, at least initially. The reason you may have reexperiencing symptoms is so that your body remains on alert. Your mind may continue sending danger signals in response to perceived threat. Reminding you of the trauma through intrusive thoughts and memories may be a way to keep you alert and safe at first. Avoidance of trauma-related information or cues also makes sense—it's good to stay away from things that are dangerous! It also makes sense for your body to be at a heightened state of arousal or readiness, in case the danger reappears—you want to be ready to react if this happens. So how do we move from a normal response to an ongoing problem? Part of what happens may be that your system does not adjust for the fact that the traumatic event is over. The event does not get processed or resolved as with other experiences we have. When something is not resolved, we tend to keep thinking about it, even when we don't want to. (**Can you think of an example [other than the trauma] in which you continued to think about an issue or problem because it wasn't quite resolved?**) Another problem is that these fear responses generalize to stimuli that are somehow associated with the traumatic event but are not dangerous in and of themselves. For example, a combat veteran may begin to respond with fear to sights and sounds that remind him or her of the combat experience, including a car backfiring, walking into the woods, or hearing fireworks. A rape victim may begin to fear men who resemble the rapist, cars that are similar to the one she was raped in, the scent of the cologne the rapist was wearing, etc. These stimuli, that are inherently not dangerous, become cues or triggers of the traumatic event. If you are responding with fear to these cues, you will likely start to avoid them. Escaping the feelings of fear and avoiding the trauma cues will likely initially cause you to feel relief but over the longer term only serves to maintain the problem. You don't have the opportunity to learn that things like cars and cologne are not dangerous. (**Are you aware of anything that might be a cue for the traumatic event?**) [See Appendix A.]

The therapist should also provide information about other areas that may be affected by the traumatic event.

Other negative consequences of trauma may include panic attacks, increased substance use, feelings of sadness or depression, anxiety, problems relating to other people, and sleep disturbance. The way we think about ourselves, other people, and the world may also change following a trauma, especially in the areas of powerlessness, esteem, safety, intimacy, and trust. (**Have you noticed a change in the way you think about yourself? People around you? Do you see the world differently?**) Although these difficulties are not uncommon in individuals who report experiencing a trauma, the good news is that many of the problems may go away on their own over time. Also, there are treatments available that have been shown to be quite effective in treating many of these difficulties. Finally, many people show resiliency when faced with a trauma and are able to find meaning in what they experienced. [See Appendix A.]

Nightmares

During this discussion, nightmares are identified as one of several potential reexperiencing symptoms, and the therapist reiterates to clients that experiencing nightmares is not necessarily an indicator that an individual meets criteria for PTSD. The following specific information is provided to clients, and, as above, this process is interactive with additional information sought from the clients about their particular experiences of nightmares.

Research studies suggest that approximately 5% of the population suffers from nightmares at any one time, and the rates are much higher, about 50% to 88%, for those who have experienced a trauma and have PTSD. Nightmares and sleep disturbances are considered the hallmark of PTSD and more people with PTSD report nightmares than those without PTSD. Experiencing a traumatic event may initiate or exacerbate the occurrence of nightmares. **(Did you have nightmares before the traumatic event? If yes, did the nightmares change in frequency, severity, or content after the traumatic event?)** The increased variability in heart rate and respiratory rate that often accompanies nightmares is consistent with the physiological arousal to cues seen in PTSD as well as physiological arousal symptoms of panic attacks. These responses, along with dream content associated with a traumatic event, may themselves also serve as trauma cues that further heighten the level of arousal and distress in individuals with PTSD. Nightmares may cause considerable sleep disruption, which could lead to distress during the day, potentially increasing the opportunity for more nightmares and disruption in functioning.

A number of theories provide possible explanations for the occurrence of nightmares. As discussed above, having nightmares is one of the reexperiencing symptoms of PTSD. It is thought that the memories of the traumatic event are not appropriately processed or stored in the brain because of the impact of the high level of distress and arousal experienced at the time of the trauma and its resulting impact on the brain. It may be that the mind is attempting to process information during the daytime through flashbacks and intrusive thoughts and at night through nightmares. Indeed, some researchers believe that chronic nightmares may reflect specific cognitive or emotional aspects of the trauma that remain unresolved. Continued experiencing of the nightmares may be the mind's attempt to gain mastery over those particular aspects of the traumatic event or its aftermath.

Another theory suggests that an individual's imagery system is initially disrupted by the overwhelming nature of the traumatic event. Individuals may then become particularly uncomfortable with imagery because of what they have been through. They may have learned through intrusive memories, flashbacks, and nightmares to engage in primarily verbal thought instead and try to avoid imagery at all times (including daydreams and imagining solutions to problems), as they don't know when a flashback or intrusion may occur. Nightmares typically have a natural capacity and inclination to change—most people who experience a trauma will have nightmares initially, then the nightmares change and fade over time. This process happens with non-trauma-related nightmares as well—we may have a nightmare, and through the night the images and story will change and morph into something else, other dreams; however, if a person is avoiding imagery and wakes up from the nightmare with significant distress, there is no opportunity for self-correction or change, and the nightmares continue.

Dreams and nightmares also have been conceptualized as visual metaphors for primary emotions (e.g., fear, terror, guilt). If your primary emotion is fear, then your mind will create a story line for that emotion. Your mind may also associate your nightmare with other times in which you were afraid, but things turned out okay. It is thought that this may be how nightmares end up changing over time, becoming less scary and less disturbing, and the information is integrated with other thoughts and memories. However, this does not appear to happen with chronic nightmares, particularly those that replay the traumatic event. Something seems to be keeping the nightmare isolated, so that these other connections are not made, and the nightmare does not change. It is possible that, because people wake up from the nightmares, they do not experience habituation—the decrease of fear that typically accompanies exposure to a feared stimulus—and may even become more sensitized to fear cues and more prone to avoiding trauma and nightmare cues, including avoiding sleep.

Finally, while nightmares may begin following a traumatic event, they may become separate from the trauma over time and become a problem in and of themselves. If we believe that they are initially helpful, by trying to help us to process the trauma or keep us vigilant, at some point that doesn't seem to be the case anymore. Why would nightmares continue for so long? For some people, the nightmares may become the thing to be afraid of, instead of or in addition to the trauma. [See Appendix A]

The information above can be overwhelming to clients; it is important for the therapist to query the clients and ascertain how much they are taking in, as illustrated in the following case example.

Case Example

Therapist: So, there are a lot of ways that therapists and researchers are thinking about how and why nightmares develop. We're still not sure how it all works. What do you think about the different ideas of how nightmares develop?

Client: I'm not sure—there are so many different ways to look at it.

T: That's true. It could be that each theory is correct to some degree.

C: Yeah, I can see that. They do seem to go together. Could different theories be accurate for different people?

T: Absolutely! It is unlikely that there is just one pathway for everyone. There are likely a number of factors that may make some of us more vulnerable to developing nightmares after a trauma.

C: That's true—if not everyone has them, then something else must be going on.

T: Right. And even among all the people who develop nightmares, all trauma-related nightmares are not the same for everyone, and they may not be the same for any individual over time. Nightmares may initially be just like the traumatic event, almost a reenactment of the trauma. What are your nightmares like? Do they seem to be replaying the traumatic event, have some similarities to the trauma, or seem unrelated?

C: Well, at first—for like 3 years after the rape, it seemed almost exactly the same. I'm sure something could have been different, but it seemed the same. The way I felt, the place, everything seemed the same. His voice was the same and what he said never changed.

T: So it was pretty much the rape over and over again?

C: Yes, it was like being raped almost every night for 3 years.

T: So it sounds like it must have changed then, after those first 3 years. What have the nightmares been like since then?

C: I remember that they started to change when I got married. They became even worse—sometimes instead of the guy who raped me, it would be my husband hurting me.

T: That must have been really hard—to dream of someone you love being the one to hurt you.

That nightmares change over time is not unusual. Clients often report that the nightmares will at some point begin to include other aspects of life and more recent stressors. They may include people, places, or situations that were not involved in the original trauma. The nightmares may also change over time to reflect potent, unresolved issues related to trauma (e.g., powerlessness, esteem, safety, intimacy, trust). Thus, it is important for the therapist to understand if and how the nightmares have changed over time, as this may provide an indication of issues clients are coping with.

At this point, the "vicious cycle" of nightmare maintenance is introduced (Davis, 2003; Davis & Wright, 2007), as described in chapter 3.

Regardless of the specific mechanism by which the nightmare develops, it is thought to be maintained over time through various channels, with avoidance being the primary component. The experience of the nightmare itself often results in a high level of arousal, distress, fear, and panic symptoms upon awakening (including racing heart, sweating, trembling, hyperventilating or feeling unable to breathe). Clients often do not return to sleep at all or for significant lengths of time due to either a fear of returning to sleep ("I may have another nightmare") or difficulty returning to sleep due to high physiological and/or cognitive arousal. Indeed, physiological responses, negative cognitions, and dream content associated with the traumatic event may themselves serve as trauma cues that further heighten the level of arousal and distress, perhaps especially for those individuals with PTSD.

> Nightmares in and of themselves are quite disturbing and disruptive. Nightmares may also impact other areas of functioning. For example, because survivors grow to fear having a nightmare, their sleep habits become affected. Survivors may anticipate having a nightmare when they begin to feel tired and get ready to go to bed. They may worry about having a nightmare and become anxious, aroused and distressed, increasing the chance that they will have a nightmare. This may also increase the amount of time between getting ready to go to sleep and actually falling asleep. (**Do you find yourself distressed before going to bed? What is this like for you?**) Experiencing nightmares may also increase your level of arousal and distress during the day, as you may be remembering aspects of the nightmare and the trauma. (**Do you experience more distress than usual the day after a nightmare? What is that like for you? How do you cope with the distress?**) [See Appendix A.]

Over time, the nightmares and resulting sleep disturbances may result in sleep deprivation. Sleep deprivation can have significant and sometimes debilitating effects, including confusion, memory loss, irritability, difficulties engaging in creative thinking, lowered response inhibition, and emotional highs and lows. In addition to the manifestations of sleep deprivation, clients likely experience increased daytime arousal due to a lack of sleep, memories of the nightmare content, and possibly memories of the trauma itself. Clients often respond to this distress through increased avoidance. Specifically regarding the nightmare, many of our clients have never told anyone of the content of their nightmares prior to their involvement in our studies.

As the time to get ready for sleep the next evening approaches, clients may experience anticipatory anxiety. Increased anxiety or fear about going to sleep may lead to increased arousal (indeed, some believe that this may be a major part of the maintenance of nightmares). The increased arousal may be exacerbated by distorted cognitions and negative self-talk (e.g., "Why can't I get over this?"; "I'm never going to be able to sleep peacefully"; "Why am I powerless to stop this?").

Clients often engage in maladaptive sleep habits in order to try to get to sleep or to avoid sleep. These may include using substances (e.g., alcohol, sleeping pills) at night to promote sleep, watching television or reading in bed to try to forget about the nightmare, and staying active very late to delay sleep and increase the chance of falling asleep quickly. While these activities may be helpful in the short term, their continued use is likely to maintain the problems over time. More information is provided on the impact of maladaptive sleep habits below.

Finally, there appears to be a very potent cognitive component to the maintenance of nightmares—a sense of profound powerlessness. Most people believe that they have little control over what happens during sleep, and survivors of trauma often believe they have little control over their lives in general. It is not surprising, then, that so few believe that they can do anything about their nightmares. They may not mention them or seek treatment for them because they truly believe that nothing can be done. Others may believe that the nightmares are not going to go away until they are able to process the trauma as a whole (Krakow, 2004)—in other words, "Once I deal with what happened to me, the nightmares and other distress will go away." This may be true for many people, but we point out to clients that the results of the treatment suggest that working with the nightmare component has a positive impact on other symptoms of distress.

Therapists may want to incorporate this more in-depth description of nightmare maintenance or may choose to simplify the explanation.

It's no wonder survivors report feeling distress! Between the nightmares themselves, disrupted sleep, increased arousal and distress during the day because of the nightmares, as well as having difficulty getting to sleep because of fearing and worrying about having nightmares, it would be very difficult to not have your functioning impaired. What you are experiencing is a vicious cycle of intrusive experiences, distress, and increased arousal creating more intrusive experiences. This treatment will help you break this cycle and will hopefully result in increased functioning in many different areas. [See Appendix A.]

Sleep Hygiene

The notion of sleep habits changing related to anticipatory anxiety is then expanded upon.

One of the primary ways in which nightmares may impact your functioning is by affecting the quality and quantity of sleep you get each night. As was discussed above, you may be getting less sleep overall, obtaining a poorer quality of sleep, feeling anxious when it is time to get ready for sleep, and feeling sleep deprived during the day. Because of these problems, many people who suffer from nightmares alter their sleep habits to try to improve their sleep. (**Think about your own situation—what do you do if you have trouble getting to sleep at night? When you have a nightmare, what do you do to try to return to sleep?**)

Some of the behaviors that people engage in to improve their sleep may be helpful in the short term, but often are not helpful in the long term. These sleep behaviors, or habits, eventually mess up your sleep cycle and may create significant problems in terms of increasing distress, contributing to other sleep problems, and actually increase problems related to sleep deprivation and the chance of having a nightmare. Next we will review a list of "dos and don'ts" related to sleep. As we go through the list, identify those behaviors that you engage in that may be helpful and those that may not be helpful. [See Appendix A.]

We then present information on helpful and unhelpful sleep habits (the list is provided in Appendix A) that incorporates aspects of both sleep hygiene and stimulus control and explain why they are helpful or unhelpful. We ask clients to identify three helpful and three unhelpful sleep habits they currently engage in. We then ask them to choose one unhelpful sleep habit to target for change over the following week. While some clients may readily accept our explanation and engage in planning to change their sleep habits, many others are more reluctant. Often, clients are very wedded to their sleep habits, erroneously believing that they are helpful long term and fear giving them up. As with any other change clients would be asked to make in therapy, it is important to not overwhelm them with the amount of change requested in a short period of time. One way to ease clients into the change is to develop a hierarchy of steps leading to the changed behavior. This step-by-step method breaks the change down into smaller, more attainable goals that they can actually see themselves able to complete. For example, if a client chooses to change the habit of smoking right up until he or she gets into bed, the therapist can encourage him or her to start with not smoking 10 minutes prior to bedtime the first 2 nights, 15 minutes the second 2 nights, and so forth. When considering altering sleep habits, it is also important to keep in mind that stimulus control appears quite helpful in restoring appropriate sleep (Morin, Culbert, & Schwartz, 1994; although see Broomfield, Gumley, & Espie, 2005, for discussion), so therapists may want to encourage changes using this principle. Stimulus control specifically refers to establishing discriminative stimuli for the sleeping environment, including using the bed only for sleeping and sexual activity, waking at the same time every day, lying down only when sleepy, getting out of bed if unable to fall asleep within 15 to 20 minutes, and returning only when sleepy (Bootzin & Epstein, 2000). All participants are encouraged to engage in these strategies.

Case Example[1]

Therapist: Some of the behaviors that people engage in to improve their sleep may be helpful in the short term but often are not helpful in the long term. These sleep behaviors or habits eventually mess up your sleep cycle and may create significant problems in terms of distress, contributing to other sleep problems and actually increasing problems related to sleep deprivation and the chance that you will have a nightmare. So after reviewing this list of dos and don'ts, what are some sleep habits that you engage in that are healthy?

Client: Well, I read before bed, but I don't actually read in the bed—I read in the front room until I get tired and then go to bed.

T: Do you find that reading relaxes you before you go to bed?

C: Oh yes, I not only read before bed, but I also read whenever I wake up in the middle of the night after having a nightmare, which helps me go back to bed.

T: Very good, it sounds like you are already engaging in some healthy sleep behaviors. What type of books do you read before bed?

---

[1] Thanks to Patricia Byrd for this case example.

C: Well, my favorite types of books to read are Stephen King books.

T: Hmmm. The healthy part of reading before bed is to relax you, and I don't know if reading horror novels would meet that purpose

C: Yeah, that's true, because often after I have read one of those books, I have to leave the light on in the bedroom to get to sleep!

T: Well, how about if we replace the Stephen King books with something that would be a little calmer. Does that sound like something you can do?

C: Yeah, I could do that.

T: Good. Are there any other healthy sleep behaviors from the list that you are currently doing?

C: Well, I don't drink caffeine after noon, and I don't eat heavy meals after 8:00 p.m.

T: Those are all good things. Now look at the not-so-healthy sleep habits. Are there any of those that you regularly do?

C: I sleep with the TV on in my bedroom, but I am not going to change that because I can't sleep without the TV on.

T: Okay, what happens, though, is that our mind gets ready and turns itself on whenever it is expecting to pay attention to something instead of starting to turn itself off so you can get some sleep.

C: I have had other people tell me not to sleep with the TV on, and I have tried it and it was awful. I got the worst night's sleep in my life. I am telling you I am different, the TV helps me sleep.

T: When you tried in the past to sleep without the TV on, what happened?

C: Well I just laid there worrying, I need the TV to distract me.

T: Were there specific things that you were worrying about?

C: I don't remember—well, actually, I was scared someone was in the room with me, like in the closet or something, and I got myself all freaked out!

T: So when the TV is on, you don't worry about such things as that?

C: No, because when the TV is on, I can see pretty much everything in my room, so there are no dark places for someone to hide.

T: So maybe the TV helps you sleep because it keeps the room from being completely dark.

C: Yeah, I guess so. I had never really thought this out before, but yeah, the light from the TV is what relaxes me.

T: Then what would you think about trying not to watch TV in bed and instead getting a night-light so that you still have the comfort of the light in your room?

C: Okay, I guess I could try that, it doesn't sound too bad.

T: Well, are there other possibly unhealthy sleep behaviors that you iden-tify with on the list?

C: I smoke right before bed, and I drink lots of water right before bed, too.

T: Alright, well, maybe these can be other habits that we work on through-out the treatment. How about for this week, we just work on reading more relaxing books before bed instead of horror novels and getting a night-light so that next week you can try sleeping in your bed without the TV on.

C: Alright, that sounds good.

Sometimes clients will describe difficulty going to sleep because they are worrying about various things (e.g., what they have to do the next day, how to cope with some stressor). We encourage these individuals to keep a pad of paper by their bed at night and write down what they are concerned about. Then, they will not forget about their worries in the morning. We even encourage some people to set aside time during the day to worry, so that they do not have to do it right before going to sleep.

PROGRESSIVE MUSCLE RELAXATION

Although their specific traumatic events are not discussed in much detail in Session 1, clients may be emotionally aroused by talking about trauma and symptoms in general. It is important to reduce their arousal and dis-tress before they leave the session. Thus, Session 1 ends with instruction and practice of PMR. A variety of PMR scripts are available for use, and many bookstores sell various relaxation audio cds and tapes. We use a comprehensive script that incorporates muscle tension and relaxation, deep breathing, association of breathing with calming words, and guided imagery.

Before starting relaxation, the use of subjective units of distress (SUDs) is explained. The therapist describes SUDs as a 0-to-100-point scale in which a score of 0 means clients are completely calm and relaxed, 50 indicates clients are moderately anxious, and 100 represents an intol-erable level of anxiety. After this explanation, the therapist asks clients to rate their SUDs prior to demonstrating the relaxation procedure so that they will have a way to compare how they felt before and after the relaxation procedure.

> Many people find it difficult to relax, particularly those who are experiencing a great deal of stress or are battling some emotional problems. In this treatment, you will learn different types of relaxation procedures that have been used in numerous treatments for anxiety and other types of difficulties. The first one that you will learn today is called progressive muscle relaxation, or PMR. PMR refers to alternately tensing and relaxing different muscle groups in your body. This technique helps people to learn the difference between feelings of tension and relaxation. We will go through this procedure together during session, and then you will be provided a CD of PMR to use at home. As with any new behavior, it may require that you do the exercises a few times to gain the full benefit. One of the things you will be asked to do over the next week is to rate your level of anxiety before and after doing PMR so that you and the therapist can assess how well it is helping you. Some people have significant difficulty relaxing, and engaging in relaxation procedures may actually make them feel more tense. If this is the case for you, make sure you let your therapist know. [See Appendix A.]

We conduct the full PMR script in session for several reasons. First, this allows clients to ask questions about the procedure. Second, some individuals have such a difficult time relaxing that they may experience relaxation-induced anxiety (Adler, Craske, & Barlow, 1987), particularly those prone to panic attacks (Cohen, Barlow, & Blanchard, 1985). Conducting PMR in session allows us to ascertain if PMR actually increases, rather than decreases, anxiety levels. Finally, we use PMR to initiate in the clients a belief in their ability to have some control over their emotions. Clients almost always report a decrease in SUDs ratings following PMR. Usually this is by quite a bit, but sometimes it is only a slight decrease. Regardless of how much the SUDs ratings changed, it is important to point out to the clients that it did change. We make a point of this to introduce the notion that they have much more control over their distress than they probably believe.

Case Example

Therapist: Now that we have finished the relaxation, can you give me a SUDs rating?
Client: I'm at about a 45.

T: Wow—that's great! Sometimes we go through life thinking that we have no control of our emotions—that we get distressed or anxious and can't do much about it—but you've just shown how much control you do have! In just 20 minutes, you were able to take your anxiety from a 75 to a 45—that's very impressive!!

C: Yeah, I guess it did decrease a lot. I was even starting to get sleepy!

T: This is one of the most important things you will learn in this treatment—how much control you actually have over your emotions AND your nightmares!

HOMEWORK

Before assigning the actual homework, the therapist should again empha-size the importance of completing it. We do this by stressing that what happens outside of the actual session can create the most improvement—you get out of the treatment what you put into it. We also encourage clients to contact the therapist if they have any questions or concerns about completing the assignments.

For homework, we ask them to practice PMR with a tape or CD (that we provide) each night before they go to sleep and to monitor their SUDs before and after the exercise. We explain to them that we will use the rating scale to determine how well PMR is working for them. We also ask them to complete the Daily Sleep Activities Log (Thompson, Hamilton, & West, 1995) each morning when they wake up. This again allows clients and the therapist to assess any changes in the frequency and intensity of the nightmares as well as the quality and quantity of sleep they are getting. As discussed above, clients choose one unhelpful sleep habit and alter it over the next week, and they use the Sleep Habit Log to monitor what sleep habit they are trying to change and what they do to change it. Lastly, we have them complete the Daily PTSD Symptom Log (Falsetti & Resnick, 2000). Although not everyone involved in this treatment meets criteria for PTSD, many will have symptoms of PTSD. Completing the PTSD Symptom Log will help the clients and the therapist to determine if the therapy is helping to reduce these symptoms.

A lot of information is packed into this initial session; it may be more feasible for some to break this material into two sessions. This could be accomplished with one session strictly devoted to psychoeducation of trauma reactions and the second devoted to education on nightmares and sleep hygiene. However, if the information is distributed across sessions, we highly recommend that the initial session end with the re-laxation procedure due to the potential for increased distress. Modifying the treatment protocol is discussed further in chapter 9, and a sample extended treatment outline is provided.

Many clients find the information from the first session very infor-mative and helpful. Many feel isolated and alone in their experience of trauma and nightmares. After the first session, this sense of isolation seems greatly decreased, which is a step toward facing the nightmare head on. Of course, not everyone will progress at the same pace, and it is important for the therapist to check distress levels prior to the clients' leaving and to determine if the clients have questions about anything from the session. We encourage clients to read over Session 1 of their manuals and to bring any questions to the next session. They may also contact the therapist between sessions if they have questions or any concerns or difficulties with the homework assignments.

7 Session 2

The second session is the longest and most intensive of the three sessions. Session 2 begins with a completion of the weekly measures, review of the previous week's homework, resolution of any concerns related to the homework, provision of a rationale for exposure to the nightmare, and instructions for exposure to the nightmare. The exposure to the nightmare is first done in writing, then orally. After the clients complete the written version of the nightmare and read it aloud, the therapist helps the clients identify potential trauma themes within the nightmare. A rationale for rescription of the nightmare is then presented, and the clients rescript the nightmare. The rescription is done both in writing and orally. The session ends with instruction and practice of diaphragmatic breathing and the assignment of homework for the coming week.

HOMEWORK REVIEW

Session 2 begins with a review of the homework assignments. The therapist should visually review each component of the homework assigned, including relaxation monitoring forms, sleep habit logs, PTSD checklist, and daily sleep logs. In particular, it is important to determine whether clients did PMR using the tape/CD, whether they experienced any

139

problems with it, and whether their SUDs ratings decreased following the relaxation procedures. The need to assess for induction of panic symptoms (panicogenic) in response to the relaxation procedure is underlined by research findings that such responses are associated with poorer treatment outcome (e.g., Borkovec et al., 1987). Some studies suggest that relaxation-induced anxiety may be related to a fear of losing control, which is not uncommon among trauma survivors, or to sensitivity to the sensory effects of relaxation (Brown, O'Leary, & Barlow, 2001; Heide & Borkovec, 1983, 1984). This may be particularly true for clients with nightmares, as they may already be conditioned to perceive the sensation of physical relaxation as a threatening or uncomfortable cue due to experiencing terrifying nightmares during the relaxed state of sleep.

Case Example

Therapist: I see from your relaxation record that the first 2 nights you did the relaxation tape, you were only able to do part of it, and it seemed to increase rather than decrease your anxiety.

Client: Yes—I just couldn't finish it.

T: Tell me what you were experiencing during the relaxation procedure.

C: Well, I felt my body becoming heavier and weaker, and I would just get really uncomfortable until I couldn't stand it anymore.

T: Were there particular thoughts going through your head while this was happening?

C: Um, I'm not sure—I know that I just didn't feel safe or comfortable. I felt better when I turned off the CD and got up and moved around.

T: I'm wondering if your mind is making a connection between feeling relaxed and going to sleep. Perhaps when you are listening to the CD and starting to relax, you start to feel anxious—similar to how your anxiety increases before going to sleep because you are worried about having a nightmare.

C: I don't know, I haven't really thought about it.

T: Well, the physiological sensations are quite similar—your body feels heavier, your mind starts to drift, you may feel somewhat dizzy. These sensations may be more pronounced or come on quicker for someone who is sleep deprived.

C: Yeah, I guess they are similar.

T: We talked last week about some of the things you do when you start to fall asleep—do you remember?

C: I get up and do busy work around the house, usually, until I am utterly exhausted and just drop.

T: Why do you think you do that?

C: Because I don't want to go to sleep—even just feeling like I'm drifting off makes me scared. I don't want to have a nightmare, so I just try to stay awake.

T: Right, so by trying to avoid sleep and waiting until you are completely exhausted to go to bed, you may be avoiding the sensations of falling asleep because they happen so quickly when you're totally worn out. Unfortunately, by continuing to avoid those relaxing sensations as you are falling asleep, you are maintaining the fear of those sensations. This is just like other things that you said you were avoiding because they were uncomfortable—things related to the trauma. Do you find yourself avoiding relaxing at other times?

C: Well, most people who know me would say I just don't relax—it's not in me.

T: Okay—so what we need to do now is help you be able to be relaxed and feel safe doing it.

If clients report that PMR initiates panicogenic responses, Brown and colleagues (2001) recommend that the therapist inform them that the response is likely a transient one that will diminish with continued practice of the technique. If clients continue to have difficulties, the procedure can be modified—including having the clients keep their eyes open during the relaxation. Clients also may benefit from graded exposure to the sensations of relaxation. Comparable to interoceptive exposure, which attempts to reduce fear of physiological symptoms similar to those experienced during a panic attack through exposure to those symptoms (Craske & Barlow, 2001), gradual exposure to sensations of relaxation may aid in habituating individuals to these sensations. As with most exposure techniques, it is very important that clients engage in consistent, repeated practice of the techniques and remain with their uncomfortable emotions until their anxiety has significantly decreased.

The therapist should also assess the progress that clients have made on modifying their sleep habits. If clients are having difficulties with the modification, the therapist will want to examine the steps developed to determine if the clients were trying to do too much too soon. Creating additional "mini steps" may reduce some of the anxiety related to making these changes. Clients should be given a lot of credit for any step taken to modify their behavior. It is often helpful to remind them that they may have been engaging in this behavior for quite sometime, possibly years; therefore, it may take some time for them to get used to doing it another way and for them to start feeling the benefits. In our experience, although a minority of people report having some trouble modifying sleep habits, most people find it much easier than they thought, and they progress through the steps more quickly than anticipated.

The clients' sleep quality and quantity is reviewed from their daily sleep logs as well as any changes in nightmare frequency, severity, or content. Interestingly, at this point in the treatment—after only one session— a number of clients report that some change has occurred. For example, one participant was quite happy at the beginning of the second session and reported, "I had several nightmares through the week, but I didn't have *the* nightmare." She went on to explain that she had not had a single night, much less a week, without dreaming about the trauma for as long as she could remember. Another participant reported fewer nightmares and experienced a dream that was not a nightmare for the first time in a long time. PTSD symptoms should also be reviewed; in particular, if there seems to be a pattern between frequency of PTSD symptoms and reported sleep problems and nightmares, the therapist can ask about the context of this association and reinforce previous discussions by pointing out the patterns of life events, symptoms of distress, and poor sleep.

Case Example

Therapist: I noticed that you had a lot of trouble sleeping Tuesday and Wednesday.

Client: Yeah, it took forever to go to sleep, and I had nightmares both nights. Wednesday, I just couldn't get back to sleep.

T: It looks like you also indicated a number of PTSD symptoms on those days. Can you tell me what was going on?

C: I had dinner with a friend from college who was in town. We started talking about old friends and . . . I don't know . . . a lot of memories just came flooding back.

T: Memories of the assault?

C: Yeah, and everything that happened afterward. I haven't really thought about it for a long time.

T: So you had a lot of memories on those days, and your anxiety was pretty high. Then you found it difficult to sleep that night.

C: Yeah, I mean, I usually have trouble sleeping, but this was worse. I hadn't really connected it to seeing Lisa, though. I guess that makes sense.

EXPOSURE TO THE NIGHTMARE

The idea of coming face to face with a fearful stimulus that an individual has been actively avoiding is challenging, both for the clients and the therapist. While the fact that the clients are in treatment suggests they are somewhat aware that coping through avoidance has not been successful in the long term, they may continue to experience short-term negative reinforcement that provides some reassurance and comfort. This comfort, although ineffective and short-lived, may be quite difficult to abandon and may be perceived as better than the unknown. The therapist can do a few things to assist with this process. First, the therapist can draw on the motivation that brought the clients into treatment in the first place by reviewing their initial complaints and using them to reinforce the goals of treatment. Second, the therapist should provide a clear and comprehensive rationale for using exposure techniques and reassure clients of the effectiveness of the techniques. Suggestions for framing the rationale are presented below. Third, the confidence and support of the therapist will likely play a significant role in the clients' willingness to trust the therapist enough to engage in an anxiety-provoking activity (Zayfert & Becker, 2007). Therapists need to be aware and in control of their own emotions. Although these issues are addressed more fully in chapter 9, it is important to note here that working with trauma survivors can be challenging. The therapist bears witness to very difficult information through hearing about the traumatic event and sitting in the presence of clients who might be very distressed. It is essential for the therapist to be present and calm in order to help the clients sit with their anxiety.

Finally, some therapists are reluctant to "induce distress" in their clients and shy away from exposure techniques. However, temporary increases in distress in therapy are probably more the rule than the exception. Whenever the therapist hits upon sensitive issues in session, the clients' anxiety and distress are likely to increase; this phenomenon is not trauma specific. See chapter 9 for additional information on concerns about exposure techniques.

Rationale for Exposure

It is important to provide clients with a comprehensive rationale for engaging in exposure work to enhance their motivation and enable them to make fully informed decisions to continue with the treatment. This rationale should incorporate the information provided in the first session on reactions to trauma and theories of the development and maintenance of nightmares, as demonstrated in the case example below. We generally ask clients if they have discussed the nightmares with anyone, if they spend time thinking about or visualizing the nightmares, and if they have ever kept a dream log or journal of their nightmares. Most of our clients have not talked or written about their nightmares and report that they avoid thinking about them the next day. Further, if a visual image of the nightmare enters their mind during the day, they try to turn it off immediately.

Case Example

Therapist: As we discussed in the first session, there are a number of reasons why you may be experiencing nightmares. Your mind may be trying to process the traumatic event, you may have developed sleep habits that promote restless sleep and nightmares, or your mind may be creating a story line to match your emotional state. Regardless of the reason for your nightmares, you are currently in a vicious cycle of experiencing nightmares, increased daytime distress related to the nightmares, anticipatory anxiety about the nightmares, and more nightmares. Because of the distress that the nightmares cause, many people avoid thinking about or talking about the nightmares. Have you ever told anyone about the nightmares?

Client: Well, my wife knows that I have them, because I talk and yell a lot during them, but I've never told her what they are about.

T: What has stopped you from telling her?

C: I guess part of it is that I just don't want to talk about it—I'm worried that she'd start asking me questions about the molestation. I mean, she knows that it happened, but doesn't know any details. I just don't want to go there.

T: Do you think about the nightmares during the day?

C: No . . . well, I mean, scenes of the nightmare will sometimes flash in my mind the next day—but I try to get real busy when that happens, push it out of my head.

T: Have you ever visualized the nightmare start to finish during the day or written it down?

C: No—it's bad enough having them at night, I don't want to deal with it during the day.

T: So it sounds like you are really working hard to avoid thinking or talking about the nightmares during the day—even just visualizing it or writing it down seems like it might be uncomfortable.

C: Definitely—it's just so horrible, I just want to forget!

T: That makes sense! When something is really distressing, it is pretty normal to try to avoid it. When you get a flash of a scene from the nightmare in your mind, how do you feel?

C: Awful—dirty.

T: And when you get busy and are able to push it out of your mind, how do you feel?

C: Relieved . . . better. Well, for a while anyway. The discomfort seems to stay with me the whole day, even if I'm not thinking about it at that moment. There's just a sense of being tired—like something is off.

T: Unfortunately, that is the way that avoidance tends to work. As we talked about last session, avoiding addressing the nightmares may be helpful in the short term in that it allows you some decreased distress, some relief, but avoiding actually maintains the problem in the long term. Just as with PTSD, if you continue to avoid reminders of the trauma, you don't allow yourself to work through the thoughts and feelings related to the trauma, and you don't fully recover.

C: That's true—and by the time I get home from work, I am already thinking about going to sleep that night and dreading it.

T: That's the vicious cycle of nightmares. What you are experiencing is actually common for many types of fears and anxieties. The good news is that there are ways to break the cycle—indeed, researchers have found that one of the most helpful ways to deal with many different types of fears is to face them head on.

The next step is to provide the rationale for using exposure techniques. The rationale for exposure should include several main points. First, nightmares, as well as other PTSD symptoms, are thought to develop in part because the traumatic event is not processed in the same way as other types of experiences. The ineffective processing may result in continually reexperiencing symptoms, as the mind continues to try to understand and make sense of the traumatic events and posttraumatic events. The fear that originated with the trauma becomes increasingly generalized to other people, places, and situations. The nightmare becomes a primary source of distress, and this distress is further generalized to stimuli related to the nightmare (e.g., sleep, bed, relaxation). Because of this distress, individuals begin engaging in various coping mechanisms to deal with the distress. One mechanism is to avoid those things that are creating the distress. So individuals increasingly avoid those people, places, and situations that produce the fear. Avoidance is maintained overtime because it is associated with immediate feelings of relief and escaping the distress. Foa and Kozak (1986) suggest that this avoidance maintains the distress by not allowing for corrective learning to take place. For example, the woman in the previous chapter reported continued avoidance of the place where her assault occurred. She reported that her avoidance and distress increased, rather than decreased, over time, and she began parking farther away from the site of the rape. By not approaching the site, she did not learn that the place in and of itself was not harmful, so it remained a source of significant distress. The avoidance of nightmare content may result in similar processes, as there is no chance to think it through and try to really understand what it means. Without the opportunity to assimilate the nightmare, it is likely to be maintained and become a chronic problem. In session, we provide a specific example of the habituation process unrelated to the person's particular trauma.

Case Example

Therapist: For example, if you were bitten by a dog, you would likely become afraid of that dog and maybe even other dogs as well. If you never allowed yourself to interact with a dog again, avoiding them at all costs, you would never learn that not all dogs are mean and bite. You would continue to feel afraid every time you encountered a dog. What if, instead of avoiding dogs, you interacted with dogs after that event—how do you think you would feel?

Client: At first I'd probably be terrified!

T: Right, the first time you approached a dog after having been bit, you might be pretty scared. How do you think you'd feel if you were to pet that dog for 30 minutes?

C: If nothing bad happened, I'd probably feel less afraid. It would be hard to be that scared for 30 minutes if nothing was happening.

T: Right. How about if you then spent time petting other types of dogs— what would happen to your anxiety?

C: I wouldn't be afraid of them after awhile.

T: Exactly. This is a process called habituation—becoming less afraid of something through repeated exposure to it. You are learning new information—that not all dogs bite, and you don't need to be afraid of all dogs. The same process works with other types of fears. If you face what you are afraid of in a safe environment until your anxiety goes down, your fear will diminish.

Written and verbal exposure to the nightmare may also allow the mind to better process the nightmare and may increase the sense of control one has over the nightmare (Davis & Wright, 2007; Foa & Rothbaum, 1998). Individuals will learn that remembering is not the same as reexperiencing and that they can remember without feeling the full intensity of distress associated with the traumatic event. Facing the nightmare directly will promote a sense of mastery, and clients will learn that they can handle the distress. This process also allows clients to begin to differentiate those things that are safe although not pleasant (the nightmare) from those things that are truly dangerous (the traumatic event; Foa & Rothbaum, 1998).

Other important information to provide to clients is that, although distress may increase during the exposure, the increase will be temporary, and repeated exposures should decrease clients' distress levels significantly. Although remembering, thinking, or visualizing the nightmare may continue to make them somewhat uncomfortable or sad, it is unlikely to create the intensity of distress that they are currently feeling. Finally, it's often helpful to provide information about the extensive empirical support for exposure techniques with many different anxiety problems, corroborating its use for trauma-related nightmares.

Instructions for Written Exposure

After presenting the rationale for the exposure, the therapist provides specific instructions for writing the nightmare. There are several steps to this component that are modeled on other exposure-based therapies (e.g., Prolonged Exposure, Multiple Channel Exposure Therapy, and Cognitive Processing Therapy). The first step is choosing which nightmare to write out. Many people report having multiple types of nightmares, although most will identify a primary, most disturbing nightmare. There are differing ideas in the literature about which nightmare clients should work on. For example, Krakow, Hollifield and colleagues (2001) discourage participants in their studies from working with the most disturbing nightmare, while Forbes et al. (2003) allow the participants to choose which nightmare to target. ERRT encourages clients to choose the most disturbing nightmare for two primary reasons. First, the treatment is brief, and we believe it is important for the clients to work on the hardest aspects while in therapy and receiving formal support. Second, if they work on another nightmare in treatment—even if it is successful—they may choose to continue avoiding the worst nightmare once they are finished with treatment and, therefore, continue to have problems. We have found that most clients do not need to do the exposure to and rescripting of each nightmare they have—addressing the most disturbing nightmare tends to have a generalized impact on other nightmares.

The second step in the exposure is to be true to the nightmare. It is important that clients make their written accounts as similar to the actual nightmares as possible in order to fully engage them emotionally and cognitively in the task. This involves writing in the present tense, as if the nightmare were occurring right now; including as much sensory information as possible, such as what the clients are seeing, smelling, hearing, feeling, and tasting; and including as much detail about the nightmare as they can recall.

> In this session, you will take a big step toward confronting the nightmares. You will begin to work on this through writing out the nightmare. You will be doing this in session, so we will be here if you find yourself becoming upset. As you begin writing, keep a few things in mind. First, remember that although it may seem as if the nightmare is real or the traumatic event is happening all over again, it is only a dream—it is not real and cannot hurt you. Telling yourself that it is not real and that you are safe can help you to start feeling some control over your emotions related to the nightmare and the trauma. Second, it is important to make the written account of the nightmare as similar to the nightmare as possible. To do this, you should write the nightmare in present tense, as if it is happening right now. Also, try to use all of your senses when writing—include descriptions of what you see, smell, hear, feel, and taste. [See Appendix A.]

We also provide them with examples of "right" and "wrong" ways to write out the nightmares to illustrate the differences in emotional impact and engagement in the two versions.

> For example, instead of writing:
> *I ran up the stairs into the bedroom and slammed the door shut. He ran up behind me, broke through the door, and told me I was in big trouble now.*
> you could write:
> *I am running up the stairs. I can feel the sweat running down my face, blurring my vision. I hear him starting up the stairs behind me. My heart is pounding, and I am very afraid. I see the bedroom door and hope that I will make it inside before he catches up to me. I am running into the bedroom,*

and I turn around and slam the door shut. I know that it won't keep him out, but it gives me a minute to think. The pictures of our family on the nightstand seem to mock me, presenting such a false picture of a normal happy family. I hear him running down the hall, hear his boots on the floor, hear him breathing hard. He slams into the door, and it opens. He is standing there in front of me, glaring at me while smiling at the same time. He tells me, "You are in big trouble now." [See Appendix A.]

Before the clients begin writing, the therapist will ask the clients for SUDs ratings to determine how anxious they are. Most clients will rate themselves fairly high at this point. We then give them approximately 10 to 20 minutes to write out the nightmare. If clients are having a difficult time during the exposure, the therapist may provide verbal encouragement (e.g., "This is really hard, but you're doing great," and so forth). The therapist may also instruct the clients in grounding techniques to assist them as they write out the nightmare. When the clients are finished writing out the nightmare, the therapist asks for another SUDs rating. Although people will respond in many different ways to the written exposure, SUDs ratings tend to remain high following the written exposure component if the clients are engaged. Some clients may have higher ratings than before they started, while others can be significantly lower. It is important to normalize their distress and remind them that the distress will dissipate.

Many of you will probably feel more anxiety after writing the nightmare. This is to be expected—the first few times you face something you fear, you are likely to feel some anxiety and distress. Don't let this discourage you—it is normal, and it won't last. The more you expose yourself to the nightmare, through writing about it, reading it, thinking about it, and talking about it, the less distress you will feel. [See Appendix A.]

IDENTIFICATION OF TRAUMA THEMES

After the participants have written out the nightmare, the trauma themes that were briefly mentioned in Session 1 are discussed more fully. These themes are drawn from information processing theory (see chapter 1). Essentially, information processing theory purports that trauma-exposed individuals sometimes develop problematic belief systems or schema. Schema are defined as ways of thinking about one's self, others, and the world that influence the way people think and feel, as well as how they respond to stimuli in their environment (McCann, Sakheim, & Abrahamson, 1988; Resick & Schnicke, 1993). Common responses following trauma are thought to be partly related to difficulties incorporating trauma experiences into existing belief systems (Resick & Schnicke, 1993). When individuals experience or encounter a schema-incongruent event, one that does not fit with their previous conceptualizations of the world, the experience and its accompanying emotions may be overwhelming. At this point, individuals must either alter the information to fit the schema (assimilation) or alter the schema to fit the information (accommodation; Resick & Schnicke, 1993). Trauma is thought to negatively affect schema related to one or more of these five areas: safety, trust, power, esteem, and intimacy (McCann et al., 1988; Resick & Schnicke, 1993).

For example, John used to believe that he was in control over what happened in his life, particularly to his own body. He was tall and muscular and was rarely concerned for his own physical safety. One night while partying at a friend's house, he became quite intoxicated and was physically attacked and raped by several men. This experience was directly counter to what he had always believed—that rape only happened to women, that he could protect himself. John might *assimilate*, or alter, the information by convincing himself that some part of him must have wanted the rape to happen, because he allowed it to happen. By contrast, if John were to *accommodate* the information, he might change his schema to incorporate the possibilities that even a man can be bodily overcome and that he is not always in control. A third response noted by Resick and Schnicke (1993) is *over-accommodation*, an extreme distortion in schema. For example, instead of changing his schema to include the possibility that in some situations he does not have control over what happens to his body or in his life, John might change his schema to suggest that he is never in control, does not have any power in his life, and is vulnerable at all times. Over-accommodation may result in dichotomized thought processes and restrict the cognitive flexibility with which individuals interpret and evaluate future information.

Domhoff (2000) suggests that trauma-related nightmares "deal, quite obviously, with emotional problems that have overwhelmed the person. . . . [T]o the degree that the experience is gradually assimilated, to that degree the dreams decrease in frequency and become altered in content." ERRT focuses on the above identified themes: power/control, safety, intimacy, trust, and esteem. Resick and Schnicke (1993) suggest that conflicting beliefs or strong negative beliefs in these areas represent "stuck points" that may be associated with significant negative emotions and behaviors. We suggest that the stuck points may also be evidenced in nightmares.

After discussing the themes and identifying them as potential stuck points, clients are provided the opportunity to read their nightmares aloud. No one is forced to read the nightmare aloud, although we encourage all clients to do this whether in individual or group therapy. Since developing ERRT, the author has had very few people who declined to read their nightmares aloud, 1 of whom later in the session reported that she regretted not reading it. Reading aloud is yet another form of exposure, which also allows for others in the group to connect with the clients and may help to reduce feelings of isolation and provide perspective for other group members. Following the reading, the clients are asked whether they can identify any relevant trauma themes in the nightmares. Although it may be more significant and meaningful for the clients to determine the themes on their own, if the individual clients struggle to identify the themes, the group and therapist can help to identify them. Once identified, the therapist may query whether the clients can see a connection between the themes identified in their nightmares and the traumatic events they experienced. Approximately 30% of our participants reported that their nightmares were dissimilar to the trauma they experienced. However, we have found that even though the content of the nightmares may not reflect the trauma, the themes are still appropriate. We also inquire as to whether the clients have noticed those particular themes playing out in their waking lives. Clients write down the three primary themes and are encouraged to pay attention to the themes for the next section of the treatment.

RESCRIPTION

After everyone has identified the primary trauma themes in their nightmares, we introduce the rescription process. Clients are asked to note their SUDs ratings before and after writing the rescriptions.

> What we would like you to do is to rewrite your nightmare. You can change any part you want—the beginning, the middle, or the end. In order for the treatment to work, however, we believe that it is important for it to be somewhat similar to the nightmare. For example, if you are having nightmares about being in a serious car accident, you may want to write the nightmare

up to the point of the actual accident and then change it so that you don't crash, but get away safely. How you rewrite it is up to you and will depend on the stuck points that you identified above. For example, if your nightmare has the theme of feeling powerless in the situation, you might want to change the dream in such a way that you are acting in a powerful manner. [See Appendix A.]

In our experience, we find that people choose a wide variety of ways to alter their nightmares. Some people use humor, some incorporate other powerful or supportive people to help them in the situation, and some develop special powers. Although we believe that it is best if the clients come up with the ideas for the rescriptions themselves, some people struggle. If this occurs, the group or therapist can assist by generating a number of options—taking care to address the primary trauma themes. For example, Sam was physically assaulted by several men at a young age. He had been having the same nightmare about the event several times per week for 23 years. In his nightmare, he was able to see their bodies and fists and flashes of the scene around him, but not their faces. The primary trauma theme identified was powerlessness. The fact that he could not remember their faces was terrifying to him, and he struggled with a way to rescript the nightmare. The group came up with a number of ideas, including that when he was in the nightmare, he could open his eyes and put cartoon faces on them, turn them into people he trusted, and make the situation a tickling match instead of an assault; or he could dress the men in Playboy bunny outfits, complete with furry tail and ears. When "Playboy bunny outfits" were mentioned, Sam began laughing heartily. Somehow that image had struck a chord with him—he laughed all the way through the rescription and later reported never having the nightmare again. Examples of several different rescriptions of a nightmare are provided at the end of this chapter.

Some individuals may experience what they consider to be nightmares but have no memory of the content of the nightmares, or they may only remember fragments. As writing out the memory is essential to the treatment, this scenario constitutes a significant obstacle. If the individuals have no memory of the nightmares, the therapist should consider whether they might actually be experiencing night terrors in which they wake up disoriented and terrified but with little-to-no memory of their dreams' content and usually little recall in the morning of the incident. Night terrors may represent a different mechanism at work and may benefit from a broader trauma-focused treatment. ERRT may still be a feasible approach for those who recall only fragments of their nightmares. One of our participants, Claire, presented with a history of early child sexual abuse and had suffered from nightmares since the age of 5. When she would awaken from a nightmare, she would only be able to recall fragments of the content. For example, she would remember large hands coming toward her or seeing a light turned on in the hallway outside her bedroom. We proceeded with treatment as structured and had her write out the fragments that she could recall and rescript each fragment. For example, she rescripted the large hands coming toward her as large hands holding a big bouquet of her favorite flowers. This approach was successful, and her nightmares decreased significantly in frequency and severity.

Finally, the participants are asked to read the rescripted versions of the nightmares aloud, giving SUDs ratings before and after the readings. By the time they have finished the rescriptions, most clients are at fairly low levels of anxiety. We take note of these declines in anxiety to maximize the clients' sense of control and mastery over their emotions, as we did following PMR. We also specifically address that they have just completed the hardest part of the treatment, and not only did they do well, they were able to face their nightmares and lower their level of distress. What generally happens over the course of this session is that the clients learn they are able to confront one of the scariest things in their lives and remain okay. Many clients report that this realization is very powerful—sometimes at the time, sometimes upon reflection. We believe that it is very important to recognize the clients' courage and bravery in confronting the nightmares and working through them. As Briere (1992) states, "The courage should be directly acknowledged by the therapist—such recognition not only reassures the client that the therapist is aware of the arduousness of the therapy process for the survivor, but also helps the therapist to develop and maintain the respect and supportiveness required of those who work with former child abuse victims" (p. 88).

DIAPHRAGMATIC BREATHING

Ending the session with another relaxation exercise helps relieve any remaining distress. Based on *Mastery of Your Anxiety and Panic* (Barlow

& Craske, 1989) and Multiple Channel Exposure Therapy (Falsetti & Resnick, 2000), we ask clients to breathe normally with one hand on their chests and another on their stomachs to determine which hand is moving more. Clients are briefly informed about "right" and "wrong" ways to breathe, and then we take them through an exercise of deep breathing, focusing on moving the diaphragm, counting on the inhalation, and thinking "relax" or "calm" on the exhalation. This is generally done 10 to 20 times. Diaphragmatic breathing also provides clients with a mobile technique for relaxing, as it may be quite challenging (and not recommended!) to do PMR while driving in rush-hour traffic.

HOMEWORK

The final component of Session 2 is assigning homework. Clients are instructed to rehearse their rescripted dreams each night before they go to sleep. They read them over and visualize them in their minds, making the images as real and vivid as possible, for a full 15 minutes. After imaginally rehearsing the rescriptions, clients do the PMR procedures with their tape/CD. Clients are also asked to practice diaphragmatic breathing for 10 minutes twice per day, rating their SUDs before and after each practice, and to work on changing another sleep habit. All the monitoring from the previous week will continue this week.

RESCRIPTION EXAMPLES

I asked three students who were trained in the nightmare treatment to independently rescript the nightmare in the manual and also on pages 148–149. What follows are their various rescriptions.

Rescription Example #1

I am running up the stairs. I can feel the sweat running down my face, blurring my vision. I hear him starting up the stairs behind me, his boots pounding against the floor. He's breathing hard, trying to catch up with me. But I have put a good distance between us. My heart is pounding, and I feel strong. As he is racing up the stairs, he has his head down, facing the floor so he doesn't see me waiting. I hear his new girlfriend giggling as she follows him up the stairs. Right before he reaches the top of the staircase, I lift my leg, with my knee bent upward, and my foot lands squarely in the middle of his chest. I see the look of shock on his face, and it makes me smile. Then I push the heel of my boot hard, sending him flailing down the stairs, knocking into the girlfriend, who starts to roll as well. I give a little wave good-bye as he and his unfortunate new girlfriend go toppling down the stairs, rolling out the front door into a large mud puddle. I calmly walk down the stairs and close the door.

Rescription Example #2

I am running up the stairs. I can feel the sweat running down my face, blurring my vision. I hear him starting up the stairs behind me. My heart is pounding, and I am very afraid. I see the bedroom door and hope that I will make it inside before he catches up to me. I run into the bedroom, and I turn around and slam the door shut. As I slam it shut, I notice there are brand-new double-bolted locks lined up and down the door, from top to bottom. I start to lock the first one, and they all simultaneously lock into place with the turn of the first lock. I am safe for the time being and have some time to think. The pictures of our family on the nightstand remind me of how much I am loved by so many people. I feel reassured and brave and remember that other areas of my life are happy and peaceful. I am reminded that normalcy is just around the corner. I hear his new girlfriend running up the stairs, calling out with concern for me. She sounds aggravated with him and shouts out that she's contacting the police. Her concern overwhelms me with feelings of security and triumph. I hear him running down the hall, hear his boots on the floor, hear him breathing hard. He slams into the door, but it doesn't budge. I suddenly hear barking dogs, and I hear him screaming. The police have arrived, and I hear them arrest him and tell him, "You are in big trouble now." I unlock and open the door, and I'm greeted by his new girlfriend hugging me, saying, "Let's get out of here once and for all!"

Rescription Example #3

I am running up the stairs. I can feel the sweat running down my face, blurring my vision. I hear him starting up the stairs behind me. My heart is pounding, and I am very afraid. I see the bedroom door and hope that I will make it inside before he catches up to me. I run into the bedroom, and I turn around and slam the door shut. I know that it won't keep him out, but it gives me a minute to think. The pictures of our family on the nightstand seem to mock me, presenting such a false picture of a normal happy family. I hear his new girlfriend laughing as she also runs up the stairs. I push the large dresser against the door to stall them both. I go out the bedroom window and climb up on the roof of the house. I scream for help as loud as I can.

A neighbor a few houses down runs over and asks what is going on. I tell him, and he calls 911 with his cell phone. My ex and his girlfriend hear me talking to the neighbor and run out of the house into their car and speed off. The police arrive soon after, and my ex and his girlfriend are arrested a few blocks down the street. I am helped down from the roof by the handsome neighbor, who looks very similar to Viggo Mortensen!!! I cry with relief in his arms and thank him. He comforts me and also gets my phone number so we can go on a date!

8 Session 3

The third and final session consists of a review of the previous week's homework, identifying any changes in symptoms over the past week, troubleshooting any areas of difficulty, teaching slowed breathing, and discussing maintenance planning. The session ends with recommendations for continued work and scheduling a posttreatment assessment.

HOMEWORK REVIEW

The homework review proceeds as in the second session, with each assignment discussed. The review in this session also includes assessing how well the clients were able to complete the breathing exercises and the imagery of their rescriptions. The clients were asked to practice the diaphragmatic breathing twice per day. In our experience, difficulty completing the breathing homework typically relates to difficulty setting aside the time to do the exercises. The therapist may need to review the rationale for doing breathing retraining and help the clients devise a way to secure time for this exercise.

We assess difficulties with rescripting, as well as changes in quality and quantity of sleep; the nature, frequency, and intensity of the target nightmare and other nightmares; the occurrence of dreams that were not nightmares; changes in PTSD symptoms; and changes in the clients' feelings about the nightmares and feelings about the traumas themselves. We do not expect necessarily that the target nightmare or other nightmares will be completely ameliorated at this point; however, the vast majority of clients do report significant reduction in the frequency and severity of not only the target nightmares but also other nightmares as well. It is rare in our experience that clients will report actually dreaming the rescripted dreams; however, many individuals report having dreams that are not nightmares, which they may not have had previously or had infrequently. It seems that as the nightmares continue to decrease in frequency and severity, and the clients are able to obtain better quality and quantity of sleep at night, their related symptoms also continue to improve. For individuals who report no change at the third session, it is important to assess compliance with each of the treatment components and assignments. Any difficulties with engaging in or completing assignments should be addressed. While the treatment is not expected to work for everyone, it is important to assess for specific factors that may contribute to the lack of response to the treatment.

TROUBLESHOOTING

Difficulties With Rescription

Although most clients do not report any difficulties with the rescripting process, a small minority may require additional assistance. The therapist will want to ensure that the clients were able to fully engage in imagining their rescriptions. Some clients may continue to engage in avoidance of anything related to the trauma, including nightmares. For these individuals, the therapist will need to determine what might be maintaining their avoidance. Some reasons may be that the clients fear related distress, loss of emotional control, or believe that imagining the rescriptions may increase the chance that they will have the nightmares.

Depending on the reason for the avoidance, the therapist has several options for intervention. The therapists can review the rationale for making the rescriptions approximate the nightmares somewhat, so that the mind is aware that they are related and can process the rescriptions (new information) in relation to the nightmares (part of the fear network). The therapist can also provide reassurance that no clients have experienced an exacerbation of nightmares from doing the rescriptions; rather, the majority of clients experience a decrease in the frequency or intensity of their nightmares. It will be important for the therapist to provide continued support and empathy to the clients and reassure them that they are in a safe place. For example, the therapist can have the clients engage in the rescription imagery while in the therapist's office and provide supportive statements (e.g., "You're doing great," or, "I know that this is tough, but you are in my office and you are safe"). The clients can then engage in self-statements when they are doing this at home. Conducting imaginal imagery in session will also allow the therapist to ascertain whether there are specific parts of the rescriptions that are particularly challenging and address those directly.

It may also be helpful to teach clients grounding techniques to increase their sense of control as they engage in the homework. One approach is to teach clients to focus on other sensory information to keep them grounded. For example, when clients are at home doing the rescriptions before going to sleep, they can be instructed to hold on to favorite pillows or blankets; if they begin feeling significantly distressed during the rescriptions, they can focus briefly on the sensation of holding the objects to remind themselves that they are in safe places, that these are stories they made up that cannot harm them, and that the nightmares or traumatic events are not happening again. Finally, it may be helpful to review the rationale for doing exposure techniques, including the safety of the technique and the evidence for its use.

Sometimes the original rescriptions may not fully address the important trauma themes or not address them sufficiently, and thus they may not be helpful to the clients.

Case Example

Sandy had been physically and sexually abused by her husband for most of the 6 years they were married. He divorced her and married another woman with whom he had been having an affair. Sandy entered treatment 1 year after the divorce. Although she rarely saw or heard from her ex-husband anymore, she continued to experience nightmares 3 to 4 nights per week. She described her nightmares as being fairly accurate portrayals of the abuse. In a typical nightmare, Sandy would be sitting in the kitchen, straining to hear the sound of her husband's car pulling into the driveway. She would be very anxious, as she never knew what he would be like when he got home. She would hear his car pull in; her heart would speed up, and she would start to shake. Her husband would enter the kitchen and immediately start berating her for something. The verbal abuse would quickly turn to physical abuse and then sexual abuse. As he would throw her on the bed and she would scream, Sandy would look out the window and see the neighbor's shades being drawn. She would feel very ashamed, scared, and alone, and she believed she would never escape this man or the abuse.

Sandy identified the primary theme of her nightmare as feeling unsafe. In her initial rescription, she is sitting in the kitchen, waiting for her husband. He enters the house and starts verbally and physically abusing her. She runs to the phone and calls the police, and then she makes it to the bedroom and locks the door before he reaches her. He is banging on the bedroom door when the police arrive. They arrest him and drive off. At the third session, Sandy reported that, while her nightmares seemed somewhat less intense, they were still very frightening and just as frequent.

Therapist: Last week you identified a lack of safety as being a primary theme of your nightmare. I am wondering if you think the rescription addresses that sense of constant danger.

Sandy: I thought it did when I wrote it out, but all week while I was imagining it, I just kept thinking of all those stories I've heard about abusers being taken away, spending a night in jail, then coming back the next day even more angry at the woman.

T: So even though he was taken away, you were pretty sure he would be coming back?

S: Yes. Of course, that made me afraid all over again.

T: I wonder if there is a way to change it so that you know that he is not going to come back, or maybe that he changes and is no longer abusive?

S: Ha! Change? Him? Don't think so. I feel sorry for his new wife—if he hasn't started with her yet, he will soon enough. He put his first wife in the hospital for a week, because she threatened to tell the cops that he was dealing drugs.

T: Okay, so changing him seems like a stretch.

S: Yes, but maybe when he gets arrested, they'll find out about his first wife and the drugs and put him away for a really long time.

T: How would you feel if you imagined that?

S: Pretty good, I think!

T: I'm also wondering about your sense of being alone—not having anyone to rely on or help you out. In your nightmare, your neighbor even closes the shade so she doesn't have to see or hear what is going on.

S: Yeah. No one ever even called the cops—and I know they must have heard what was happening. And I've never told my family—they live so far away, there is nothing they could have done, and I didn't want to worry them.

T: Is there any way that you can incorporate something into the rescription to address that sense of being alone?

S: I have some ideas.

In Sandy's revised rescription, she is sitting in the kitchen, straining to hear the sound of her husband's car pulling into the driveway. She is very anxious, as she never knows what he will be like when he gets home. She hears his car pull in, and her heart speeds up. The police are already there—she had been beaten the night before, and her neighbor drove her to the police station while her husband was at work to report the incident. Her father and brother had driven all night and were also waiting with her in the kitchen. Her husband enters the kitchen and immediately starts berating her for something. Then he realizes that the family and police are there. Before they take him away, the cops tell her that her husband is wanted on several other charges and will not be getting out of prison . . . ever!

For Sandy, it was important in her rescription not only that she get out of the immediate situation but also that she feel safe in the long term. It was also very important to address her sense of isolation and feeling that she could not count on others to be there for her. This rescription proved much more effective in ameliorating Sandy's nightmares. At a follow-up session, she reported that, while she knew there was always a chance her ex-husband could come back and harm her again, she was able to better cope with that possibility during the day and was no longer tormented by the past at night.

Some clients may not have fully engaged in the homework due to difficulties sustaining images of the rescription for a full 15 minutes. Again, this may be due to many factors. Some clients may have avoided imagery due to the negative experiences with flashbacks and nightmares, engaging primarily in verbal thought, and may have difficulty reengaging the imagery system (Krakow, 2004). Therapists may need to walk through the rescription with the clients step by step to determine whether there is a particular aspect of the imagery that is more troublesome. If a particularly troubling part is identified, the therapist can help the clients to determine why this may be more difficult, including whether there is a particular theme present in part of the dream that is not adequately dealt with in the new narrative. Therapists can also help the clients include additional details in the rescriptions to enhance the vividness of the narrative. In addition, the clients can be assigned to read the rescriptions repeatedly at the beginning and to try to incorporate the imagery more gradually.

At times, we find that clients have trouble extracting themselves from their notions of the reality of the situations. For example, women in domestic violence relationships may have difficulty rescripting their nightmares, because they cannot imagine their husbands or the situations being any different. Thompson, Hamilton, and West (1995) suggest that resistance may represent an underlying feeling of guilt related to trauma experiences. It may also be that the nightmares represent sources of protection in that they serve to keep the clients vigilant to danger. If clients are hesitant or having a difficult time, it is important to remind them that we are not trying to alter a reality—their nightmares are not a reality, they are dream experiences. Often, the group will do this spontaneously. If the clients continue to be uncertain, I may have the group give additional ideas for rewriting the nightmares to see if anything strikes the clients as more plausible while still addressing the themes. Finally, I may ask the clients to give it a try, even if they do not buy into the rescriptions. It is important to acknowledge that the technique may or may not work for them, but we can approach it as an experiment to test it out. Finally, it may be most feasible to have the client start with changing one small aspect of the nightmare (e.g., the color of the shirt they are wearing, the direction they are facing, the type of vehicle they are driving). Making this small change may be sufficient to jump-start the natural imagery process of nightmares changing and morphing over time.

Another form of resistance we encountered was a woman in a substance treatment program. Jane had experienced significant trauma in her life and had recurrent nightmares for years. When she achieved sobriety, her nightmares changed to "using" nightmares in which she dreamed that she returned to using cocaine and suffered the physical, psychological, and social consequences of using again. Jane initially sought help for the nightmares; however, after the assessment and before treatment began, she recognized that she did not actually want to get rid of them, as they served an important function in helping her to remain sober. She would awaken from her nightmares with increased determination to continue with her substance abuse treatment and to not return to a life of using.

For some individuals, additional work may be required on underlying issues before clients are ready to face their nightmares and change them. It is important that the therapist not assume that the clients are being "difficult" or that the therapy needs to be forsaken, but that instead the therapist may need to slow down and take the time to ascertain what might be going on and to work with the clients to address any salient issues. For example, Mark was a Vietnam veteran who had experienced nightmares two to three times per week since his return from Vietnam 3 decades earlier. He reported that he would occasionally have a few months' reprieve during which he would not experience the nightmares, but eventually they would return. At the beginning of the war in Iraq, the nightmares returned, and he had experienced them multiple times per week since 2003. His nightmares primarily involved losing several of his close friends in battle. Mark initially was uncomfortable engaging in the rescription, because he felt it would be disloyal to his buddies, and, ultimately, he did not want to say good-bye to them. He was afraid he would not dream about them anymore, and it would be like losing them all over again. We worked with Mark on more adaptive ways of remembering and honoring his comrades. He was then able to successfully rescript his nightmares to depict more positive memories of his buddies, and the nightmares ceased.

A final issue that a few clients have reported is boredom with the rescriptions. Some people find that a few nights of imagery are sufficient to decrease the anxiety related to the nightmares and, subsequently, the frequency and severity of the nightmares, so they become disinterested in continuing with the imagery. We believe that it is important for the clients to engage in the imagery for at least a full week and have recommended that clients enhance their rescriptions to be more powerful narratives or to add additional details to supplement their original rescriptions, particularly if they are still experiencing the nightmares. The enhanced rescriptions should continue to focus on relevant themes. If the individuals are no longer experiencing the nightmares, the work they have done may be sufficient, and they may not need to continue. At this point, however, the optimal dose of imagery is unknown and likely differs widely from person to person. Indeed, some people may not need rescripting at all, as the exposure component may be sufficient to reduce their nightmares' frequency and severity. Although the specific mechanism of change in ERRT is unknown, possibilities are addressed further in chapter 10.

SLOW BREATHING

Following the review of the homework and troubleshooting ongoing difficulties, we instruct the clients to slow their breathing. Essentially, this is engaging in the deep diaphragmatic breathing that they learned in Session 2 and extending the time to take each breath, exhaling twice as long as inhaling, to enhance the sense of relaxation. Clients are also encouraged to use the breathing technique in various situations and places to extend the benefits of relaxation.

MAINTENANCE PLANNING

The final session ends with maintenance planning and relapse prevention. As the treatment is so brief, this component is considered particularly important. Some clients may feel that such a brief treatment may not have long-term effects and fear that they may slide back to previous symptoms and habits. We discuss the findings of our research, which suggest that not only do most people tend to maintain treatment gains over time, but they actually improve as they continue to apply the skills they have learned in new and different ways.

Maintenance planning involves several steps, including reviewing changes across treatment, identifying techniques that were particularly effective or ineffective, discussing continued use of skills learned in treatment, anticipating high-risk times, and problem solving. We ask clients to describe how they are different in terms of their sleep and nightmares—not only behaviorally but also in terms of how they think about sleep and their nightmares.

Case Example

Therapist: I would like for you to think about anything that may have changed over the past 3 weeks. How are you compared to when you started?

Client: I can't believe this is only the third session—it has felt like a whirlwind.

T: Yes, this is a brief treatment, and it may seem as though we've packed a lot of information into three sessions.

C: That's for sure! Well, I haven't had the nightmare in 8 days—that's a big change!

T: When was the last time you went that long without having the night-mare?

C: I've had it every night or every other night since I can remember.

T: So this is a big change! Has your sleep changed as well?

C: Yes—I'm actually sleeping through the night, at least so far. It is actually kind of weird.

T: Even good changes can take some getting used to. Do you think about sleep or your nightmares differently now?

C: Hmm, well, the first night that I had to do the rescription, I remember going to bed a bit earlier than usual—I wasn't dreading it as much, because I was focused on doing the rescription. I guess that I'm dreading it less each night, but it's not totally gone—part of me is waiting for the nightmare to come back.

T: How are you handling that part of you?

C: Well, I guess I'm just taking it 1 night at a time. I feel lucky each morning that I wake up without having it. But I also don't feel the same way about the nightmare. I used to get so anxious and upset when an image from the nightmare would pop into my head during the day, but now when it happens, I find myself thinking about what we talked about last week—how I feel out of control, and that's coming through in my nightmare.

T: Does that change how you think and feel about the nightmare?

C: Yes—I'm now thinking of the nightmare as a kind of reminder that I need to pay attention to certain things going on in my life instead of as a dark terrible thing. I am starting to look at what's going on in my waking life.

T: So you've already noticed some changes in both your sleep and wake times. Not everyone is where you are at the end of the treatment; some may notice some small changes already, some may notice large changes, and some may feel about the same as when they started. An important aspect of this treatment is that you should continue to improve in terms of how you feel, your quality of sleep, and the nightmares, as time goes on, as long as you continue to practice those things you have learned. For some people, this simply takes a bit longer than for others. Some people believe that once they leave treatment, especially a time-limited treatment, they will start having frequent nightmares and sleeping poorly again. However, reports from previous clients suggest that this does not typically happen. The skills you have learned can be applied to other areas in your life and will assist you in identifying and adjusting what you do to impact how you feel. Of the different parts of the treatment, what do you think were the most and least helpful for you?

C: I don't know that anything was unhelpful . . . I guess hearing all that information about PTSD and trauma at the beginning was a bit overwhelming. I had to go back through the manual and reread the information a few times. I'm glad I have it all there in case I need to look back. The most helpful part, I think, was writing out the nightmare and talking about it. I just didn't think I could do it . . . it was hard. But once I did, and we talked about the lack of control and powerlessness, I don't know—it kind of made sense.

T: It seems like you're not reacting as emotionally to the nightmare but rather are thinking about it, considering it on a more cognitive level.

C: Yeah—I can actually sit and think about it now. I never used to do that.

T: You also mentioned thinking more about your waking life.

C: Yes—I am starting to see how similar issues seem to play out during the day as well, particularly in my job and in my relationships.

We then discuss how to continue utilizing the skills learned in treatment. The clients are provided with a manual of their own, so at any time they are able to look back and review the information and techniques that were taught. We also suggest that the techniques may be helpful for other situations in their lives, particularly in times of difficulty and increased stress.

The skills you have learned can be applied to other areas in your life and will assist you in identifying and adjusting what you do, which will impact how you feel. Continue to use the skills you have learned and try to avoid falling back into maladaptive patterns (sleep habits, avoidance of feared situations, etc.). There are times and situations, however, in which you may be at higher risk for falling back into old routines, feeling greater distress, even having nightmares again. These high-risk times may come when you are under significant stress or experience another traumatic event. If you do find yourself distressed, or if you have another nightmare, it is important to keep it in perspective. If you are having a hard time, try looking back through this manual and increasing the amount of time that you are practicing the breathing activities and PMR. If you have another nightmare, repeat the procedure we used on your original nightmare—exposure through writing it out and reading it and rescripting. It is very important to try not to fall back into maladaptive sleep habits and coping strategies. [See Appendix A.]

We end the session by discussing the possibility that the clients may want to seek additional help in the future. This may include a booster session to focus on sleep and nightmares, or they may choose to work on other problems.

> Although reviewing the material in this manual and practicing the procedures you have learned should significantly help your level of distress and experience of nightmares, there may come a time when you consider seeking additional treatment. Remember, although you may have been experiencing distress in a number of areas—PTSD, nightmares, depression—this treatment was designed to lower the frequency and intensity of your nightmares. Although we expect that your overall level of distress will also decrease, and your sleep quality will increase, it is not likely to relieve you of all symptoms. Seeking additional treatment should not be viewed as a failure but rather an opportunity to further process important events in your life and improve your level of functioning. [See Appendix A.]

9 Treatment Considerations

Now that you are more familiar with the treatment, we turn to various issues to consider when thinking about using ERRT. As with any treatment, ERRT may not be the most appropriate approach for every client. Below, we review what is currently known about implementing similar treatments with various clients—when is it indicated, and when is it contraindicated. But first, we start with several issues specific to therapists.

THERAPIST CONSIDERATIONS

Appropriate Training

While the procedures utilized in ERRT may appear simple and straightforward, we believe that professionals without appropriate training should not attempt to implement this treatment. As we have stated previously, "We recommend that therapists wanting to utilize this protocol have background education in cognitive behavioral theory and techniques, trauma, and sleep disorders, as well as specific training, including supervised experience, in the assessment and treatment of trauma (see also Foa, Keane, & Friedman, 2000, for practice guidelines for treating PTSD)" (Davis & Wright, 2006, p. 14).

ERRT is concerned primarily with addressing chronic nightmares, but it is likely that other issues related to the trauma experience may arise during treatment. Therefore, therapists need to be well versed in all aspects of trauma treatment. Some excellent resources for additional readings in trauma treatment are included in Table 9.1. I have also included several important resources in Table 9.2 for those who want to further their knowledge in treating sleep-related disorders.

Another way to keep up with the latest information on trauma and sleep treatments, receive additional training, and consult with the experts is through attending professional conferences. Several conferences may include issues related to trauma treatment, treatment of sleep problems, and use of cognitive behavioral techniques in particular. Several of these professional organizations and their Web sites are included in Table 9.3.

Vicarious Trauma

As most therapists are aware, it can be quite challenging to leave work at the office. Whether it is a particular client or a particular problem area, sometimes it is more difficult to separate ourselves from the stories we hear and the struggles we bear witness to. This may be especially salient for trauma therapists who are consistently exposed to stories and depictions of the worst of humanity. When our work begins to negatively influence our beliefs, perceptions, and interactions with others, we may be experiencing what is referred to as *vicarious traumatization*. Saakvitne and Pearlman (1996) provide the following definition: "Vicarious traumatization is the transformation of the therapist's or helper's inner experience as a result of empathic engagement with survivor clients and their trauma material. Simply put, when we open our hearts to hear someone's story of devastation or betrayal, our cherished beliefs are challenged, and we are changed" (p. 25).

During the first clinical trial, we were in the midst of a heavy recruiting push for participants. An ad had been run on the local National Public Radio station, and we were getting numerous inquiries. As it was summer, and my students had not yet returned to school, I was conducting all of the phone screens. I screened close to 60 people in a 2-week period, asking them about their nightmares and inquiring about their trauma histories. Over the course of those 2 weeks, I found myself becoming increasingly irritable and down. For a while, I did not connect what I

Table 9.1

SELECT RESOURCES FOR ADDITIONAL READINGS IN TRAUMA TREATMENT

Briere, J. (1992). *Child abuse trauma: Theory and treatment of the last effects.* Newbury Park, CA: Sage Publications.

Briere, J. (1996). *Therapy for adults molested as children: Beyond survival* (2nd ed.). New York: Springer Publishing Company.

Foa, E. B., Keane, T. M., & Friedman, M. J. (Eds.). (2000). *Effective treatments for PTSD: Practice guidelines from the International Society for Traumatic Stress Studies.* New York: Guilford Press.

Foa, E. B., Keane, T. M., & Friedman, M. J. (2005). Guidelines for treatment of PTSD. *Journal of Traumatic Stress, 13,* 539–588.

Foa, E. B., & Rothbaum, B. O. (1998). *Treating the trauma of rape: Cognitive-behavioral therapy for PTSD.* New York: Guilford Press.

Follette, V. M., Ruzek, J. I., & Abueg, F. R. (1998). *Cognitive-behavioral therapies for trauma.* New York: Guilford Press.

Linehan, M. M. (1993). *Cognitive behavioral therapy of borderline personality disorder.* New York: Guilford Press.

Linehan, M. M. (1993). *Skills training manual for treating borderline personality disorder.* New York: Guilford Press.

Najavits, L. M. (2002). *Seeking safety: A treatment manual for PTSD and substance abuse.* New York: Guilford.

Pearlman, L. A., & Saakvitne, K. W. (1995). *Trauma and the therapist: Countertransference and vicarious traumatization in psychotherapy with incest survivors.* New York: W.W. Norton.

Resick, P. A., Monson, C. M., & Chard, K. M. (2007). *Cognitive processing therapy: Veteran/military version.* Washington, DC: Department of Veterans Affairs.

Resick, P. A., & Schnike, M. K. (1993). *Cognitive processing therapy for rape victims: A treatment manual.* London: Sage Publishers.

Zayfert, C., & Becker, C. B. (2007). *Cognitive-behavioral therapy for PTSD: A case formulation approach.* New York: Guilford Press.

Table 9.2

SELECT RESOURCES FOR ADDITIONAL READINGS ON TREATING SLEEP PROBLEMS

Bootzin, R. R., Epstein, D., & Wood, J. M. (1991). Stimulus control instructions. In P. Hauri (Ed.), *Case studies in insomnia* (pp. 19–28). New York: Plenum Press.

Bootzin, R. R., Manber, R., Loewy, D. H., Kuo, T. F., & Franzen, P. L. (2004). Sleep disorders. In H. E. Adams & P. B. Sutker (Eds.), *Comprehensive handbook of psychopathology* (3rd ed., pp. 671–711). New York: Springer Science + Business Media, Inc.

Currie, S. R., Wilson, K. G., Pontefract, A. J., & de Laplante, L. (2000). Cognitive-behavioral treatment of insomnia secondary to chronic pain. *Journal of Consulting and Clinical Psychology, 68*, 407–416.

Edinger, J. D., Hoelscher, T. J., Marsh, G. R., Ionescu-Pioggia, M., & Lipper, S. (1992). A cognitive-behavioral therapy for sleep-maintenance insomnia in older adults. *Psychology of Aging, 7*, 282–289.

Kryger, M. H., Roth, T., & Dement, W. C. (2005). *Principles and practices of sleep medicine* (4th ed.). Philadelphia: Elsevier Sanders.

Lavie, P., Pillar, G., & Malhotra, A. (2002). *Sleep disorders: Diagnosis, management and treatment*. London: Martin Dunitz Publishers.

Lichstein, K. L., & Morin, C. M. (Eds.). (2000). *Treatment of late-life insomnia*. Thousand Oaks, CA: Sage Publishers.

Lichstein, K. L., Wilson, N. M., & Johnson, C. T. (2000). Psychological treatment of secondary insomnia. *Psychology and Aging, 15*, 232–240.

Lynch, A. M. (2007). State of the art reviews: Nonpharmacologic approaches to the treatment of insomnia. *American Journal of Lifestyle Medicine, 1*, 274–282.

Morin, C. M. (1993). *Insomnia: Psychological assessment and management*. New York: Guilford Press.

Morin, C. M., Blais, F., & Savard, J. (2002). Are changes in beliefs and attitudes about sleep related to sleep improvements in the treatment of insomnia? *Behaviour Research and Therapy, 40*, 741–752.

Morin, C. M., & Espie, C. A. (2003). *Insomnia: A clinical guide to assessment and treatment*. New York: Springer-Verlag.

Morin, C. M., Hauri, P. J., Espie, C. A., Spielman, A., Buysee, D. J., & Bootzin, R. R. (1999). Nonpharmocologic treatment of chronic insomnia: An American Academy of Sleep Medicine review. *Sleep, 22*, 1–25.

Table 9.2

(CONTINUED)

Perlis, M. L., & Lichstein, K. L. (2003). *Treating sleep disorders: Principles and practice of behavioral sleep medicine.* Hoboken, NJ: John Wiley & Sons, Inc.

Spielman, A. J., Saskin, P., & Thorpy, M. J. (1987). Treatment of chronic insomnia by restriction of time in bed. *Sleep, 10,* 45–56.

Summers, M. O., Crisostomo, M. I., & Stepanski, E. J. (2006). Recent developments in the classification, evaluation, and treatment of insomnia. *Chest, 130,* 276–286.

was feeling to all of the stories that I was hearing. Once I made the connection, I was able to consult with colleagues who do similar work, which was immensely helpful. There are a number of ways to cope with vicarious trauma, but the first step is to identify it. This is easier said than done, as sometimes, even when we know it is happening, it may be difficult to admit. Therapists working with trauma-exposed clients should establish a professional network of colleagues with whom they can consult. Often, the sharing of common struggles may be enough to get a therapist back on track. If needed, however, therapists may want to seek out formal supervision with someone who has extensive experience with similar clientele. Other strategies include those we encourage our clients to utilize—taking care of ourselves, getting adequate sleep, and taking time away from work to engage in pleasurable activities, to name a few.

Briere (1992) addresses other issues that therapists may face when working with trauma survivors, including overidentification, boundary confusion, projection, and countertransference. These are probably less likely to be issues if therapists are only engaging in a brief, focused therapy, such as ERRT. However, we encourage therapists who are using ERRT as a component of a broader trauma treatment to consult additional resources for information on how to handle these concerns.

CONCERNS ABOUT USING EXPOSURE

A key to using exposure therapy—or, really, any therapy—is comfort and confidence in your abilities to administer the treatment (Foy et al., 1996;

Table 9.3

PROFESSIONAL ORGANIZATIONS

African Society for Traumatic Stress Studies (AfSTSS): http://www.istss.org/organization/affiliates.cfm

American Professional Society on the Abuse of Children: http://www.apsac.org

American Psychiatric Association: http://www.psych.org

American Psychological Association: http://www.apa.org

American Psychological Society: http://www.psychologicalscience.org

Anxiety Disorders of America Association: http://www.adaa.org

Association de Langue Française pour l'Etude du Stress et du Traumatisme (ALFEST): http://www.trauma-alfest.com

Association for Behavioral and Cognitive Therapies: http://www.aabt.org

Australasian Society for Traumatic Stress Studies (ASTSS): http://www.astss.org.au

Canadian Traumatic Stress Network (CTSN): http://www.ctsn-rcst.ca

Deutschsprachige Gesellschaft für Psychotraumatologie e.V. (DeGPT): http://www.degpt.de

European Society for Traumatic Stress Studies (ESTSS): http://www.estss.org

Institute on Violence, Abuse and Trauma (IVAT): http://www.ivatcenters.org

International Society for Traumatic Stress Studies (ISTSS): http://www.istss.org

International Society for the Study of Trauma and Dissociation (ISSTD): http://www.isst-d.org

Japanese Society for Traumatic Stress Studies (JSTSS): http://www.jstss.org

Sociedad Argentina dePsicotrauma (SAPsi): http://www.psicotrauma.org.ar

South African Institute for Traumatic Stress: http://www.saits.org.za

Zayfert & Becker, 2007). If the therapist appears nervous or uncertain about what is happening, it is unlikely that the clients will have high expectations for the technique or, indeed, trust in the therapist's competence. Imagine for a moment going skydiving for the first time, feeling quite apprehensive, and then realizing your instructor looks just as nervous. This would be enough to keep most of us firmly on the ground! As Zayfert and Becker (2007) point out, there are numerous ways of increasing your confidence and skill, including obtaining additional training, doing cotherapy with a colleague with more experience, reading about the techniques, seeking supervision from an expert, and having a good professional support system.

As with any type of therapy, direct exposure techniques are not appropriate for every client (Litz, Blake, Gerardi, & Keane, 1990). However, clinical decisions are often based on incomplete or nonexistent evidence (e.g., exposure therapy makes people worse; Feeny, Hembree, & Zoellner, 2003). Of course, this phenomenon is not restricted to exposure-based therapies (e.g., Barlow, Levitt, & Bufka, 1999). In spite of the wealth of data supporting its use, sometimes concerns about using exposure techniques continue, even among highly trained therapists. In a survey of therapists, Becker, Zayfert, and Anderson (2004) found that only a minority of the total sample had received training in exposure therapies. About half of the therapists with training and experience used exposure techniques with most of their PTSD clients. Participants reported not wanting to use manualized treatments and worrying about participants' exacerbation of symptoms. In an effort to address some of the misperceptions surrounding exposure-based therapies, a number of articles were published that describe the issues and present data regarding the veracity of the perceived contraindications for exposure therapy.

To address concerns about the tolerability of exposure therapy, specifically the issue of exacerbation of distress, Foa, Zoellner, Feeny, Hembree, and Alvarez-Conrad (2002) evaluated: (1) reliable deterioration in symptoms, and (2) whether deterioration was associated with treatment outcome. Participants were 76 female victims of assault. Results indicated that a minority of individuals demonstrated a relatively small increase in symptoms following the initiation of imaginal exposure (9.2% depression, 10.5% PTSD symptoms, 21.1% anxiety). However, individuals who experienced exacerbation did not differ from those who did not experience exacerbation in terms of drop out or treatment outcome.

Moreover, it is worth evaluating the premise that any symptom exacerbation should be avoided to begin with. Clients often enter therapy long after troubles have begun and coping strategies are no longer effective. While the ultimate goal of treatment is to improve client functioning, therapy is hard work! When hot-button issues are addressed and clients confront significant concerns, their anxiety and distress are likely to increase temporarily, regardless of the specific technique being used. Though an increase in distress may not be necessary for improved functioning, it is also not always a sign of decompensation. Of course, unbridled progression with any therapy—including exposure—without consideration of increased symptoms is to be avoided. This begs the question of when to consider a different course—or, how much exacerbation is too much? Briere (1992) addresses this issue in his work, *Child Abuse Trauma: Theory and Treatment of the Lasting Effects.* He suggests that when clients do not seem to be getting better, therapists should consider the following hypotheses: "(a) The treatment *is* having negative effects, either by virtue of technical errors or as a result of countertransferential difficulties; (b) treatment is working, but process issues, such as pacing, intensity control, or consolidation, require more attention; and/or (c) therapy is proceeding as it should, and the exacerbation is a natural, transitory effect of clinical improvement" (p. 144). Ways of handling increased distress are discussed more fully below.

To further address the issue of the tolerability of exposure therapy, Hembree and colleagues (2003) note that if clients had significant difficulties tolerating exposure procedures, one would expect significantly higher drop-out rates from therapies that use them. To address this question, these investigators examined drop-out rates in 25 published studies evaluating the efficacy of cognitive behavioral treatments for PTSD. Drop-out rates of active treatments ranged from 18.9% to 26.9%. Results indicated that exposure therapies did not yield higher drop-out rates than non-exposure-based therapies, suggesting that exposure techniques are well tolerated. Further, the authors cite drop-out rates from treatments of other types of disorders and find that rates for exposure therapies for PTSD are comparatively low. Specific to treatments targeting nightmares, one study investigating a self-exposure treatment reported approximately 60% drop-out rate in the exposure group (Burgess, Gill, & Marks, 1998). Reported rates of dropout from Imagery Rehearsal Therapy (IRT) range from 18% to 44% (Wittmann, Schredl, & Kramer, 2007). In many cases, however, it is unclear how "drop out" is being defined. Krakow (2004) reports that one third of participants dropped out before treatment began or early in treatment. In our first randomized clinical trial (RCT), 26% of participants dropped out of the study. Dropouts were defined as participants who either did not complete the second evaluation (wait-list control group) or attended at least one session and did not return to complete treatment (treatment group). To date, the reasons for not initiating treatment or dropping out of treatment for nightmares have not been systematically investigated. Given the brief and effective nature of treatments for nightmares and their chronic condition, it seems an important next step to determine why people choose not to engage in or complete treatment and to explore ways to enhance the number of people who do complete treatment.

Another prominent myth is that clients do not like and are resistant to exposure techniques. Overall, findings suggest that exposure techniques are well tolerated (Foa et al., 2002; Hembree et al., 2003) and perceived as helpful (e.g., Davis & Wright, 2007). For example, at the 6-month follow-up in the first RCT of ERRT, we asked participants to rate the various components of ERRT on a scale from "not at all helpful" to "very helpful." The written-exposure component was rated as "helpful" or "very helpful" by 100% of participants (Davis & Wright, 2007). Zoellner, Feeny, Cochran, and Pruitt (2003) conducted a study to explore the choices people make in terms of mental-health treatment following a traumatic event. The investigators administered a scenario of a sexual assault and rationales for prolonged exposure and Sertraline (Zoloft) to 273 undergraduate women. They were asked to rate the credibility of each treatment and to choose the one they would engage in, stating why they made that choice. Over half of the sample reported an experience of trauma. Results indicated that 87.4% of the sample chose prolonged exposure, 6.9% chose Sertraline, and 5.7% chose no treatment. Of those who had experienced a traumatic event, 18% met criteria for PTSD. Of these, 74.1% chose prolonged exposure, 22.2% chose Sertraline, and 3.1% chose no treatment. Overall, the participants reported that "perceived mechanism/effectiveness" of the treatments and the side effects influenced their decisions. Of course, the participants were undergraduates and not seeking treatment; it would be intriguing to replicate this study in a clinical population.

Another myth is that "exposure therapy is rigid and insensitive to clients' needs" (Feeny et al., 2003, p. 85). Feeny and colleagues believe that this myth may relate to the misperception about the use of treatment manuals (cf. Kendall, 1998). While interventions should follow the guidelines and steps of the treatment, that does not mean that adjustments cannot or should not be made or that basic clinical skills are not utilized. Every client is different, and some adjustments to interventions may be required along the way. Below, we address particular modifications to be considered with specific types of client presentations and a case example of a modification.

As reported above, rarely is PTSD or nightmares the only presenting complaint. Most individuals who have experienced a traumatic event will have multiple concerns with various degrees of severity. A common misperception about exposure therapies is that the research on which they are based does not employ "real world" clients—those with multiple problem areas that demand attention. Further, many believe that exposure techniques are not sufficient to handle multiple problems (Feeny et al., 2003; Kendall, 1998). While many early-treatment-outcome studies were more restrictive in who was allowed to be in the study, more recent efficacy studies are increasingly inclusive to approximate general clinical populations (e.g., Davis & Wright, 2007; Foa et al., 1999). Further, effectiveness studies conducted on exposure therapies suggest that they are highly translatable to nonacademic settings, as community therapists have outcomes comparable to clinical research therapists (see Foa et al., 2005).

Clinical lore suggests that individuals with comorbid Axis I and Axis II disorders would be less successful in treatments focusing on Axis I conditions, however there is little evidence to suggest that this is true. For example, two studies found no difference on PTSD status posttreatment between individuals with and without personality disorders, although those without personality disorders were more likely to reach good end-state functioning on a combined score of posttraumatic, depressive, and anxious symptoms (e.g., Feeny, Zoellner, & Foa, 2002; Hembree, Cahill, & Foa, 2004). Studies also find promising results in the use of exposure therapies with clients with PTSD and comorbid Axis I disorders (e.g., Falsetti, Resnick, & Davis, 2005). Finally, research finds that increasing complexity of presenting complaints does not necessitate increasing complexity of treatment approaches (e.g., Feeny et al., 2003; Foa et al., 2005). Exposure techniques tend to impact more than just PTSD symptoms. Often, when the PTSD symptoms start to abate, improvement occurs in other areas as well. Similarly, studies of IRT and ERRT find that many other indices of distress are favorably affected, including PTSD symptoms, anxiety, depression, and sleep quality and quantity (e.g., Davis & Wright, 2007; Krakow, Hollifield, et al., 2001). These findings speak to the importance of conducting multiple assessments throughout treatment. If, toward the end of treatment, other difficulties are still prominent, then it may be appropriate to incorporate approaches specific to the remaining difficulties or to refer to another therapist for more in-depth attention to those other areas if they are outside your area of expertise.

The above discussion of the myths of exposure therapy is not intended to suggest that exposure therapies should be utilized with everyone. Indeed, as Becker and colleagues (2004) point out, some therapists may be using exposure techniques in cases that are contraindicated. A review of the evidence regarding who may not benefit from exposure therapy is presented in the following section.

CLIENT CONSIDERATIONS

Therapists may not be alone in their concern about utilizing exposure therapies. When the use of exposure techniques is first discussed, clients may have some apprehension. Of course, any therapies designed to address trauma-related issues will necessarily have to address the trauma on some level, and it is likely that clients will be apprehensive regardless of the manner in which this is done. As Briere (1992) states, the manner of coping that most survivors of trauma engage in typically incorporate attempts to avoid thinking about or experiencing the negative effect associated with the trauma. Such strategies may be healthy and adaptive for situations in which the individual has limited control, such as prolonged, ongoing child abuse. Finding ways of escaping temporarily may be the only way that many people are able to make it through horrendous circumstances.

Kim was a 32-year-old clerk at an auto parts store. She had an extensive history of physical and sexual abuse perpetrated by a number of her mother's boyfriends as she was growing up. Her mother, although loving toward Kim, was an alcoholic and was frequently not emotionally available to her because of the alcohol or her time spent with men. Kim's mother was not aware of the abuse that Kim suffered, and Kim never disclosed it, as she did not want to burden her mother. When Kim came to therapy, she reported an increase in her use of alcohol to cope with feelings of shame and anger regarding her past abuse. As a child, during the abuse she would escape mentally, disconnecting from the experience. In early adolescence, she tried to spend as much time as possible away from home and wound up developing friendships with older teenagers who were heavy users of various drugs and alcohol. Kim began drinking at the age of 13 and using marijuana at age 14, quickly progressing to harder substances. She stopped using drugs in her mid-20s but increasingly relied on alcohol to get by.

Kim's experience is not uncommon. She had tried numerous strategies to cope with the terrible situation at home. At some point, however, she determined that the strategies—alcohol and drug use—were no longer sufficient to cope or were starting to interfere too much with work or relationships to continue. People like Kim may experience additional shame and guilt for how they chose to cope with their traumas, further compounding the negative effects of the trauma itself. It is important for the therapist to acknowledge that the individuals did what they had to do to get through terrible situations, while balancing and affirming the clients' recognition and need for different coping strategies to move forward. While many individuals will recognize at some level that previous coping strategies are no longer working, they may still remain quite reluctant to give them up and fully face the negative thoughts, memories, and emotions they have been trying to dampen for so long. Thus, most are likely to feel significant apprehension about entering therapy to address the issues.

While ERRT has been found to be effective for many individuals (see chapter 10), the research has not progressed to the point that we can determine who may and may not benefit from this treatment. The treatment studies that have been conducted with ERRT have employed liberal inclusion criteria, treating individuals with multiple types of traumatic events, numerous diagnoses, and a range of education levels and socioeconomic statuses. Although we have not yet conducted extensive analyses to determine if there are particular demographic or mental-health factors that result in decreased efficacy for the treatment, clinically we have not noted an identifiable pattern, other than those factors that would be expected for any treatment. Specifically, those individuals who continue to avoid trauma-related stimuli, miss sessions, and are not compliant with homework tend to not experience as much benefit from the treatment.

Safety considerations should be prominent and paramount in developing treatment plans for individuals with any presenting problem, including nightmares. Clients with limited affect tolerance, significant emotional instability, few resources and coping skills, and little support may need interventions focused on these areas before attempting ERRT or other symptom-specific interventions. The nature of a clinical research trial naturally restricts the degree to which clinical researchers can stray from the treatment being evaluated. In clinical practice, however, it would probably not be a matter of not conducting the therapy but rather of doing some additional sessions to establish safety first before continuing with the therapy. Below, I review the literature on several client characteristics that may pose additional challenges for conducting ERRT.

In general, cognitive behavioral therapies are considered to be a less optimal choice for individuals with significant cognitive impairments without substantial modifications. IRT, however, was used successfully with a 10-year-old child with nightmares and considerable cognitive impairment and psychiatric difficulties (Peirce, 2006). This case study utilized five sessions, as opposed to the standard three sessions, and did not appear to include the psychoeducation or cognitive restructuring and behavioral components used in IRT and ERRT. Such modifications warrant additional research attention.

Extreme anger, overwhelming anxiety, and emotional numbing are three conditions in which exposure therapy may not be indicated, may be less effective, or may require modifications to typical protocols, although contradictory evidence exists in the empirical literature. Strategies for handling these situations specifically for use with PTSD treatment are highlighted by Jaycox and Foa (1996) are detailed below.

The theory underlying exposure techniques suggests that, in order for exposure to be successful, the client needs to engage the memory of the traumatic event or nightmare. Regardless of the mode of exposure (e.g., written, imaginal), exposure techniques require that the representation of the event or stimulus evoke an affect similar to that experienced in the presence of the actual stimulus (Foa & Kozak, 1986; Lang, Melamed, & Hart, 1970; Wolpe, 1958). Extreme anger is thought to hinder engagement with fear related to trauma memories or nightmares, lessening the efficacy of or serving as a contraindication for exposure therapies. Currently there is evidence both for this assertion (e.g., Foa, Riggs, Massie, & Yarczower, 1995; Vaughan & Tarrier, 1992) and against it (e.g., Stapleton, Taylor, & Asmundson, 2006; Cahill, Rauch, Hembree, & Foa, 2003; van Minnen, Arntz, & Keijsers, 2002). While extreme anger may be conceptualized as a defense against feelings of vulnerability and powerlessness, it may also serve to maintain posttrauma difficulties by not allowing the individual to engage the fear related to the trauma. Engaging the trauma memories or nightmares may further fuel the anger, and the therapist should closely monitor the client's potential for harm to self or others. Therapists will need to determine the best course depending on the nature of the anger and the manner in which it affects treatment. For example, the therapist may try to empathize with the clients and reframe the anger as justified but an obstacle to recovery. If the clients are unable to put aside their anger long enough to engage with the trauma memories or nightmares, the therapist may try cognitive restructuring techniques focused on the anger first or anger management skills (Jaycox & Foa, 1996; Zayfert & Becker, 2007). Unfortunately, at this time there is little empirical evidence available to suggest one course over another.

Another way of not being able to fully access trauma memories or nightmares is via emotional numbing or severe dissociation. Again, these serve to inhibit engagement with the trauma memories or nightmares, interfering with treatment. The treatment may also increase the use of numbing or dissociation as a coping mechanism (Jaycox & Foa, 1996). Again, cognitive techniques may be helpful, depending on the issues underlying the numbing response. Often, clients will reveal a fear of not being able to handle the expected overwhelming emotion if they were to fully engage in the memories or nightmares. Exploring these concerns, modifying distorted thoughts, initiating additional coping skills (e.g., relaxation), and instituting modifications to the protocol (e.g., making exposure more gradual) may increase the confidence of the clients in their abilities to face the nightmares (Jaycox & Foa, 1996).

While studies show that higher pretreatment psychological reaction (Foa, Riggs, et al., 1995) and physiological reaction (heart rate) to fear (Lang et al., 1970) is associated with positive treatment response, it remains unclear at what level this is no longer the case. At what point is the response too high? People may be overengaged with the trauma memories or nightmares and overanxious during exposure, and this may interfere with the ability to fully process and gain control over the memories or nightmares. They also may increasingly engage in maladaptive coping strategies, including dissociating, to try to control their high level of anxiety (Jaycox & Foa, 1996). While overengagement is relatively uncommon in our experience, there are several strategies we recommend if this does occur. We suggest a graduated approach, such as having clients write out smaller portions of their nightmares and rescript them in these smaller segments. The individuals might also be able to write out the nightmares in a more distant manner—as if they are watching them on television—instead of as the standard protocol instructs, as if the nightmares are happening right now. The level of detail included could also be lessened or more time with breaks could be allotted to the exposure portion of the session. These strategies may allow clients enough distance to gain control and a greater sense of comfort. If clients have more than one nightmare, they may also want to start with the less distressing one. Once they have mastered these modified techniques, clients may have the confidence to address their nightmares more directly. Skills training in affect regulation may also be implemented prior to exposure work for individuals who have difficulty tolerating intense affect (see Cloitre, Kocnen, Cohen, & Han, 2002).

There is contradictory information in the literature about whether exposure alone is appropriate for clients struggling with significant guilt and shame. While some studies suggest that exposure-based therapies lead to worsening guilt (Pitman et al., 1991) others find that exposure therapies reduce guilt and do not differ in outcome from other approaches (e.g., Stapleton, Taylor, et al., 2006; van Minnen et al., 2002). Specific to treating nightmares, Ziarnowski and Broida (1984) suggest that more may be needed for veterans with significant guilt feelings, as "just making the dreams go away does not resolve the guilt issues" (p. 68). This indication has yet to be empirically determined, however, and there still may be clinical utility to mitigating the nightmares, as this may allow more coping resources to deal with the remaining issues. Thompson, Hamilton, and West (1995) also report more difficulties in using IRT with veterans who reported significant guilt related to their combat experiences and, subsequently, their nightmares. This may be another area to consider using cognitive restructuring prior to exposure work.

While many of the above factors do not warrant exclusion from exposure treatments, they may warrant closer monitoring and openness on the part of the therapist to modify protocols if they seem to be interfering with treatment. An example from the authors' practice illustrates a modification used specifically with ERRT. Allan, a veteran of the Korean War, was treated for nightmares related to combat. He had numerous difficulties and severe PTSD upon returning from his tour but had improved considerably prior to 2003. During the lead up to and following the invasion of Iraq by American troops, Allan's symptoms returned, almost to previous levels. He experienced nightmares four to five times per week. While they differed considerably in content, they revolved around a similar theme of losing friends and comrades during the war. In the second session of the treatment, while writing out the nightmare, Allan began to weep intractably and did not want to continue with the exposure. He described the tremendous guilt he experienced in being one of the only soldiers in his unit to make it home, particularly as he was in charge of his unit. Cognitive restructuring was initiated for four sessions, after which, Allan reported sufficiently reduced feelings of guilt. Treatment of the nightmares commenced successfully.

THERAPY CONSIDERATIONS

Modifications of the Protocol

The ERRT manual included in Appendix A was standardized for research adherence and ease of dissemination among therapists. Therapists may feel free to utilize the manual as is in practice. However, as described above, therapists should also employ professional discretion and use client presentation to modify ERRT, not only the time allocated for each topic but also the format. Each modification of the protocol should be assessed, however, to determine potential impact on efficacy, as outlined in chapter 5. Indeed, even without significant modification of the protocol, it is recommended that therapists utilize ongoing assessment and monitoring of client symptoms.

Timing. ERRT, as presently practiced, is conducted in three sessions of approximately 1.5 to 2 hours each. While this format has been successful with numerous participants, therapists may determine that extending the number of sessions may be appropriate. As discussed above, several client factors may indicate that other interventions should be added to the treatment, including cognitive impairment, anger, guilt, and over- and underengagement. A sample extended protocol is provided in Table 9.4.

Table 9.4

SAMPLE EXTENDED TREATMENT	
Session 1	Psychoeducation about trauma and nightmares PMR
Session 2	Psychoeducation about sleep PMR
Session 3	Rationale for exposure Written/oral exposure to nightmare Diaphragmatic breathing
Session 4	Rescripting the nightmare Slowed breathing
Session 5	Troubleshooting Relapse prevention

Nightmares as Only Part of the Puzzle. Although ERRT is found to be efficacious with reducing nightmares and related distress, including PTSD
symptoms, we are not suggesting that ERRT be administered in place
of a broader intervention approach. Determining when and how to use
ERRT will depend in large part on the particular case formulation. If
nightmares seem to be a minor aspect of the presenting concerns, ERRT
should not be the first or only treatment administered, and, indeed, the
nightmares may resolve with broader treatment of PTSD. For example,
if clients present with full-blown PTSD and nightmares appear to be
just part of this picture, then it may be in the clients' best interests to
administer one of the first-line treatments for PTSD. However, it may
be helpful to add in components of ERRT to address the nightmares
and sleep disturbances, as these have been shown to be resistant to various psychological and pharmacological treatments (Davis, DeArellano,
Falsetti, & Resnick, 2003; Forbes, Creamer, & Biddle, 2001; Johnson
et al., 1996; Scurfield, Kenderdine, & Pollard, 1990; Zayfert & DeViva,
2004). If nightmares appear to be the primary problem and the driving force behind other concerns, then ERRT is a quick, cost-effective
intervention to apply. As stated in chapter 5, we strongly recommend
that therapists conduct comprehensive assessments at baseline and posttreatment. This approach will assist the therapist in determining whether
ERRT was sufficient or whether additional treatment is required.

Therapists also need to consider the influence of other sleep-related
disorders. For example, chapter 1 described findings suggesting that SDB
is highly prevalent with PTSD and nightmares (Krakow et al., 2006). A
referral to a sleep medicine specialist is recommended if the therapist
suspects that other conditions may be contributing to the nightmares and
sleep disturbances.

Choice of Nightmare. As described in chapter 7, we encourage participants
to choose their worst nightmares to work on in treatment, while other
researchers actively encourage clients to start with a lower intensity nightmare. "Worst" is generally considered to be the nightmare resulting in
the greatest distress or impairment in functioning. While we have not
seen significant difficulties with our approach, it is possible that starting
with the worst may be too intense for some people. If the clients choose
to start with lower intensity nightmares, and the "worst" nightmare is
not resolved in the process, we would strongly recommend extending
the treatment to allow them to work on the worst while in treatment.
Given the chronicity of nightmares and the avoidance inherent in coping

with trauma, clients may never tackle these nightmares on their own and continue to suffer.

A Note of Caution. Several writers have indicated that certain recurring themes or particular content within dreams may be signs that such events actually occurred. While the veracity of this notion is yet to be empirically determined, it does suggest potential for harm if therapists make interpretations based on these themes.

We reviewed literature in chapter 2 that suggests trauma may be associated with particular themes or stuck points in a people's waking and sleeping lives. It is equally possible that these themes may become evident in the absence of traumatic events. We reviewed literature in chapter 2 that states that recurring themes in dreams may be an indication of some ongoing problem. This is still an empirical question. Further, we are aware of no solid empirical data supporting the notion that certain recurring themes are indications of previous abuse or trauma. While Belicki and Cuddy (1996) report finding some differences between sexually abused, physically abused, and nonabused individuals in patterns of sleep and dream disturbance and content of participants' "worst" nightmares, they also caution that "these patterns of sleep disturbance are insufficient evidence to indicate a history of sexual abuse" (p. 55).

Research has indicated that a false dream interpretation may result in individuals' believing that certain things happened in childhood, although they had no previous memories of these events (Mazzoni & Loftus, 1998). ERRT does *not* involve an interpretation of dreams or nightmares and does not make claims to be able to identify previous events—traumatic or otherwise. We caution anyone using this procedure to *not* engage in the suggestion of possible abuse or trauma that clients may be unaware of or have not reported. We believe that even nightmares that appear to be exact replications of actual traumatic events likely incorporate some aspects that were not a part of the traumas. Nightmares are dream events that may incorporate aspects of real events to varying degrees. The point of the treatment is to directly confront and change trauma-related nightmares to help individuals process them, not to uncover other traumatic events or interpret the meaning of dreams for participants.

Efficacy of Exposure, Relaxation, and Rescripting Therapy

Davis, Rhudy, Byrd, and Wright

EFFICACY

The efficacy of ERRT has been assessed via a case study, case series, and an RCT. We are currently in the process of analyzing data from our second RCT. As described in chapter 5, the development of the treatment began with the case study. Intrigued by the findings, we followed this with a case series (Davis & Wright, 2005). Four people (3 women and 1 man) were treated individually over the course of 4 months. The participants ranged in age from 28 to 56. They reported various histories of trauma, including sexual assault in childhood, rape, physical assault, motor vehicle accidents, natural disaster, and domestic violence. All participants reported experiencing more than one type of trauma. The duration of participants' nightmares ranged from 5 to 25 years and were experienced at least once per week for most of that time. The participants were administered the treatment and were assessed at pretreatment, posttreatment, and 3- and 6-month follow-ups (1 person was not able to attend the 6-month follow-up).

Results indicated that all participants reported reduced nightmare severity. Three out of 4 reported reduced frequency of nightmares (the 1 person who was still having an average of one nightmare per week described them as much less severe). Three out of 4 reported decreased PTSD symptoms (1 person's PTSD symptom frequency stayed the same but symptom severity decreased). Finally, 3 out of 4 also reported decreased depression and overall number of sleep problems (Davis & Wright, 2005).

The next step toward assessing the efficacy of ERRT was to conduct a randomized controlled trial (Davis & Wright, 2007). We advertised for this study via flyers, radio ads, and e-mail. The inclusion criteria included having a minimum of one nightmare per week for the previous 3 months and experiencing a traumatic event no less than 3 months prior to beginning the study. The 3-month posttrauma criterion is fairly standard in the trauma treatment literature and allows time for natural recovery processes to occur. Exclusion criteria included apparent psychosis, mental retardation, an age of 17 or younger, active suicidality or recent parasuicidal behaviors, or current drug/alcohol dependence. A total of 49 individuals were initially randomized into either a treatment group or a wait-list control group. The participants were primarily women (82%), Caucasian (75%), employed full time (37%), and had at least some college education (63%). The participants reported an average of 4.6 traumatic events over their lifetimes. At baseline, participants reported an average frequency of 4.4 nightmares per week and an average severity rating of 2.96 (possible range 0–4; Trauma-Related Nightmare Survey; Davis et al., 2001). Nearly one third reported taking over an hour to fall asleep at night, and participants reported obtaining an average of 5.5 hours of sleep per night. Participants in the treatment group were assessed at baseline, 1 week posttreatment, and then at 3- and 6-month follow-ups. The control group was assessed at baseline and 4 weeks later and then was offered the treatment.

Intent-to-treat analyses (a conservative measure of outcome using all participants initially assigned to the control group and those in the treatment group who completed at least one treatment session, regardless of subsequent dropout) and completer analyses (using all participants in the control group who completed the second evaluation and those in the treatment group who completed the treatment) indicated that the treatment group reported significantly better scores for frequency and severity of nightmares, sleep problems, PTSD-symptom frequency and severity, feelings of restfulness upon awakening, and depression. Finally, changes from baseline to follow-up were examined for all participants who completed the treatment and either the 3-month or 6-month follow-up assessments ($n = 19$). At the follow-up assessment only 16% of participants ($n = 3$) reported experiencing a nightmare in the past week, and only 21% ($n = 4$) experienced a nightmare in the past month. Statistically significant positive findings were also found for severity of nightmares,

Table 10.1

PERCENTAGE OF PARTICIPANTS RATING TREATMENT COMPONENTS AS HELPFUL OR VERY HELPFUL

Writing out the nightmare	100
Sleep education	100
Insights from group/therapist	100
Reading nightmare aloud	92
Rescripting nightmare	83
Nightmare education	81
PMR	74
Diaphragmatic breathing	74
PTSD education	63

PTSD symptoms, sleep quality and quantity, number of sleep problems, fear of sleep, depression upon awakening, Beck Depression Inventory scores, and a subjective feeling of restfulness upon awakening. Finally, 53% of the 19 participants met criteria for PTSD at baseline, whereas only 21% met criteria at the 6-month follow-up (Davis & Wright, 2007). To obtain a better understanding of the clinical significance of our findings, we also examined the outcome via end-state functioning. Good end-state functioning was defined as scoring in the nonclinical range on each of the outcome measures or as empirically defined by the authors of the measures used. The only exception was nightmare frequency; we used the absence of nightmares in the past week as the criterion to determine good end-state functioning. The following met criteria for good end-state functioning: 84% for nightmares, 79% for PTSD diagnosis, 74% for depression, and 53% for sleep quality at the 6-month assessment. Finally, we queried the participants at the 6-month follow-up about the perceived helpfulness of all the treatment components. Specifically, participants were asked to rate nine treatment components on a scale of 1 (*very unhelpful*) to 5 (*very helpful*). Table 10.1 shows the percentage of participants who rated each component as "helpful" or "very helpful" (Davis & Wright, 2007).

Thus far, the research indicates that the treatment seems to be quite effective. One limitation of our research program was the reliance on self-reported outcomes. In an effort to more fully understand the nature of post-trauma nightmares and to determine the impact of the treatment on the physiological concomitants of fear, we assessed several physiological indices in a second randomized controlled trial (see Foa & Kozak, 1986; Orr & Roth, 2000). We reasoned that if ERRT is successful at reducing the frequency and intensity of post-trauma nightmares, then nightmare-related negative affect and its physiological effects (i.e., sympathetic activation) should also be diminished. The method and procedures for this study were essentially the same as the initial RCT, with the addition of a physiological assessment component.

To assess physiological reactivity, a script-driven imagery paradigm was employed. A brief narrative, or "script," of each participant's nightmare content was generated from data obtained by a standardized interview conducted at the initial evaluation prior to treatment. The interview asked specifically about subjective and sensory content of the participant's nightmare. That content was then used to generate a 30-second script of approximately 100 words that was recorded onto a computer. In addition, other nonpersonal, emotionally charged scripts (such as pleasant, neutral, action, or frightening) were also recorded. During each physiological assessment session, participants sat comfortably in a reclining chair while the computer presented the personal nightmare script and the standard scripts to the participants over headphones in a random order. Immediately after the computer presented each script, the participants were asked to imagine themselves in the scene described by the script "as if it were happening to them at that moment." Physiological measures that index negative affect and autonomic arousal were assessed before and during each script-driven imagery task.

Facial electromyogram (EMG) was used to assess the electrical activity of muscles associated with facial displays of negative affect and fear. The corrugator muscle is involved with pulling down the inner part of the eyebrow toward the nose to make a frown. Greater corrugator muscle activity, as assessed from EMG, was used to index greater negative affect (displeasure). The lateral frontalis muscle is involved with pulling the outer part of the eyebrow upwards during facial displays of fear. Therefore, greater frontalis muscle activity, as assessed from EMG, was also used to assess negative affect. Autonomic reactions were assessed from heart rate and skin conductance. Heart rate (HR) was assessed from electrocardiogram (ECG) sensors attached to each forearm. Skin conductance was determined by passing an imperceptible electric current through the participants' fingers to assess changes in the electrical conductivity of the skin. The conductivity of the skin is affected by activity of sweat glands (and sweating), which is controlled by the sympathetic branch of the autonomic nervous system. Sympathetic arousal promotes sweating in the palms of the hands and soles of the feet and increases the conductivity of the skin during the initiation of the flight or fight response. Skin conductance level (SCL) was used to assess changes in sympathetic activation and arousal. In addition to these physiological measures, subjective reports of pleasure/displeasure, arousal, and negative affect in response to the imagery were also obtained. It was hypothesized that nightmare imagery would lead to the greatest physiological-emotional reactivity and that treatment of nightmares would reduce subsequent physiological and emotional reactions.

Preliminary results of this second RCT suggest the effect of treatment on the traditional self-report outcomes mirrors those of the original study. Treatment led to improvements in nightmare frequency and severity, depression, panic symptoms upon waking from a nightmare, sleep quality, and PTSD symptoms. Findings from the physiological assessments also suggest treatment is efficacious. Prior to treatment, personal nightmare imagery led to significant physiological-emotional arousal (Rhudy, Davis, Williams, McCabe, & Byrd, 2008). Relative to standard script imagery, nightmare imagery elicited significantly greater corrugator muscle activity, HR, and SCL, as well as subjective arousal, displeasure, and negative affect. These effects were not dependent on current diagnosis of PTSD, as physiological-emotional reactivity to nightmare imagery was present and similar in persons with and without PTSD. This is an important finding, because nightmare-related thoughts appear to have physiological consequences even for persons without clinically significant trauma-related psychopathology. Moreover, the degree of physiological-emotional reactivity elicited by nightmare imagery was positively associated with nightmare-related symptomatology (severity/number of sleep problems, fewer hours slept per night and, panic upon awakening; Rhudy, Davis, Williams, McCabe, & Byrd, 2008).

Of greatest importance, a comparison of physiological data from pre- and posttreatment assessments suggests ERRT led to significant reductions in all physiological (corrugator EMG, lateral frontalis EMG, HR, SCL) and subjective (displeasure, arousal, fear, anger, and sadness) reactions to nightmare imagery (Rhudy, Davis, Williams, McCabe, Bartley, Byrd, & Pruiksma, under review). In fact, group means for persons in the treatment group suggest physiological reactivity to the nightmare imagery was nearly abolished at the posttreatment assessment. These treatment gains were not solely due to the passage of time or repeated exposure to nightmare imagery, because reductions in physiological-emotional reactivity were not present in the control group who did not receive treatment but whose assessments were yoked to the treatment group. Moreover, physiological reactions to a standard fear script were not impacted by treatment. Therefore, it would appear that ERRT leads to reductions in physiological-emotional reactions specific to nightmare-related thoughts/imagery. We are in the process of determining whether these treatment gains are sustained at the 3- and 6-month follow-ups. In addition, it will be important to determine whether post-treatment reductions in physiological-emotional reactivity predict long-term gains in self-reported nightmare and trauma-related symptomatology.

CRITICAL COMPONENTS AND MECHANISMS OF CHANGE

While evidence suggests ERRT and IRT are efficacious in improving sleep and in reducing nightmare frequency, severity, and related distress, not enough is known about the relative fit of the various models of nightmare development to further our understanding of the critical components and mechanisms of change of these direct treatments. Although there are several possibilities that stem from the theories of nightmare development and maintenance and the broader trauma literature, at this time there is insufficient empirical data to fully understand the specificity of the treatment. Marks (1978) describes components that were important to consider in imagery rehearsal's impact on nightmares: exposure, abreaction, and mastery. ERRT combines all three of these aspects, as well as additional components. Next, we discuss the potential contribution of these components and others.

Exposure and Abreaction

Empirical evidence from the broader anxiety literature suggests that exposure is likely a key component for alleviating fear and anxiety (e.g., Foa, Keane, & Friedman, 2000). Foa and Kozak (1986) suggest that two processes are necessary for exposure to work: The fear structure must be activated, and information counter to those pathological aspects of the fear network must be provided. Part of the corrective information may come from habituation. Exposure allows clients to face the fear of the nightmare content in a safe place—the therapist's office—and habituate to the anxiety. Clients learn that they can sit with the anxiety—that they can handle it and not fall apart. Even if they do experience some distress, exposure and habituation correct the erroneous notion that anxiety will continue indefinitely without escape or that something horrible will happen. Without the ability to escape and avoid, there is no negative reinforcement for these behaviors. Also, conducting exposure in a safe, therapeutic environment incorporates new safety information into the fear structure (Foa & Kozak, 1986; Foa & McNally, 1995; Rothbaum & Mellman, 2001).

Although minimized in some Imagery Rehearsal Therapy (IRT) protocols, some authors have identified exposure as a possible critical component in IRT/ERRT (Davis & Wright, 2007; Forbes, Phelps, & McHugh, 2001; Marks, 1978). In many studies assessing IRT or ERRT, participants are exposed to their nightmares through writing them out, reading them aloud, and/or discussing them with the therapist or other group members (e.g., Krakow, Kellner, Pathak, & Lambert, 1996). In a study with male veterans, Hartmann (1984) found that the nightmares decreased as they were discussed in groups, although relapses were common when a new stressor was encountered. Many of the nightmares in the study of ERRT described above incorporated some aspects of the traumatic event, providing opportunities for participants to discuss the trauma indirectly. Further, the rescriptions included at least some original images of the nightmare. Thus, participants are exposed to original images through nightly repetition of the rescripted nightmares as well as to the trauma indirectly (for trauma similar nightmares) or directly (for replicative nightmares) through writing and reading the nightmares in session. Similarly, the identification of trauma themes within the nightmares also generated significant discussion of the traumas themselves among group members. These procedures may have allowed the participants to habituate to the anxiety through engaging in the exposure techniques throughout the session and through homework.

One question that arises is the extent to which exposure is effective in reducing nightmares if the content of the nightmare is only peripherally related or is unrelated to a traumatic event. We believe that even nightmares that do not represent the trauma directly by manifest content may include themes that reflect conflicts initiated or promoted by the traumatic event. Further, over time the nightmares themselves evolve to become the fear stimulus in addition to the original traumatic event. Conceptualized in this way, conducting exposure to the nightmare content (part of the trauma fear structure) should extinguish the fear response to the nightmares, thus reducing nightmare-related problems.

Interestingly, both ERRT and IRT show generalized effects in that other indices of distress (e.g., depressive and PTSD symptoms) improve following treatment, although they were not directly addressed in treatment. Spoormaker, Schredl, and van den Bout (2006) propose that the findings that direct nightmare treatments reduce a wide array of symptoms "suggest that nightmares are a key element of PTSD and may, together with other [REM] sleep disturbances, very well be the hallmark of PTSD, as suggested by Ross et al." (p. 26). Forbes, Phelps, et al. (2001) suggest that the reported reductions in PTSD symptoms following treatment "may be related to modification of the trauma memory network" (Foa, Steketee, & Rothbaum, 1989). The intervention involves alteration to the nightmare content with associated changes in affect, and alteration to the perception of the power, importance, and controllability of the nightmare. These processes may combine to modify aspects of the stimulus, response, and meaning propositions in the trauma memory network" (p. 440). Perhaps exposure to any part of the fear structure is enough to initiate change of response to trauma-specific imagery, not necessarily nightmare imagery alone.

Numerous studies have described the benefits of writing about stressful events. Studies have found improved health benefits in college students and people with physical health conditions, including rheumatoid arthritis and asthma. Other health benefits noted include fewer doctor visits, improved immune functioning, reduced blood pressure, improved lung and liver function, and fewer days in the hospital. The typical protocol involves participants writing about stressful situations or events over a period of time. While many studies report an increase in negative emotion pre- to postwriting within session, at follow-up weeks later, participants report improved physical health and, to a lesser degree, psychological health. Studies examining the benefits of expressive writing with trauma-exposed individuals, however, are equivocal. While some studies found improvements in symptoms in nonclinical samples (e.g., Largo-Marsh & Spates, 2002; Schoutrop, Lange, Hanewald, Davidovich, & Salomon, 2002; Pennebaker, Kiecolt-Glaser, & Glaser, 1988), others found no differences (e.g., Batten, Follette, Rasmussen Hall, & Palm, 2002) or negative effects (e.g., Gidron, Peri, Connolly, & Shalev, 1996). Many of these studies followed Pennebaker et al's (1988) protocol of writing for 3 days, 20 minutes per day. This length and duration is likely insufficient as a stand-alone intervention for a trauma population. However, several treatments, including Cognitive Processing Therapy (Resick & Schnicke, 1993) and Multiple Channel Exposure Therapy (Falsetti, Resnick, &

Davis, 2005), have included written exposure as part of broader PTSD protocols with success.

Clinically we have observed that the process of writing out the nightmare seems to take the power out of the nightmare. It is akin to thinking that there is a monster under the bed and turning the light on and looking—you may see some scary dust bunnies, but no monsters. Somehow, the nightmares are not as frightening for some people when they get them out of that dark place in their minds and look at them on paper in the light of day. This process seems to put the nightmares into perspective. One participant, after writing out her nightmare, was staring at her writing with an odd expression on her face. When asked about this, she said incredulously, "This is it? This is what I've been afraid of all this time?"

Several researchers have investigated possible mechanisms responsible for positive findings of expressive-writing interventions. For example, one study found that emotional expression (catharsis) was not sufficient. The key aspect of expressive writing appears to be writing about both cognitive and emotional aspects of an event (Pennebaker & Graybeal, 2001). For example, one study found that the use of positive emotion words was related to health improvement, while negative emotion words were not. Further, the increased use of cognitive words across writing sessions was associated with significantly greater health improvements (Pennebaker, Mayne, & Francis, 1997; Petrie, Booth, & Pennebaker, 1998).

Several authors suggest that through repeated writings of stressful events, the participants develop a more coherent and organized narrative of the event (e.g., Foa, Molnar, & Cashman, 1995; Koopman et al., 2005). For example, Foa, Molnar, and Cashman (1995) evaluated changes in the narratives of rape victims pre- to posttreatment. They found that posttreatment narratives were longer, incorporated less action or talking, and included more thoughts and feelings about the sexual assault, although fragmentation of the narratives did not significantly change. Interestingly, an increase in organization was related to decreased depression but not anxiety, while a decrease in fragmentation was related to decreased anxiety but not depression. It is unlikely that such narrative changes are salient for ERRT, as participants only write the nightmares out one time. However, the simple process of putting something that typically resides in the dark corners of the psyche on paper, with instructions to write it as it happened and with great detail, may provide an element of organization that previously was not there. This notion is speculative at this time, however, and warrants empirical investigation.

Overall, while there is clear support for the role of exposure-based techniques and expressive writing in improving functioning, it is unclear what role these play in the current treatment. ERRT uses both written and oral exposure to the original nightmare, but these are only done one time in one session. Participants are not assigned to write or talk about their nightmares outside of session (although they are assigned to imagine the rescripted dream). This approach differs significantly from classic exposure techniques that require prolonged and repeated sessions of exposure. Further, other groups use variants of IRT that specifically minimize the exposure component and have achieved very promising results (see chapter 5). For example, Krakow and colleagues probably use the least amount of exposure in their approach (cf. Krakow & Zadra, 2006). Their protocol instructs clients to select a less intense dream (one that is not replicative of the trauma), to change it any way they want, and to rehearse the changed dream imaginally a few times per day. Thus, the specific dosage of exposure that is sufficient to produce long-term, clinically meaningful changes in nightmares, sleep quality, and daytime functioning remains an empirical question. We next briefly review several studies that have compared various components of nightmare treatments and degrees of exposure to determine potential specific mechanisms of change.

Comparison Studies

In one of the earliest comparison studies, Cellucci and Lawrence (1978) evaluated systematic desensitization, a nightmare discussion control condition, and self-monitoring in 29 undergraduates reporting an average of two or more nightmares per week. Treatment lasted 5 weeks and, at follow-up, results indicated that all three groups differed from each other for *frequency* of nightmares, with the desensitization group demonstrating the greatest reduction, followed by the discussion group. For *intensity* of nightmares, however, only the desensitization group reported significantly less intense nightmares than the self-monitoring group. Interestingly, sleep-onset latency was reduced across all groups. No difference in treatment outcome was found between individuals with post-trauma and those with idiopathic nightmares.

Miller and DiPilato (1983) examined the efficacy of three approaches in the treatment of "repeated nightmares" (p. 871) with a minimum frequency of one nightmare per month (53% of the sample reported recurrent nightmares, and 28% reported post-trauma nightmares). Thirty-two individuals were randomly assigned to systematic desensitization (including relaxation), PMR, or a wait-list control group. Each treatment group received six sessions of therapy, with the systematic desensitization group having somewhat longer sessions. Results at the 9-week follow-up found that both treatment groups reported a greater decrease in nightmare frequency than the control group, though no difference was found for the intensity of the nightmares. The treatment groups did not differ from each other. At the 19-week follow-up, after the control group had been treated, nightmare frequency continued to improve, and no differences were found among groups (38% reported an absence of nightmares); however, the intensity of the nightmares was less for those in the desensitization group who still reported nightmares. No differential treatment effect was found for quantity of sleep, time to fall asleep, or mood.

Kellner, Neidhardt, Krakow, and Pathak (1992) treated 28 individuals randomly assigned to one session of either desensitization or rescription and rehearsal. The desensitization group was instructed to write out their nightmares, to practice imagining the nightmares and relaxing when they felt tension, and then to practice relaxation before going to sleep. The second group was instructed to write down recent nightmares, to rescript them any way they wanted, and then to write down the rescripted versions and rehearse the rescripted versions while relaxed. Overall, at the 4- and 7-month follow-ups, participants reported reduced frequency of nightmares, and no treatment differences were found. Intensity of emotions during and upon waking from nightmares decreased in the desensitization group but not the rehearsal group, and no differential treatment effect was reported. Decreases in physiological response upon waking from a nightmare and scores on somatic scales did not change in either group, while ratings of depression, anxiety, and hostility decreased for both. As both groups included exposure to some degree (either of the original nightmare or the changed version), findings suggest it may be exposure, not rescripting, that is the key ingredient.

Neidhardt, Krakow, Kellner, and Pathak (1992) randomly assigned 20 individuals to either recording and rehearsal/rescription or just recording of nightmares for 1 month. At the 3-month follow-up, nightmare frequency decreased in both groups, and there were no differences by treatment type, but the recording plus rehearsal/rescripting group also decreased in a number of measures of distress (not nightmare distress). Again, it appears that exposure alone (recording) does have a positive effect on the frequency of nightmares; however, only the group that conducted additional exposure through rehearsal and rescripted their nightmares had a generalized effect on reduction of distress. Krakow, Kellner, Neidhardt, Pathak, and Lambert (1993) followed the participants in the Neidhardt study over a period of 30 months. Those who had been in the recording-only group were subsequently offered IRT. Treatment gains were maintained for frequency of nightmares and general distress at the 30-month follow-up. The original IRT group appeared to fare better in this study, as the addition of IRT to the recording group after a 3-month follow-up did not increase their functioning beyond the recording intervention alone.

These studies suggest that while many approaches (e.g., relaxation, discussion, recording) are successful in reducing the *frequency* of nightmares, something else (e.g., desensitization, rescripting and rehearsal) is needed to impact the *intensity* of nightmares and more general indices of distress. This supports previous findings reported in chapter 2 that suggest that frequency and intensity of nightmares are minimally related, different mechanisms may be responsible for each, and different treatment approaches may be warranted. These findings are particularly important given the influence of nightmare intensity on related pathology (Krakow & Zadra, 2006). While questions remain regarding whether exposure is necessary or sufficient for optimal treatment gains, the success of the varying protocols used and the complexity of the relationship among sleep disorders, nightmares, anxiety, posttraumatic symptoms, and depression beg the question whether and to what extent other factors may contribute.

Rescripting

A good laugh and a long sleep are the best cures in the doctor's book.
—Irish Proverb

Imagery modification has been used extensively in therapy across various orientations. Some researchers and therapists believe that engaging and modifying images may provide corrective information in a way that strict verbal therapies may not (Beck, Freeman, & Associates, 1990). For example, imaginal exposure and rescripting has been used to treat difficulties related to child sexual abuse (Smucker & Niederee, 1995). In this intervention, the clients repeatedly imagine the traumatic events and gradually incorporate imaginal rescriptions of the events to change what happened via mastery imagery. The treatment's developers contend that many people will have experienced a trauma at an age too young to encode the event verbally. They state that if an event is encoded largely in images, a technique that directly deals with the images may be the most effective in helping the client recover (Smucker, Dancu, Foa, & Niederee, 2002). The few studies that have evaluated imagery rehearsal have found promising findings (e.g., Arntz, Tiesema, & Kindt, 2007; Dancu, Foa, & Smucker, 1993; Grunert, Weis, Smucker, & Christianson, 2007; Rusch, Grunert, Mendelsohn, & Smucker 2000).

In Rusch and colleagues (2000) study of imaginal exposure, rescripting, and cognitive restructuring, they noted that many in their sample changed their imagery in a way that made it humorous. We have also found that in our own research. While we tell our clients to rescript their nightmares to directly confront the primary themes identified in the nightmares, we do not tell them how to change them (although if a person is having difficulty, the group or therapist may make some suggestions). Many choose to interject humor in some part of the story line, which seems to take the power out of the nightmare.

Mary was a 62-year-old with a long history of domestic violence and numerous nightmares per week. While aspects of the nightmares would change, the main story line was that she was lying in bed and heard someone come into the house and approach her bedroom. She was frozen in her bed, unable to move, knowing that she was about to die. She peered over her blankets to make sure the door was locked, knowing it would not keep the intruder out. In her rescription, she was again lying in bed and heard someone come in the house and close the door; she did not leave the bed but peered under the blankets to make sure she was wearing her best negligee, as she waited with great anticipation for Richard Gere to join her.

Similar to the *Riddikulus* curse invoked in *Harry Potter and the Prisoner of Azkaban* (Rowling, 1999), the use of humor appears to change not only the image but also the way that we think about the object of fear (i.e., the nightmare). As Professor Lupin notes, "The charm that repels a boggart is simple, yet it requires force of mind. You see, the thing that really finishes a boggart is *laughter.* What you need to do is force it to assume a shape that you find amusing" (Rowling, 1999, p. 134). As Rusch and colleagues (2000) suggest, this use of humor and resulting positive affect may reflect a type of reciprocal inhibition, may increase feelings of control over the images themselves and the accompanying affect, and may incorporate corrective information into the fear network.

Ehlers and Clark (2000) suggest that intrusions include appraisals, sensations, and emotions present at the time of the trauma that do not reflect any change in appraisal of the event, as though they are stuck. They are largely maintained in this manner through avoidance. An important part of therapy, whether through cognitive restructuring or rescripting, is to reevaluate those original appraisals. This may be an important way of providing corrective information (Hackmann & Holmes, 2004). The provision of corrective information or the alteration of appraisals may be an avenue through which rescription promotes change in nightmares.

Cognitive Changes

Cognitive changes may stem from several aspects of ERRT, including the modification of presleep cognitive activity, psychoeducation, thematic exploration, and the enhancement of one's sense of mastery and control. Alteration of presleep cognitive activity is thought to be a primary mechanism of change for the treatment of insomnia and may be a significant contributor to improvements reported in ERRT. ERRT may accomplish this through the PMR script we use, which includes guided imagery and a focus on deep breathing. Participants are asked to listen to a CD of the 20-minute script each night before sleep. For the clients, engaging in the imagery and focusing on breathing may inhibit cognitive arousal and anxious anticipation. After the second session, participants also focus on imagining their rescripted dreams, which may perhaps inhibit other cognitive activity. Participants are also instructed that if they are spending time worrying during sleep, they should write down their worries and set aside time in the morning to either take care of what they were concerned about or just time to worry about it some more. We have not tracked the extent to which individuals are doing this, however, so it is uncertain whether this plays a role in the outcome.

The psychoeducation provided in Sessions 1 and 2 likely helps to reframe perspectives that people have regarding their sleep and nightmares. Increased knowledge of the potential mechanisms underlying nightmares and what maintains them over time may provide a sense of controllability that was absent previously. Further, providing relatively simple instructions to begin modifying sleep and nightmares (e.g., modification of sleep hygiene) may also be empowering and alter the way that participants perceive their difficulties with sleep and nightmares.

Thematic Exploration

The thematic exploration of nightmares is one of the components that differentiate ERRT from other nightmare treatments. Studies examining schema or themes in trauma-exposed individuals have found that distressed individuals evidenced more unresolved themes (Littleton, 2007; Newman, Riggs, & Roth, 1997). It is possible that identifying the primary themes noted in nightmares, particularly recurring themes, may help participants to identify those areas that are salient for them. These themes may be trauma specific or may be more general themes in the individuals' lives. Often, participants will point out ways in which these themes also impact their waking lives. Identifying these themes allows participants to begin to address them, not only in their nightmares and rescriptions, but also in how they think and process information about these themes during the day, and begin to modify related dysfunctional beliefs.

Control/Mastery

A very potent clinical observation noted in our own studies as well as others (Krakow & Zadra, 2006) is that many individuals enter treatment with the strong belief that they have no control over their nightmares or, indeed, many other aspects of their lives. Most have attempted numerous other treatments to rid themselves of their nightmares and approach our treatment as a "last-ditch effort." Indeed, after listening to the overview of the treatment, one participant noted that she had "already tried all of those things" and had even "followed the advice of Dr. Phil," all to no avail. Skepticism is not uncommon at the beginning of treatment, which would seem to stack the deck against the treatment, given the strong evidence in the literature about the importance of treatment expectations (e.g., Lambert & Barley, 2001). Numerous research groups (e.g., Bishay, 1985; Krakow et al., 1996; Forbes, Phelps, et al., 2001; Marks, 1978, 1987) have speculated that an increased sense of mastery may be a primary mechanism of change, perhaps directly addressing this sense of skepticism.

Germain, Krakow, and colleagues (2004) evaluated scripts from 44 sexually assaulted women involved in IRT to assess degree of mastery and negative content. Nightmare and new dream scripts were evaluated using the Hall and Van de Castle (1966) dream-scoring system and the Multidimensional Mastery Scale developed by two of the authors. Results indicated that new dream scripts were rated higher on the positive subscales and lower on the negative subscales of the Hall and Van de Castle system. Further, some differences were found for mastery subscales, with new dream scripts incorporating significantly more elements of social mastery and environmental mastery and less avoidance than nightmares. The investigation did not assess whether the nature or degree of the shift in mastery was related to improvement in terms of nightmares and sleep functioning. This is an important area for future study, particularly as it is not clear whether the increase in control and mastery needs to be evidenced in the dream itself for change to occur. Indeed, the majority of individuals who participated in our treatment report not experiencing the rescripted dreams but rather continuing to have the nightmares without the emotional intensity or just not having the nightmares anymore. This finding was also reported by Krakow and colleagues (1993).

If mastery is a component of healing, it may be in the form of covert modeling (Lueger, 2001). Clients may achieve a real sense of mastery through repeated imagining of handling a very difficult situation. Also, clients may experience a sense of mastery and control through "conquering" the nightmares by writing them out and rescripting them and having that sense of increased control reflected in the absence of nightmares. Several groups, however, report not having participants write out the original nightmares (e.g., Bishay, 1985; Krakow & Zadra, 2006) and provide various instructions for how to do the rescriptions, yet they still achieve positive results. This raises the question of whether mastery comes from exposure, rescription, or insertion of mastery into the new dream. Krakow (2004) uses the instruction to "change it any way you wish" and report that, while most participants change aspects of their nightmares to positive elements, it is unclear if this represents "mastery." Bishay (1985) has participants rescript specifically with a triumphant ending. Further, Kellner, Singh, and Irigoyen-Rascon (1991) report a case series of 4 patients using IRT. They found that 3 of the individuals experienced improved functioning following IRT, and none had changed the nightmare to a masterful or happy ending. While more study is needed, it appears that mastery may happen not through specific elements incorporated in a dream, but through the process of working through the nightmares. Be it rescription, exposure, humor, mastery elements, or relaxation, the fact that clients are able to face and conquer something terrifying may enhance their sense of competency and strength.

Susan was a 55-year-old law clerk who had a long history of domestic violence. She and her husband were now divorced, but he continued to show up at her home at least once per week to verbally and emotionally torment her. Her nightmares were similar to his typical visits and involved him coming to the house, sometimes with his new girlfriend, and yelling at Susan and humiliating her. She never felt able to kick him out or talk back to him, even though they had been divorced for a number of years. Her rescription centered on standing up to him, telling him off, and kicking him out of her house, knowing that he would not return. The treatment was successful, and she reported no longer having that nightmare or any other nightmares. When she came in for her 6-month follow-up evaluation, she jubilantly reported that she had actually done what she had rescripted and had not seen her ex-husband in more than a month. She was amazed and excited about the new sense of power and control over her life.

Our clinical observations suggest that it is incredibly powerful for people to realize that they have some control over things they believed were far beyond their range of control. Participants may experience enhanced control over daytime distress through reduction in anxiety via relaxation procedures and then through changes in nightmares through rescripting/exposure. This, in turn, may enhance their coping resources and partly explain the generalized impact of the treatment.

Modification of Sleep Habits

Sleep-hygiene education and sleep-habit modification (e.g., stimulus control, sleep restriction, modification of sleep hygiene) are important components of most behavioral interventions for sleep problems (Morin, 2005). While the modifications will naturally differ depending on the specific habits, all participants are instructed in stimulus control, which has support in the treatment of insomnia. The theory underlying stimulus control is that, over time, the sleep environment itself may become a conditioned cue for nightmares and poor sleep. The very act of getting ready for bed and the bedroom environment itself may elicit worries about having nightmares. Thus, participants are encouraged only to go to bed when sleepy, to leave their beds if they do not fall asleep within 20 minutes of lying down, to return only when sleepy, and to limit activity in bed to sleep and sexual activity. We have found this last suggestion to be particularly challenging for people, as many report engaging in various sleep-avoidant activities in bed, including watching television and working on their laptops. Another tricky situation is reading in bed. Many people report reading to get sleepy and have a strong preference for doing this in bed. We encourage people to read in another location and only use the bed for sleep. A variety of other sleep-hygiene changes are made, depending on the particular person's sleep habits. While there is not much evidence for the efficacy of modifying sleep habits as stand-alone treatments, this may be an important component of the overall approach.

The notion that modifying sleep habits may play a significant role in decreasing nightmares goes back to the vicious cycle discussed in chapter 3. Although the habits that develop, often over many years, may be helpful in the short term to initiate or maintain sleep, they tend to be unhelpful in the long term. By providing education about and modifying these sleep habits, individuals may make important behavioral changes that contribute to better and longer sleep. It may be the increase in the quality and quantity of sleep that provides clients with the energy and clarity to see and cope with the remaining problems or distress in a new way. Mellman (2006) states that "insomnia is a prospective risk factor for psychiatric disorders, including anxiety disorders. . . . [T]herefore, in addition to alleviating distress from insomnia, amelioration of sleep disturbances possibly can have therapeutic impact on other symptoms and serve to prevent relapse and exacerbation" (p. 1053). ERRT's function in increasing the quality and quantity of sleep may also account for the generalized, broader improvement in symptoms.

Relaxation

The relaxation component of the treatment focuses on decreasing physiological anxiety, tension, and cognitive activity prior to sleep. PMR may help to reduce anticipatory anxiety regarding going to sleep by relaxing the body and mind, perhaps clearing the mind of thoughts that may increase the chance of having a nightmare. During treatment, many people reported falling asleep to the relaxation tape, so it is likely that they did not have time to worry about nightmares and sleeping. Coren (1988) suggests that physiological and cognitive arousal are separable phenomena and have differential impact on sleep, with cognitive arousal showing worse impact (e.g., Nicassio, Mendlowitz, Fussell, & Petras, 1985). Treatments that utilize relaxation methods to reduce anticipatory anxiety or cognitive arousal often find improvements in sleep. As stated above, the script we use incorporates PMR as well as mental imagery, thus potentially impacting both cognitive arousal and somatic arousal presleep. However, the specific action is yet to be determined.

Evidence suggests that relaxation is a helpful component of treating anxiety disorders and sleep disorders. However, it is unlikely to be powerful enough to reduce nightmares on its own. Busby and De Koninck (1980) examined the use of transcendental meditation or relaxation for 5 weeks on mood and dream content. They found no differences between the groups, and both groups reported decreases in trait anxiety and presleep anxiety and slight increases in pleasant themes in dreams. The authors suggest these findings support the notion of a continuation between waking and sleeping "activity." Specific to nightmares, Miller and DiPilato (1983) found that, while relaxation had an impact on nightmare frequency, it did not affect intensity, nor did it generalize to other indices of distress.

SUMMARY

Even for such a brief treatment, understanding the critical components and mechanisms of change is a complex issue, particularly given the chronic nature of nightmares in most of the participants we have treated. While single component treatments may address some of the issues, it may be that broader improvement will require multicomponent treatments. The particular approach taken will also depend on relevant predisposing, precipitating, and perpetuating factors discussed in chapter 3. Particularly relevant is the degree to which the traumatic event is still a viable precipitating factor, or whether the nightmares are driven more through the perpetuating factors. And, of course, this treatment approach may not work for everyone. Future studies will need to extend our understanding by exploring who benefits and under what circumstances.

CONCLUSION AND FUTURE DIRECTIONS

As reported in chapter 1, Woodward and colleagues (2007) found that individuals who participated in psychophysiological studies, compared to nonparticipants, reported lower severity on several measures, which differed depending on the requirements of the specific studies. This calls into question the representative nature of participants in treatment studies as well. As effective as nightmare treatments are found to be, we still may not be accessing those with the most significant problems. Indeed, a proportion of the individuals who call and state interest in the study and are invited to participate based on the phone screen do not present for an evaluation. This finding is not uncommon for studies evaluating treatments for sleep disorders or trauma-related problems. The reluctance to engage in treatment may suggest skepticism about the treatment's ability to bring about change. It also likely reflects continued avoidance coping.

Direct nightmare treatments also report somewhat high drop-out rates, though these vary considerably depending on how "dropout" is defined. In our own studies, we find that approximately 26% of people who enter the treatment do not complete it. While this is not out of the range for drop-out rates of other treatment studies, as noted in chapter 9, it is an area for continued study to determine if changes can be made or other interventions added that might increase the number of people willing to complete treatment.

Few studies have compared differing components of the available treatments for nightmares. As a number of approaches that vary in specific components report positive findings, it will be an important next step to do direct comparisons to determine if any approach is more effective in addressing nightmares, sleep, and related distress. It will also be important to conduct additional studies assessing the impact of the treatments on physiological indices and objective sleep measures (Spoormaker et al., 2006). As Krakow and Zadra (2006) note, it also is important to conduct more thorough evaluations of sleep disorders and determine which participants may fare better with specific sleep medicine approaches in addition to or instead of direct nightmare treatments.

Another potentially fruitful area for exploration is to add nightmare and sleep-specific components to already established therapies for PTSD. As a number of the components are drawn from established treatments (e.g., relaxation, rationale for exposure), the nightmare and sleep-specific components could probably be added in one or two sessions. As noted in chapter 9, previous attempts to augment exposure therapies with different techniques (e.g., cognitive restructuring) have not successfully improved responses over and above exposure alone; these combinations seem to be targeted at symptoms (e.g., maladaptive cognitions) that already are successfully improved with exposure alone. Studies have also stripped aspects of exposure in their comparison studies, potentially diminishing its potency (see Foa, Rothbaum, & Furr, 2003). Adding one or two sessions specific to nightmares and sleep—symptoms known to be treatment resistant—could prove to be an important addition without taking away from the essential components of established treatments. It may also be important to evaluate the sequence of treatments. If a trauma-exposed individual presents with primary difficulties of nightmares and sleep, it may be prudent to start with direct treatment of those problems, followed by, if necessary, components addressing other posttrauma symptoms.

Overall, the empirical investigation of nightmare treatments is in its infancy. Just as there seem to be many different profiles of nightmare sufferers and a great number of factors shown to be related to nightmares, both idiopathic and post-trauma, it is no great leap of faith to consider that there are many paths to the chronic nightmare stage. There may be as many different optimal treatment approaches. For some, simple interventions may be enough to interrupt the vicious cycle; for others, a more complex treatment regime may be required. Much more work remains to be done! It is heartening, however, that nightmares have now come to the attention of trauma and sleep experts alike, and great strides continue to be made to rid people of the malady of nightmares.

Participant Manual

Chapter 1: Introduction

AN OVERVIEW OF TREATMENT

First of all, congratulations on making a courageous decision to seek treatment for your nightmares. It takes a great deal of strength, motivation, and courage to face your nightmares head on. Exposure, Relaxation, and Rescripting Treatment (ERRT) was developed for the treatment of nightmares related to traumatic events. ERRT is a modified version of a treatment that was found to be effective for the treatment of trauma-related nightmares[1,2] and includes additional components that have been found to be helpful in treatment for anxiety difficulties[3,4,5,6] and sleep disturbances.[7]

The treatment targets three systems in which anxiety may manifest: physiological, behavioral, and cognitive. Physiological reactions to nightmares may include increased arousal close to the time you typically go to bed, panic attack symptoms upon awakening from a nightmare (e.g., racing heart, sweating, choking), symptoms of sleep deprivation during daytime hours (e.g., confusion, memory loss, irritability or emotional highs and lows, exacerbation of other emotional difficulties), and increased arousal during the daytime. The behavioral reactions to nightmares may include using substances (e.g., alcohol, sleeping pills) at night to help you get to sleep; watching television in bed to try to forget about the nightmares; and avoiding situations, places, or people that remind you of the nightmares and traumatic event (even avoiding sleep!). The cognitive reactions to nightmares may include telling yourself you will never be able to get to sleep, feeling too afraid to sleep because you fear having another nightmare, or believing that you will never "get over" the trauma because it continues to be disruptive, even while you sleep. This treatment was designed to target each of these systems.

ERRT is a three-session treatment. You may find it difficult to imagine that three sessions would be sufficient to rid you of nightmares. The purpose of the treatment is to try to reduce the frequency and intensity of your nightmares. It may also reduce your level of distress during the day as your sleep improves and you begin to understand the ways in which the trauma and the nightmares are affecting you. The treatment requires that you attend all three sessions of treatment. Homework will be assigned at the end of the first two sessions. Completion of the homework assignments is very important to your success in this treatment. We will review the homework at the beginning of each session. You will also be asked to complete additional measures at the beginning of each session. The treatment sessions and this manual will provide a guide for working through the nightmares, but it is up to you to do the work. The treatment manual is yours to keep so that you can review the material between sessions.

The treatment incorporates the use of relaxation procedures; education about trauma, posttraumatic stress disorder, nightmares, and sleep habits; relearning adaptive sleep habits; exposure to your nightmare content; and rewriting your nightmare to decrease the level of fear it generates. Next is an overview of each of the treatment sessions.

Session 1

Introduction and education about trauma, posttraumatic stress disorder, sleep habits, and nightmares. Instruction will be provided on progressive muscle relaxation (PMR) procedures.

Homework. Practice relaxation procedures with tape/CD, monitor nightmare frequency, relaxation exercises, sleep habits, and PTSD symptoms.

Session 2

Review homework. Discuss the relationship between the nightmare and the traumatic event. Write out the nightmare, and read the nightmare aloud. Learn about imagery rehearsal, rewrite the nightmare, and practice imagery rehearsal of the changed dream. Learn breathing retraining.

Homework. Practice relaxation procedures with tape/CD, rehearse the changed dream, monitor nightmare frequency, relaxation exercises, sleep habits, and PTSD symptoms.

Session 3

Review homework. Discuss relaxation procedures and imagery rehearsal. Identify any problem areas and make plans for what to continue working on. Schedule first follow-up evaluation.

A Note on Confidentiality. As you know, everyone involved in this treatment has had a traumatic event occur in his or her lifetime. In an individual therapy situation, all information would be kept confidential with several exceptions that are outlined in the copy of the informed consent form that you received. In a group situation, the therapist cannot guarantee total confidentiality, as group members will hear about the histories and concerns of the other group members over the course of treatment. It is very important for each group member to protect and respect the information he or she hears in treatment. No one should discuss any information brought up in the context of treatment or talk about who is in the group to any person outside of the group. In order for treatment to work, everyone needs to feel free to discuss sensitive matters openly, without fear that his or her information will be shared outside the group.

Chapter 2: Session 1 – Education and Relaxation

COMPLETE ASSESSMENT MATERIALS

Trauma

Everyone involved in this treatment has experienced a traumatic event. This treatment was not designed for one particular type of trauma, nor is it only for people who have experienced a single trauma. A number of different events can be considered traumatic and lead to nightmares. Traumatic events may include, but are not limited to, the sudden, unexpected death of a loved one; sexual assault; child sexual abuse; physical assault; physical abuse; car accidents; combat; and natural disasters. Although individuals who experience traumatic events often feel alone, as if they are the only ones who have experienced such events, the majority of us have experienced some type of trauma. Indeed, research has found that approximately 50% to 60% of the general population has experienced some type of traumatic event.[11]

    People respond to traumatic events in a number of ways. Some individuals feel intense distress almost immediately. Others may feel little distress at first or be in a state of shock, and then experience more difficulties later on, even years after the event. Still others report experiencing few difficulties at all. The manner in which a traumatic event may impact a person's life is quite varied. Approximately one third of individuals who experience trauma may experience symptoms of posttraumatic stress disorder (PTSD). PTSD includes three different categories of symptoms.[12] The first category includes symptoms that involve reexperiencing the traumatic event in some way, such as feeling as if the event were occurring again, nightmares about the event, and thinking about the event when you don't want to. **Do your nightmares tend to be about the trauma? Do you experience any other reexperiencing symptoms?** The second category includes the ways that people attempt to avoid people, places, situations, and things that remind them of the traumatic event. Common ways in which people try to avoid such reminders include pushing thoughts of the event out of their minds, not interacting with someone who reminds them of a perpetrator, and using substances to try to forget what happened. **Have you found yourself trying to avoid thoughts or reminders of the trauma?** The second category also includes numbing responses, such as feeling detached from other people and unable to have loving feelings. **Have you experienced emotions as strongly as you used to?** The third category of symptoms involves a heightened state of arousal. Individuals might experience physical sensations when reminded of the trauma, including an increased heart rate, breathing faster, and sweating. People may also feel as if they are always on guard, trying to be aware of possible dangers in their environment, and have difficulty falling and staying asleep. **Do you feel increased arousal if something reminds you of the trauma?**

If you think about these symptoms, they really do make sense and may be helpful, at least initially. The reason you may have reexperiencing symptoms is so your body remains on alert. Your mind may continue sending danger signals in response to perceived threat. Reminding you of the trauma through intrusive thoughts and memories may be a way to keep you alert and safe at first. Avoidance of trauma-related information or cues also makes sense—it is good to stay away from things that are dangerous! It also makes sense for your body to be at a heightened state of arousal or readiness in case the danger reappears—you want to be ready to react if this happens. So how do we move from a normal response to an ongoing problem? Part of what happens may be that your system does not adjust for the fact that the traumatic event is over. The event does not get processed or resolved as with other experiences we have. When something is not resolved, we tend to keep thinking about it, even when we don't want to. **Can you think of an example (other than the trauma) in which you continued to think about an issue or problem because it was not quite resolved?**

Another problem is that these fear responses generalize to stimuli that are somehow associated with the traumatic event but are not dangerous in and of themselves. For example, a combat veteran may begin to respond with fear to sights and sounds that remind him or her of the combat experience, including a car backfiring, walking into the woods, or hearing fireworks. A rape victim may begin to fear all men who resemble the rapist, cars that are similar to the one she was raped in, the scent of the cologne the rapist was wearing, and so forth. These stimuli, which are inherently not dangerous, become cues or triggers of the traumatic event. If you are responding with fear and terror to these cues, you will likely start to avoid them. Escaping the feelings of fear and avoiding the trauma cues will likely initially cause you to feel relief but over the long term only serves to maintain the problem. You do not have the opportunity to learn that such things as cars and cologne are not dangerous. **Are you aware of anything that might be a cue for the traumatic event?**

Other negative consequences of trauma may include panic attacks, increased substance use, feelings of sadness or depression, anxiety, problems relating to other people, and sleep disturbance.[12] The way we think about ourselves, other people, and the world may also change following a trauma, especially in the areas of powerlessness, esteem, safety, intimacy, and trust.[4,13] **Have you noticed a change in the way you think about yourself? People around you? Do you see the world differently?** Although these difficulties are not uncommon in individuals who report experiencing a trauma, the good news is that many of the problems may go away on their own over time. Also, there are treatments available that have been shown to be quite effective in treating many of these difficulties. Finally, many people show resiliency when faced with a trauma and are able to find meaning in what they experienced.

Nightmares

You are being offered this treatment because you have identified experiencing nightmares as a significant difficulty. Although experiencing nightmares is a symptom of PTSD, you do not necessarily meet all the criteria for PTSD. It is important to know that this treatment is designed to reduce the frequency and intensity of nightmares and does not directly target other symptoms of distress. However, it is our hope that, by reducing the nightmares and improving your quality of sleep, other symptoms of distress that you may be experiencing will also lessen in intensity.

Research studies suggest that approximately 5% of the population suffers from nightmares at any one time,[14] and the rates are much higher—about 50% to 88%—for those who have experienced a trauma and have PTSD. Nightmares and sleep disturbances are considered the hallmark of PTSD[15] and more people with PTSD report nightmares than those without PTSD. Experiencing a traumatic event may initiate or exacerbate the occurrence of nightmares.[16] **Did you have nightmares**

before the traumatic event? If yes, did the nightmares change in frequency, severity, or content after the traumatic event?

The increased variability in heart rate and respiratory rate that often accompanies nightmares is consistent with the physiological arousal to cues seen in PTSD as well as physiological arousal symptoms of panic attacks.[17] These responses, along with dream content associated with a traumatic event, may themselves also serve as trauma cues that further heighten the level of arousal and distress in individuals with PTSD. Additionally, nightmares may cause considerable sleep disruption, which could lead to increased distress during the day, potentially increasing the opportunity for more nightmares and disruption in functioning.

A number of theories provide possible explanations for the occurrence of nightmares. As discussed above, having nightmares is one of the reexperiencing symptoms of PTSD. It is thought that the memories of the traumatic event are not appropriately processed or stored in the brain because of the impact of the high level of distress and arousal experienced at the time of the trauma and its resulting impact on the brain.[18] It may be that the mind is attempting to process information during the daytime through flashbacks and intrusive thoughts and at night through nightmares. Indeed, some researchers believe that chronic nightmares may reflect specific cognitive or emotional aspects of the trauma that remain unresolved.[20,23] Continued experiencing of the nightmares may be the mind's attempt to gain mastery over those particular aspects of the traumatic event or its aftermath.

Another theory[19] suggests that an individual's imagery system is initially disrupted by the overwhelming nature of the traumatic event. Individuals may then become particularly uncomfortable with imagery because of what they have been through. They may have learned through intrusive memories, flashbacks, and nightmares to engage in primarily verbal thought instead and try to avoid imagery at all times (including daydreams and imagining solutions to problems), as they don't know when a flashback or intrusion may occur. Nightmares typically have a natural capacity and inclination to change—most people who experience a trauma will have nightmares initially, and then the nightmares change and fade over time. This process happens with non-trauma-related nightmares as well—we may have a nightmare, and through the night the images and story will change and morph into other dreams. However, if an individual is avoiding imagery and wakes up from the nightmare with significant distress, there is no opportunity for self-correction or change, and the nightmares continue.

Dreams and nightmares also have been conceptualized as visual metaphors for primary emotions (e.g., fear, terror, guilt). If your primary emotion is fear, your mind will create a story line for that emotion. Your mind may also associate your nightmare with other times in which you were afraid, but things turned out okay. It is thought that this may be how nightmares end up changing over time, becoming less scary and less disturbing, and the information is integrated with other thoughts and memories.[20] However, this does not appear to happen with chronic nightmares, particularly those that replay the traumatic event. Something seems to be keeping the nightmare isolated, so these other connections are not made, and the nightmare does not change. It is possible that, because people wake up from the nightmares, they do not experience habituation—the decrease of fear that typically accompanies exposure to a feared stimulus—and may even become more sensitized to fear cues and more prone to avoiding trauma and nightmare cues, including avoiding sleep.[21]

Finally, while nightmares may begin following a traumatic event, they may become separate from the trauma over time and become a problem in and of themselves. If we believe that they are initially helpful, by trying to help us to process the trauma or keep us vigilant, at some point that doesn't seem to be the case anymore. Why would nightmares continue for so long? For some people, the nightmares may become the thing to be afraid of, instead of or in addition to the trauma.

All trauma-related nightmares are not the same for everyone, and they may not be the same for any individual over time. Nightmares may initially be just like the traumatic event, almost a reenactment of the trauma. Over time, however, the nightmares may begin to include other aspects of life and more recent stressors. They may include people who were not involved in the original trauma. For example, a rape survivor reported that, after having children, her nightmares began to include them—specifically, that they were also in danger. Further, the nightmares may change to reflect potent, unresolved issues related to trauma (e.g., powerlessness, esteem, safety, intimacy, trust). **Have your nightmares stayed the same or changed over time?**

Nightmares in and of themselves are quite disturbing and disruptive. Nightmares may also impact other areas of functioning. For example, because survivors grow to fear having a nightmare, their sleep habits become affected. Survivors may anticipate having a nightmare when they begin to feel tired and get ready to go to bed. They may worry about having a nightmare and become anxious, aroused and distressed, increasing the chance that they will have a nightmare. This may also increase the amount of time between getting ready to go to sleep and actually falling asleep. **Do you find yourself distressed before going to bed? What is this like for you?** Experiencing nightmares may also increase your level of arousal and distress during the day, as you may be remembering aspects of the nightmare and the trauma. **Do you experience more distress than usual the day after a nightmare? What is that like for you? How do you cope with the distress?**

It is no wonder survivors report feeling distress! Between the nightmares themselves, disrupted sleep, increased arousal and distress during the day because of the nightmares, as well as having difficulty getting to sleep because of fearing and worrying about having nightmares, it would be very difficult to not have your functioning impaired. What you are experiencing is a vicious cycle of intrusive experiences, distress, and increased arousal, creating more intrusive experiences. This treatment will help you break this cycle and will hopefully result in increased functioning in many different areas.

Sleep Habits

One of the primary ways in which nightmares may impact your functioning is by affecting the quality and quantity of sleep you get each night. As was discussed above, you may be getting less sleep overall, experiencing poorer quality sleep, feeling anxious when it is time to get ready for sleep, and feeling sleep deprived during the day. Because of these problems, many people who suffer from nightmares alter their sleep habits to try to improve their sleep. **Think about your own situation—what do you do if you have trouble getting to sleep at night? When you have a nightmare, what do you do to try to return to sleep?**

Some of the behaviors that people engage in to improve their sleep may be helpful in the short term but often are not helpful in the long term. These sleep behaviors, or habits, eventually mess up their sleep cycles and create significant problems in terms of increasing distress, contributing to other sleep problems, and actually increasing problems related to sleep deprivation. Next, we review a list of "dos and don'ts" related to sleep.[22] As we go through the list, identify those behaviors that you engage in that may be helpful and those that may not be helpful.

- **Don't** use coffee, tea, caffeinated sodas, chocolate, alcohol, or tobacco close to your bedtime. Even though you may feel "better" and more relaxed when using these substances, many of them are stimulants and actually increase your physiological arousal, making it more difficult to fall asleep. Although alcohol is a depressant and may make it easier to fall asleep, it also causes you to wake up during the night. In fact, your body goes into withdrawal from the alcohol during the night, which may increase the chance that you will experience a nightmare.

- **Do** try to set and maintain a regular schedule for going to bed and getting up in the morning—even on weekends and vacations. Keeping a regular sleep schedule helps your body strengthen your sleep/wake cycle. Keeping this schedule also means you should avoid taking naps during the day.
- **Don't** eat heavy evening meals or drink a lot of liquid close to bedtime. Try warm milk or a light snack to help promote sleep.
- **Do** engage in relaxing activities before going to bed, including reading, taking a bath, meditating, listening to relaxing music, or doing specific relaxation exercises to help encourage sleep.
- **Don't** use your bed for activities other than sleeping or sexual activity. Engaging in other activities, such as reading, eating, or watching television, in bed will create an association in your mind between the bed and "awake" activities.
- **Do** create an environment that is conducive to sleep: Turn the lights down an hour before going to bed, set the temperature so that it is not too hot or too cold, and try to reduce the level of noise.

Identify three helpful sleep habits you engage in:

1. _____
2. _____
3. _____

Now identify three unhelpful sleep activities you engage in:

1. _____
2. _____
3. _____

You will be asked to try to change one unhelpful sleep habit per week during this treatment.

What do you do if all else fails? Many people toss and turn for hours, thinking they are just about to fall asleep, or stay awake worrying about having a nightmare or how they will feel in the morning if they do not get enough sleep. If you do not fall asleep after being in bed for about 20 minutes, it may help to get out of bed and engage in a quiet activity (reading, watching television) until you feel sleepy again. Then, return to bed. Continue this until you fall asleep. If you find it difficult to get to sleep because you are worrying about things, you may want to write down your concerns and then set aside some time during the day to think about the situation. It may take a while to break some of your unhelpful sleep habits, but try not to become discouraged. It probably took many weeks, months, or years to establish these habits, and it will take some time to break them. It will be well worth the effort, however, when your sleep increases, and you begin to get the rest you deserve!

Relaxation

Many people find it difficult to relax, particularly those who are experiencing a great deal of stress or are battling some emotional problems. In this treatment, you will learn different types of relaxation procedures that have been used in numerous treatments for anxiety and other types of difficulties. The first one that you will learn today is called *progressive muscle relaxation* or *PMR*. PMR refers to alternately tensing and relaxing different muscle groups in your body. This technique helps people to learn the difference between feelings of tension and relaxation. We will go through this procedure together during session, and then you will be provided a tape or CD of PMR to use at home. As with any new behavior, it may require that you do the exercises a few times to gain the full benefit of it. One of the things you will be asked to do over the next week is to rate your level of anxiety before and after doing PMR so that you and the therapist can assess how well it is helping you. Some people have significant difficulty relaxing, and engaging in relaxation procedures may actually make them feel more tense. If this is the case for you, make sure you let your therapist know.

Before we begin PMR, please sit quietly for a moment and try to assess how anxious you are feeling right now. You will be asked to rate your level of anxiety, or your subjective units of distress (SUDs), on a scale from 0 to 100. Zero would represent no anxiety, feeling completely calm and at peace, 50 would represent a moderate level of anxiety, and 100 would represent an intolerable level of anxiety.

HOMEWORK

As discussed earlier, homework is an essential part of this treatment. Because the treatment is quite brief, how well it will work depends largely on the effort that you put into it outside of the therapy sessions. All self-report sheets that you are asked to complete are included at the end of this chapter. If you have difficulties completing them over the next week, please feel free to call the therapist.

- Practice relaxation procedures with the tape/CD: Use the tape/CD to practice PMR each night before you go to sleep. Use the PMR rating scale to rate your SUDs before and after the exercise. Your therapist will use the rating scale to determine how well PMR is working for you.
- Fill out the Modified Daily Sleep Activities Log[2] each morning when you wake up. This will allow you and your therapist to assess any changes in the frequency and intensity of your nightmares, as well as the quality and quantity of sleep you are getting.
- Choose one unhelpful sleep habit and alter it over the next week. For example, if you typically read in bed, choose another place to read for the next week. Use the sleep habit log to monitor which sleep habit you are trying to change and what you do to change it.
- Complete the Daily PTSD Symptom Log.[3] Although not everyone involved in this treatment will have PTSD, most will have some symptoms of PTSD. Completing the PTSD log will help you and your therapist determine if the therapy is helping to reduce these symptoms.

Progressive Muscle Relaxation Record

Directions. Practice PMR using the tape/CD each night before you go to sleep, preferably in bed. Before starting PMR, rate your level of anxiety on a scale from 0 to 100, where 0 means not at all anxious, 50 means moderately anxious, and 100 means extremely anxious. After you complete PMR, rate your level of anxiety again.

Table A2.1

	SESSION 1: PROGRESSIVE MUSCLE RELAXATION RECORD	
DATE	**LEVEL OF ANXIETY BEFORE PMR (0–100)**	**LEVEL OF ANXIETY AFTER PMR (0–100)**

Sleep Habit Log

Target Sleep Habit: _____

Table A2.2

SESSION 1: SLEEP HABIT LOG	
DATE	**WAYS YOU ALTERED THE SLEEP HABIT**

Daily PTSD Symptom Checklist

Table A2.3

SESSION 1: DAILY PTSD SYMPTOM CHECKLIST							
	CHECK EACH TIME YOU HAVE THIS SYMPTOM						
	MON _/_	TUE _/_	WED _/_	THU _/_	FRI _/_	SAT _/_	SUN _/_
1. Upsetting thoughts about the event							
2. Nightmares (for previous night)							
3. Flashbacks (acting or feeling as though the event were happening again)							
4. Got very upset when reminded about the event							
5. Tried to avoid thoughts or feelings about the event							
6. Tried to avoid an activity or place that reminded me of it							
7. Did not do a free-time activity because of lost interest							
8. Felt less close to someone than before the event							
9. Felt my emotions in a situation less than before the event							
10. Thought of future plans as changed because of the event							
11. Had intense physical reactions (panic attack) to a reminder of the event							
12. Had trouble sleeping (record number of times woke up)							

Table A2.3

(CONTINUED)

	CHECK EACH TIME YOU HAVE THIS SYMPTOM						
	MON _/_	TUE _/_	WED _/_	THU _/_	FRI _/_	SAT _/_	SUN _/_
13. Got angry or irritable							
14. Had trouble concentrating							
15. Checked to see who was around me, felt on guard							
16. Was easily startled or jumpy							
17. Could not remember part of what happened during the event							

Adapted from Falsetti, S. A., & Resnick, H. S. (1997). *Multiple channel exposure therapy: Patient manual.* Charleston, SC: Medical University of South Carolina.

Chapter 3: Session 2

COMPLETE ASSESSMENT

Review of Homework

Did you complete the monitoring forms? Were there any difficulties practicing PMR? Were you able to alter a sleep habit? Did you notice any changes in your sleep? Nightmares? PTSD symptoms?

FACING THE NIGHTMARE

As we discussed in the first session, there are a number of reasons why you may be experiencing nightmares. Your mind may be trying to process the traumatic event, you may have developed sleep habits that promote restless sleep and nightmares, or your mind may be creating a story line to match your emotional state. Regardless of the reason for your nightmares, you are currently in a vicious cycle of experiencing nightmares, increased daytime distress related to the nightmares, anticipatory anxiety about the nightmares, and more nightmares.

Because of the distress that the nightmares cause, many people avoid thinking about or talking about the nightmares. Although this may be helpful in the short term in that it allows you some decreased distress, it actually maintains the problem in the long term. Just as with PTSD, if you continue to avoid reminders of the trauma, you do not allow yourself to work through the thoughts and feelings related to the trauma, and you do not fully recover. Indeed, researchers have found that one of the most helpful ways to deal with many different types of fears is to face them head on. For example, if you were bitten by a dog, you would likely become afraid of that dog and maybe even other dogs as well. If you never allowed yourself to interact with dogs again, avoiding them at all costs, you would never learn that not all dogs are mean and bite. You would continue to feel afraid every time you encountered a dog. **If you interacted with dogs after that event, however, how do you think you would feel?** The first time you pet a dog, you might still feel afraid. However, if you were to pet 20 dogs, your fear would diminish. This is a process called *habituation*—becoming less afraid of something through repeated exposure to it. You learn that not all dogs bite, and you do not need to be afraid of all dogs.

In this session, you will take a big step toward confronting the nightmares. You will begin to work on this through writing out the nightmares. You will be doing this in session, so we will be here if you find yourself becoming upset. As you begin writing, keep a few things in mind. First, remember that, although it may seem as if the nightmare is real or the traumatic event is happening all over again, it is only a dream—it is not real and cannot hurt you. Telling yourself that it is not real and that you are safe can help you to start feeling some control over your emotions related to the nightmare and the trauma. Second, it is important to make the written account of the nightmare as similar to the nightmare as possible. To do this, you should write the nightmare in present tense, as if it is happening right now. Also, try to use all of your senses when writing—include descriptions of what you see, smell, hear, feel, and taste. For example, instead of writing:

> *I ran up the stairs into the bedroom and slammed the door shut. He ran up behind me, broke through the door, and told me I was in big trouble now.*

you could write:

> *I am running up the stairs. I can feel the sweat running down my face, blurring my vision. I hear him starting up the stairs behind me. My heart is pounding, and I am very afraid. I see the bedroom door and hope that I will make it inside before he catches up to me. I am running into the bedroom, and I turn around and slam the door shut. I know that it won't keep him out, but it gives me a minute to think. The pictures of our family on the nightstand seem to mock me, presenting such a false picture of a normal happy family. I hear him running down the hall, hear his boots on the floor, hear him breathing hard. He slams into the door, and it opens. He is standing there in front of me, glaring at me while smiling at the same time. He tells me, "You are in big trouble now."*

It is important to include as many details as you can, to make the image as vivid as possible. The next few pages are for your written account of the nightmare. You will be given about 20 minutes to write down as much of the nightmare as you can. Remember, if you start becoming distressed— you are in a safe place, you are not alone, and it is only a dream. Before you begin, rate how anxious you feel from 0 to 100:_____.

My nightmare:

_____

_____

_____

_____

_____

_____

_____

_____

_____

_____

_____

_____

_____

_____

_____

_____

_____

_____

_____

_____

_____

_____

_____

_____

_____

_____

_____

_____

_____

_____

_____

_____

_____

_____

_____

_____

_____

_____

_____

_____

_____

_____

_____

_____

_____

_____

_____

_____

Now rate how you anxious you feel after writing the nightmare: _____.

Many of you will probably feel more anxiety after writing the nightmare. This is to be expected—the first few times you face something you fear, you are likely to feel some anxiety and distress. Do not let this discourage you—it is normal, and it will not last. The more you expose yourself to the nightmare, through writing about it, reading it, thinking about it, and talking about it, the less distress you will feel.

Now we will give everyone the opportunity to read their nightmares aloud. This may seem scary, but it is another form of exposure. It may also help you to feel less alone and less isolated to share your story and share others' as well. As you read your nightmare, we want you to be aware of certain themes that may be evident in your nightmare. These themes are common problems for people who have experienced a traumatic event and include: feeling unsafe, difficulties with intimacy, feeling distrust toward others, feeling powerless and not in control of yourself and your environment, and low esteem of yourself and others. Before you read the nightmare, rate how anxious you feel:_____.

After you have read your nightmare, rate how anxious you feel:_____.

What themes did you notice in your nightmare? Write them down in the spaces provided:

1. _____
2. _____
3. _____

These themes are very important to keep in mind as you continue in your efforts to face the nightmare. Several authors have suggested that difficulties with these areas may represent "stuck points"[4]—issues that you are having difficulties processing or working through. Being aware of these issues and identifying them is the first step toward dealing with them.

RESCRIPTING THE NIGHTMARE

Now that you have written out and read your nightmare, it is time to change it! What we would like you to do is to rewrite your nightmare. You can change any part you want—the beginning, the middle, or the end. In order for the treatment to work, however, we believe that it is important for it to be somewhat similar to the nightmare, so your brain makes the connection between the new version and the old version. For example, if you are having nightmares about being in a serious car accident, you may want to write the nightmare up to the point of the actual accident and then change it so that you do not crash, but get away safe. How you rewrite it is up to you and will depend on the stuck points that you identified above. For example, if your nightmare has the theme of feeling powerless in the situation, you might want to change the dream in such a way that you are acting in a powerful manner. Also, keep in mind the same guidelines that we discussed for writing out the nightmare: Write in present tense, use all of your senses, and be as detailed as possible. Before you begin, rate how anxious you feel from 0 to 100: _____.

My rescripted dream:

_____

_____

_____

_____

_____

_____

_____

_____

_____

_____

_____

_____

_____

_____

_____

_____

_____

_____

_____

_____

_____

_____

_____

_____

_____

_____

_____

_____

_____

_____

_____

_____

_____

_____

_____

_____

_____

_____

_____

_____

_____

_____

Now rate how you anxious you feel after writing the rescripted dream: _____.

Congratulations! This was probably the most difficult part of the treatment! You were able to take a very important step in facing the fear that has been causing you so much distress. You are already taking back your power and increasing the control over your life.

Again, we will give everyone the opportunity to read their rescripted dreams aloud, as this is yet another form of exposure. Similar to reading the original nightmare aloud, it may also help you to feel less alone and less isolated to share your changed story and share in others' changes as well. As you read your rescripted dream, we want you to be aware of the differences between your typical nightmare and this rescripted version. Remember, identification and incorporation of the theme(s) into your rescripted dream is an empowering experience for you and gives you control. Before you read the rescription, rate how anxious you feel: ___.

Now rate how you anxious you feel after reading the rescripted dream aloud: _____.

Before we end the session, we would like to teach you another technique for relaxing. This technique is called *diaphragmatic breathing*. Although breathing is something everyone does, many people do not do it correctly. Breathing the wrong way can create many problems over time, including increasing the chance that you will experience physical symptoms, such as hyperventilation. To check how you are currently breathing, place one hand on your stomach and the other on your chest and just breathe normally. Do you notice which hand is moving? For most people, the hand on the chest is probably moving the most. This means that they are breathing from their chest instead of from their diaphragm. Now try it again, this time concentrating on breathing from your diaphragm. Breathe through your nose, feeling the air move into your lungs, pushing down on your diaphragm, and pushing your stomach out. Try to get the hand on your stomach to move more than the hand on your chest. As you breathe in, count "1" and think "relax" as you breathe out. Take another breath and count "2" as you inhale and think "relax" as you exhale. Continue to do this up to the count of 10 and back down again.

HOMEWORK

■ Rehearse your rescripted dream each night before you go to sleep. Read it over and try to visualize it in your mind. Make the images as real as possible. Do this for 15 minutes. After rehearsing the rescripted dream, do the PMR procedures with the tape/CD. Remember to use the PMR rating scale to rate your SUDs before and after the exercise.
■ Fill out the Daily Sleep Activities Log each morning when you wake up.
■ Choose another one of your unhelpful sleep habits and alter it over the next week. Use the sleep habit log to monitor which sleep habit you are trying to change and what you do to change it.
■ Complete the Daily PTSD Symptom Log.
■ Practice breathing exercises twice per day. Use the breathing exercises log to rate your anxiety before and after each practice.

Progressive Muscle Relaxation Record

Directions. Practice PMR once a day. Before starting PMR, rate your level of anxiety on a scale from 0 to 100, where 0 means not at all anxious, 50 means moderately anxious, and 100 means extremely anxious. After you complete PMR, rerate your level of anxiety.

Table A3.1

DATE	LEVEL OF ANXIETY BEFORE PMR (0–100)	LEVEL OF ANXIETY AFTER PMR (0–100)
SESSION 2: PROGRESSIVE MUSCLE RELAXATION RECORD		

Sleep Habit Log

Target Sleep Habit: _____

Table A3.2

SESSION 2: SLEEP HABIT LOG	
DATE	**WAYS YOU ALTERED THE SLEEP HABIT**

Breathing Retraining Record

Directions. Practice breathing retraining techniques twice per day. Before starting breathing retraining, rate your level of anxiety on a scale from 0 to 100, where 0 means not at all anxious, 50 means moderately anxious, and 100 means extremely anxious. After you complete the breathing exercises, rerate your level of anxiety.

Table A3.3

SESSION 2: BREATHING RETRAINING METHOD		
DATE	**LEVEL OF ANXIETY BEFORE BREATHING RETRAINING (0–100)**	**LEVEL OF ANXIETY AFTER BREATHING RETRAINING (0–100)**
	1. 2.	1. 2.
	1. 2.	1. 2.
	1. 2.	1. 2.
	1. 2.	1. 2.
	1. 2.	1. 2.
	1. 2.	1. 2.
	1. 2.	1. 2.

Daily PTSD Symptom Checklist

Table A3.4

SESSION 2: DAILY PTSD SYMPTOM CHECKLIST							
	CHECK EACH TIME YOU HAVE THIS SYMPTOM						
	MON _/_	**TUE** _/_	**WED** _/_	**THU** _/_	**FRI** _/_	**SAT** _/_	**SUN** _/_
1. Upsetting thoughts about the event							
2. Nightmares (for previous night)							
3. Flashbacks (acting or feeling as though the event were happening again)							
4. Got very upset when reminded about the event							
5. Tried to avoid thoughts or feelings about the event							
6. Tried to avoid an activity or place that reminded me of it							
7. Did not do a free-time activity because of lost interest							
8. Felt less close to someone than before the event							
9. Felt my emotions in a situation less than before the event							
10. Thought of future plans as changed because of the event							
11. Had intense physical reactions (panic attack) to a reminder of the event							
12. Had trouble sleeping (record number of times woke up)							

Table A3.4

(CONTINUED)							
	CHECK EACH TIME YOU HAVE THIS SYMPTOM						
	MON _/_	TUE _/_	WED _/_	THU _/_	FRI _/_	SAT _/_	SUN _/_
13. Got angry or irritable							
14. Had trouble concentrating							
15. Checked to see who was around me, felt on guard							
16. Was easily startled or jumpy							
17. Could not remember part of what happened during the event							

Adapted from Falsetti, S. A., & Resnick, H. S. (1997). *Multiple channel exposure therapy: Patient manual.* Charleston, SC: Medical University of South Carolina.

Chapter 4: Session 3

COMPLETE ASSESSMENT

Review of Homework

Did you complete the monitoring forms? Were there any difficulties practicing diaphragmatic breathing? Were you able to alter a sleep habit? Did you have any problems imagining your rescripted nightmare? Did you notice any changes in your sleep? Nightmares? PTSD symptoms? Have your feelings about the nightmares changed? Have your feelings about the trauma changed?

SLOWING YOUR BREATHING

Now that you have learned how to do diaphragmatic breathing, you can enhance the level of relaxation you feel by slowing down your rate of breathing. As you continue the exercises—breathing with your diaphragm, counting on the inhalation, and saying "relax" on the exhalation—start to slow down your rate of breathing. Try to count to three on the inhalation and to six on the exhalation. Although we say such things as "take a deep breath" when we want someone to calm down and relax, the most relaxing part of breathing is actually the exhalation. So aim for exhaling twice as long as you inhale. Practice this over the next week, again noting your level of distress/anxiety before and after this exercise.

REVIEW TREATMENT

- How are you compared to when you started?
- What are the most important things you learned in this treatment?
- What were the most and least helpful parts of the treatment?

TREATMENT MAINTENANCE

This is a brief treatment, and it may seem as though we have packed a lot of information into three sessions. Think about anything that may have changed over the past 3 weeks. Some may notice small changes already, some may notice large changes, and some may feel the same. An important aspect of this treatment is that you should continue to improve in terms of how you feel, your quality of sleep, and the nightmares, as time goes on, as long as you continue to practice those things you have learned. For some people, this simply takes a bit longer than for others. Some people believe that once they leave treatment, especially a time-limited treatment, they will start having frequent nightmares and sleeping poorly again. Reports from previous clients suggest that this does not typically happen. The skills you have learned can be applied to other areas in your life and will assist you in identifying and adjusting what you do to impact how you feel. Continue to use the skills you have learned and try to avoid falling back into maladaptive patterns (sleep habits, avoidance of feared situations, and so forth).

There are times and situations, however, in which you may be at higher risk for falling back into old routines, feeling greater distress, and even having nightmares again. These high-risk times may come when you are under significant stress or experience another traumatic event. If you do find yourself distressed, or if you have another nightmare, it is important to keep it in perspective. If you are having a hard time, try looking back through this manual and increasing the amount of time that you are practicing the breathing activities and PMR. If you have another nightmare, repeat the procedure we used on your original nightmare—exposure through writing it out, reading it, and rescripting it. It is very important to try not to fall back into maladaptive sleep habits and coping strategies.

Although reviewing the material in this manual and practicing the procedures you have learned should significantly help your level of distress and experience of nightmares, there may come a time when you consider seeking additional treatment. Remember, although you may have been experiencing distress in a number of areas—PTSD, nightmares, depression—this treatment was designed to lower the frequency and intensity of your nightmares. Although we expect that your overall level of distress will also decrease and your sleep quality will increase, it is not likely to relieve you of all symptoms. Seeking additional treatment should not be viewed as a failure but rather as an opportunity to further process important events in your life and improve your level of functioning.

CONGRATULATIONS on completing this treatment and taking a giant step toward improving your future. You have shown great strength in facing your nightmare—be proud of yourself and the work you have done! Sweet dreams!

Progressive Muscle Relaxation Record

Directions. Practice PMR once a day. Before starting PMR, rate your level of anxiety on a scale from 0 to 100, where 0 means not at all anxious, 50 means moderately anxious, and 100 means extremely anxious. After you complete PMR, rerate your level of anxiety.

Table A4.1

SESSION 3: PROGRESSIVE MUSCLE RELAXATION RECORD		
DATE	LEVEL OF ANXIETY BEFORE PMR (0–100)	LEVEL OF ANXIETY AFTER PMR (0–100)

Sleep Habit Log

Target Sleep Habit: _____

Table A4.2

SESSION 3: SLEEP HABIT LOG	
DATE	**WAYS YOU ALTERED THE SLEEP HABIT**

Breathing Retraining Record

Directions. Practice breathing retraining techniques twice per day. Before starting breathing retraining, rate your level of anxiety on a scale from 0 to 100, where 0 means not at all anxious, 50 means moderately anxious, and 100 means extremely anxious. After you complete the breathing exercises, rerate your level of anxiety.

Table A4.3

SESSION 3: BREATHING RETRAINING METHOD		
DATE	LEVEL OF ANXIETY BEFORE BREATHING RETRAINING (0–100)	LEVEL OF ANXIETY AFTER BREATHING RETRAINING (0–100)
	1. 2.	1. 2.
	1. 2.	1. 2.
	1. 2.	1. 2.
	1. 2.	1. 2.
	1. 2.	1. 2.
	1. 2.	1. 2.
	1. 2.	1. 2.

Daily PTSD Symptom Checklist

Table A4.4

SESSION 3: DAILY PTSD SYMPTOM CHECKLIST							
	CHECK EACH TIME YOU HAVE THIS SYMPTOM						
	MON _/_	**TUE** _/_	**WED** _/_	**THU** _/_	**FRI** _/_	**SAT** _/_	**SUN** _/_
1. Upsetting thoughts about the event							
2. Nightmares (for previous night)							
3. Flashbacks (acting or feeling as though the event were happening again)							
4. Got very upset when reminded about the event							
5. Tried to avoid thoughts or feelings about the event							
6. Tried to avoid an activity or place that reminded me of it							
7. Did not do a free-time activity because of lost interest							
8. Felt less close to someone than before the event							
9. Felt my emotions in a situation less than before the event							
10. Thought of future plans as changed because of the event							
11. Had intense physical reactions (panic attack) to a reminder of the event							
12. Had trouble sleeping (record number of times woke up)							

Table A4.4

(CONTINUED)							
	CHECK EACH TIME YOU HAVE THIS SYMPTOM						
	MON _/_	TUE _/_	WED _/_	THU _/_	FRI _/_	SAT _/_	SUN _/_
13. Got angry or irritable							
14. Had trouble concentrating							
15. Checked to see who was around me, felt on guard							
16. Was easily startled or jumpy							
17. Could not remember part of what happened during the event							

Adapted from Falsetti, S. A., & Resnick, H. S. (1997). *Multiple channel exposure therapy: Patient manual.* Charleston, SC: Medical University of South Carolina.

REFERENCES

1. Thompson, K. E., Hamilton, M., & West, J. A. (1995). Group treatment for nightmares in veterans with combat-related PTSD. *NCP Clinical Quarterly, 13–17.*
2. Krakow, B., Kellner, R., Pathnak, D., & Lambert, L. (1996). Long term reduction of nightmares with imagery rehearsal treatment. *Behavioural and Cognitive Psychotherapy, 24,* 135–148.
3. Falsetti, S. A., & Resnick, H. S. (1997). *Multiple channel exposure therapy: Patient manual.* Charleston, SC: Medical University of South Carolina.
4. Resick, P. A., & Schnicke, M. K. (1993). *Cognitive processing therapy for rape victims: A treatment manual.* Newbury Park, CA: Sage.
5. Foa, E. B., & Rothbaum, B. O. (1998). *Treating the trauma of rape: Cognitive-behavioral therapy for PTSD.* New York: Guilford Press.
6. Craske, M. G., Barlow, D. H., & Meadows, E. A. (2000). *Mastery of your anxiety and panic (MAP-3): Therapist guide for anxiety, panic, and agoraphobia* (3rd ed.). San Antonio, TX: Psychological Corporation.
7. Morin, C. M., & Azrin, N. H. (1987). Stimulus control and imagery training in treating sleep-maintenance insomnia. *Journal of Consulting and Clinical Psychology, 55,* 260–262.
8. Lang, P. J. (1968). Fear reduction and fear behavior: Problems in treating a construct. In J. M. Schlein (Ed.), *Research in psychotherapy* (Vol. 3). Washington, DC: American Psychological Press.
9. Barlow, D. H. (1988). *Anxiety and its disorders.* New York: Guilford Press.
10. Falsetti, S. A., Resnick, H. S., & Davis, J. L. (2005). Multiple channel exposure therapy: Combining cognitive behavioral therapies for the treatment of post-traumatic stress disorder with panic attacks. *Behavior Modification, 29,* 70–94.
11. Kessler, R. C., Sonnega, A., Bromet, E., Hughes, M., & Nelson, C. B. (1995). Post-traumatic stress disorder in a national comorbidity survey. *Archives of General Psychiatry, 52,* 1048–1060.
12. American Psychiatric Association. (2000). *Diagnostic and statistical manual of mental disorders* (4th ed., Text Revision). Washington, D.C.: Author.
13. McCann, I. L., Sakheim, D. K., & Abrahamson, D. J. (1988). Trauma and victimization: A model of psychological adaptation. *Counseling Psychologist, 16,* 531–594.
14. Bixler, E., Kales, A., Soldatos, C., Kales, J., & Healey, S. (1979). Prevalence of sleep disorders in the Los Angeles metropolitan area. *American Journal of Psychiatry, 136,* 1257–1262.
15. Ross, R. J., Ball, W. A., Sullivan, K. A., & Caroff, S. N. (1989). Sleep disturbance as the hallmark of post-traumatic stress disorder. *American Journal of Psychiatry, 146,* 697–707.
16. Blanes, T., Burgess, M., & Marks, I. M. (1993). Dream anxiety disorders (nightmares): A review. *Behavioural Psychotherapy, 21*(1), 37–43.
17. Craske, M. G., & Barlow, D. H. (1993). Panic disorder and agoraphobia. In D. H. Barlow, *Clinical handbook of psychological disorders: A step-by-step treatment manual* (2nd ed., pp. 1–47). New York: Guilford Press.
18. van der Kolk, B. A. (1996). Trauma and memory. In B. A. van der Kolk, A. C. McFarlane, & L. Weisaeth (Eds.), *Traumatic stress: The effects of overwhelming experience on mind, body, and society* (pp. 279–302). New York: Guilford Press.

19. Krakow, B. (2004). Imagery Rehearsal Therapy for chronic post-traumatic night-mares: A mind's eye view. In R. I. Rosner, W. J. Lyddon, & A. Freeman (Eds.), *Cognitive therapy and dreams* (pp. 89–109). New York: Springer Publishing.
20. Hartmann, E. (1998a). *Dreams and nightmares: The origin and meaning of dreams.* Cambridge, MA: Perseus Publishing.
21. Rothbaum, B. O., & Mellman, T. A. (2001). Dreams and exposure therapy in PTSD. *Journal of Traumatic Stress, 14,* 481–490.
22. Means, M. K., & Edinger, J. D. (2006). Nonpharmacologic therapy of insomnia. In R. L. Lee-Chiong (Ed.), *Sleep: A comprehensive handbook* (pp. 133–136). Hoboken, NJ: John Wiley & Sons, Inc.
23. Foa, E. B., Rothbaum, B. O., & Steketee, G. S. (1993). Treatment of rape victims. *Journal of Interpersonal Violence, 8,* 256–276.

Posttreatment Clinical Significance Scale

Davis, Wright, Byrd, and Rhudy

POSTTREATMENT CLINICAL SIGNIFICANCE SCALE

1. How closely did you follow the techniques learned in the study (i.e., progressive muscle relaxation, changing sleep habits, etc.)? Circle one.

    Completely   Mostly   Sometimes   Rarely   Never

2. How often do you use the techniques you learned in treatment? Circle one.

    Every time   Most of the   Some of   Rarely   Never
               time   the time

    Please answer the following questions in relation to changes you believe are due to the nightmare treatment.

3. Overall, have you noticed a change in your relations with others?

0	1	2	3	4
Much Worse	Somewhat Worse	No Change	Somewhat Better	Much Better

4. Overall, have you noticed a change in your work, volunteering, or performance of duties?

0	1	2	3	4
Much Worse	Somewhat Worse	No Change	Somewhat Better	Much Better

5. Overall, have you noticed a positive change in your general activity level?

0	1	2	3	4
Much Worse	Somewhat Worse	No Change	Somewhat Better	Much Better

6. Overall, how has your sleep been since the treatment ended?

0	1	2	3	4
Much Worse	Somewhat Worse	No Change	Somewhat Better	Much Better

7. Overall, how is your level of anxiety since the treatment has ended?

0	1	2	3	4
Much Worse	Somewhat Worse	No Change	Somewhat Better	Much Better

8. Overall, how is your level of depression since the treatment has ended?

0	1	2	3	4
Much Worse	Somewhat Worse	No Change	Somewhat Better	Much Better

9. Overall, how are your PTSD symptoms?

0	1	2	3	4
Much Worse	Somewhat Worse	No Change	Somewhat Better	Much Better

10. Overall, how is your mental health?

0	1	2	3	4
Much Worse	Somewhat Worse	No Change	Somewhat Better	Much Better

11. Overall, how is your physical health?

0	1	2	3	4
Much Worse	Somewhat Worse	No Change	Somewhat Better	Much Better

12. Would you recommend this treatment to another person who was having nightmares?

Yes _____   No _____

13. Would you redo the treatment if you had the opportunity?

Yes _____   No _____

14. If you could change anything about the treatment, what would it be?

_____

_____

_____

_____

15. How comfortable did you feel with the therapist giving you the treatment?

0	1	2	3	4
Completely Uncomfortable	Somewhat Uncomfortable	Neutral	Somewhat Comfortable	Very Comfortable

16. How clear was the information presented to you in treatment?

0	1	2	3	4
Not Clear At All	Somewhat Unclear	Neither Clear nor Unclear	Somewhat Clear	Very Clear

17. Please rate the following:

Not at all helpful	Rarely helpful	Somewhat helpful	Helpful	Very helpful
0	1	2	3	4

   a. Education about PTSD _____
   b. Education about nightmares _____
   c. Education about sleep _____
   d. Changing sleep habits _____
   e. Progressive muscle relaxation _____
   f. Writing out nightmare _____
   g. Reading nightmare _____
   h. Identifying themes in nightmare _____
   i. Rescripting nightmare _____
   j. Diaphragmatic breathing _____
   k. Insights from other group members _____
   l. Other _____

18. What was the hardest aspect of treatment? Why?

_____

_____

_____

19. Did you like the format of the treatment?
   a. Group: Yes _____   No _____
   b. Individual: Yes _____   No _____

THANK YOU for SUCCESSFULLY completing the treatment and all the assessments! You have taken a huge step in the right direction, decreasing the effects of nightmares upon your life. If you continue to have problems, try using the techniques that you learned in treatment (e.g., rescripting, progressive muscle relaxation, etc.). And again, thank you and we wish you nothing but continued improvement and best wishes.

Dr. Joanne L. Davis & Dr. Jamie L. Rhudy

Members of the TRAPT Center and the Human Psychophysiological Laboratory

Bibliography

Adler, C. M., Craske, M. G., & Barlow, D. H. (1987). Relaxation induced panic (RIP): When resting isn't peaceful. *Integrative Psychiatry, 5*, 94–100.

Allen, J. G., Console, D. A., Brethour, J. R., Huntoon, J., Fultz, J., & Stein, A. B. (2000). Screening for trauma-related sleep disturbance in women admitted for specialized inpatient treatment. *Journal of Traumatic Stress, 1*, 59–83.

American Psychiatric Association. (1980). *Diagnostic and statistical manual of mental disorders* (3rd ed.). Washington, DC: Author.

American Psychiatric Association. (1994). *Diagnostic and statistical manual of mental disorders* (4th ed.). Washington, DC: Author.

American Psychiatric Association. (2000). *Diagnostic and statistical manual of mental disorders* (4th ed., Text Revision). Washington, DC: Author.

American Sleep Disorders Association. (2001). *International classification of sleep disorders, revised: Diagnostic and coding manual.* Chicago: American Academy of Sleep Medicine.

American Sleep Disorders Association. (2005). *International classification of sleep disorders* (2nd ed.). Westchester, IL: American Academy of Sleep Medicine.

Anda, R. F., Felitti, V. J., Bremner, J. D., Walker, J. D., Whitfield, C., Perry, B. D., et al. (2006). The enduring effects of abuse and related adverse experiences in childhood: A convergence of evidence from neurobiology and epidemiology. *European Archives of Psychiatry and Clinical Neuroscience, 256*, 174–186.

Archibald, H. C., Long, D. M., Miller, C., & Tuddenham, R. D. (1962). Gross stress reaction in combat—A 15-year follow-up. *American Journal of Psychiatry, 119*, 317–322.

Arntz, A., Tiesema, M., & Kindt, M. (2007). Treatment of PTSD: A comparison of imaginal exposure with and without imagery rescripting. *Journal of Behavior Therapy and Experimental Psychiatry, 38*, 345–370.

Babor, T. F., Biddle-Higgins, J. C., Saunders, J. B., & Monteiro, M. G. (2001). *AUDIT: The alcohol use disorders identification test: Guidelines for use in primary health care.* Geneva, Switzerland: World Health Organization.

Barlow, D. H. (1988). *Anxiety and its disorders.* New York: The Guilford Press.

Barlow, D. H., & Craske, M. G. (1989). *Mastery of your anxiety and panic.* Albany, NY: Graywind Publications.

Barlow, D. H., & Craske, M. G. (1994). *Mastery of your anxiety and panic II.* Albany, NY: Graywind Publications.

Barlow, D. H., Levitt, J. T., & Bufka, L. F. (1999). The dissemination of empirically supported treatments: A view to the future. *Behaviour Research and Therapy, 37,* S147–S162.

Bastien, C. H., Vallières, A., & Morin, C. M. (2001). Validation of the Insomnia Severity Index as an outcome measure for insomnia research. *Sleep Medicine, 2,* 297–307.

Batten, S. V., Follette, V. M., & Palm, K. M. (2002). Physical and psychological effects of written disclosure among sexual abuse survivors. *Behavior Therapy, 33,* 107–122.

Bear, M. F., Connors, B. W., & Paradiso, M. A. (2006). Neuroscience: Exploring the brain. New York: Lippincott, Wilkins, and Williams.

Beck, A. T., & Steer, R. A. (1993). *Beck anxiety inventory manual.* San Antonio, TX: Psychological Corporation.

Beck, A. T., Freeman, A., & Associates (1990). *Cognitive therapy of personality disorders.* New York, NY: The Guilford Press.

Beck, A. T., Steer, R. A., & Brown, G. K. (1996). *The Beck depression inventory – II.* San Antonio, TX: The Psychological Corporation.

Becker, C. B., Zayfert, C., & Anderson, E. (2004). A survey of psychologists' attitudes towards and utilization of exposure therapy for PTSD. *Behaviour Research and Therapy, 42,* 277–292.

Belicki, K. (1992). Nightmare frequency versus nightmare distress: Relations to psychopathology and cognitive style. *Journal of Abnormal Psychology, 101,* 592–597.

Belicki, K., & Belicki, D. (1986). Predisposition for nightmares: A study of hypnotic ability, vividness of imagery, and absorption. *Journal of Clinical Psychology, 42,* 714–718.

Belicki, K., & Cuddy, M. (1996). Identifying sexual trauma histories from patterns of sleep and dreams. In D. Barrett (Ed.), *Trauma and dreams* (pp. 46–55). Cambridge, MA: Harvard University Press.

Berquier, A., & Ashton, R. (1992). Characteristics of the frequent nightmare sufferer. *Journal of Abnormal Psychology, 101,* 246–250.

Bishay, N. (1985). Therapeutic manipulation of nightmares and the management of neuroses. *British Journal of Psychiatry 147,* 67–70.

Bixler, E., Kales, A., & Soldatos, C. (1979). Sleep disorders encountered in medical practice: A national survey of physicians. *Behavioral Medicine, 6,* 13–21.

Bixler, E., Kales, A., Soldatos, C., Kales, J., & Healey, S. (1979). Prevalence of sleep disorders in the Los Angeles metropolitan area. *American Journal of Psychiatry, 136,* 1257–1262.

Blagrove, M., Farmer, L., & Williams, E. (2004). The relationship of nightmare frequency and nightmare distress to well-being. *Journal of Sleep Research, 13,* 129–136.

Blake, D. K., Weathers, F. W., Nagy, L. M., Kaloupek, D. G., Klauminzer, G., & Charney, D. S., et al. (1990). A therapist rating scale for assessing current and lifetime PTSD: The CAPS-1. *Behavior Therapist, 13,* 187–188.

Bonanno, G. A. (2005). Resilience in the face of potential trauma. *Current Directions in Psychological Science, 14,* 135–138.

Bonanno, G. A., Galea, S., Bucciarelli, A., & Vlahov, D. (2006). Psychological resilience after disaster: New York City in the aftermath of the September 11th terrorist attack. *Psychological Science, 17,* 181–186.

Bootzin, R. R., & Epstein, D. R. (2000). Stimulus control. In K. L. Lichstein & C. M. Morin (Eds.), *Treatment of late life insomnia* (pp. 167–184). London: Sage.

Bootzin, R. R., Manber, R., Loewy, D. H., Kuo, T. F., & Franzen, P. L. (2004). Sleep disorders. In H. E. Adams & P. B. Sutker (Eds.), *Comprehensive handbook of psychopathology* (3rd ed., pp. 671–711). New York: Springer Science + Business Media, Inc.

Borkovec, T. D., Mathews, A. M., Chambers, A., Ebrahimi, S., Lytle, R., & Nelson, R. (1987). The effects of relaxation training with cognitive therapy or nondirective therapy and the role of relaxation in reduced anxiety in the treatment of generalized anxiety. *Journal of Consulting and Clinical Psychology, 55,* 838–888.

Boscarino, J. A. (2004). Post-traumatic stress disorder and physical illness: Results from clinical and epidemiologic studies. *Annals of the New York Academy of Science, 1032,* 141–153.

Boscarino, J. A., & Chang, J. (1999). Electrocardiogram abnormalities among men with stress-related psychiatric disorders: Implications for coronary heart disease and clinical research. *Annals of Behavioral Medicine, 61,* 378–386.

Brady, K. T., Dansky, B. S., Sonne, S. C., & Saladin, M. E. (1998). Post-traumatic stress disorder and cocaine dependence: Order of onset. *American Journal on Addictions, 7(2),* 128–135.

Breger, L. (1967). Function of dreams. *Journal of Abnormal Psychology Monograph, 72,* 1–28.

Breger, L., Hunter, I., & Lane, R. W. (1971). The effect of stress on dreams. *Psychological Issues, 7,* 27.

Bremner, J. D. (2006). Stress and brain atrophy. *CNS & Neurological Disorders Drug Targets, 5,* 503–512.

Breslau, N. (1998). Epidemiology of trauma and post-traumatic stress disorder. In R. Yehuda (Ed.), *Psychological trauma* (pp. 1–29). Washington, DC: American Psychiatric Press, Inc.

Breslau, N., Davis, G. C., Andreski, P., & Peterson, E. (1991). Traumatic events and post-traumatic stress disorder in an urban population of young adults. *Archives of General Psychiatry, 48,* 216–222.

Breslau, N., Kessler, R. C., Chilcoat, H. D., Schultz, L. R., Davis, G. C., & Andreski, P. (1998). Trauma and post-traumatic stress disorder in the community: The 1996 Detroit area survey of trauma. *Archives of General Psychiatry, 55,* 626–632.

Breslau, N., Roth, T., Burduvali, E., Kapke, A., Schultz, L., & Roehrs, T. (2004). Sleep in lifetime post-traumatic stress disorder: A community-based polysomnographic study. *Archives of General Psychiatry, 61,* 508–516.

Briere, J. (1992). *Child abuse trauma: Theory and treatment of the last effects.* Newbury Park, CA: Sage Publications.

Briere, J. (1995). *Trauma symptom inventory professional manual.* Odessa, FL: Psychological Assessment Resources.

Briere, J. (2001). *Detailed assessment of post-traumatic stress (DAPS).* Odessa, FL: Psychological Assessment Resources.

Broomfield, N. M., Gumley, A. I., & Espie, C. A. (2005). Candidate cognitive processes in psychophysiologic insomnia. *Journal of Cognitive Psychotherapy: An International Quarterly, 19,* 5–17.

Brown, T., & Boudewyns, P. (1996). Periodic limb movements of sleep in combat veterans with PTSD. *Journal of Traumatic Stress, 9,* 129–136.

Brown, R. J., & Donderi, D. C. (1986). Dream content and self-reported well-being among recurrent dreamers, past-recurrent dreamers, and nonrecurrent dreamers. *Journal of Personality and Social Psychology, 50,* 612–623.

Brown, T. A., O'Leary, T. A., & Barlow, D. H. (2001). Generalized anxiety disorder. In D. H. Barlow (Ed.), *Clinical handbook of psychological disorders* (pp. 154–208). New York: Guilford Press.

Bryant, R. A. (2000). Acute stress disorder. *PTSD Research Quarterly, 11*, 1–8.

Bryant, R. A., & Harvey, A. G. (1996). Visual imagery in post-traumatic stress disorder. *Journal of Traumatic Stress, 9*, 613–619.

Bryant, R. A., & Harvey, A. G. (1997). Acute stress disorder: A critical review of diagnostic issues. *Clinical Psychology Review, 17*, 757–773.

Brylowski, A. (1990). Nightmares in crisis: Clinical applications of lucid dreaming techniques. *Psychiatric Journal of the University of Ottawa, 15*, 79–84.

Burgess, M., Gill, M., & Marks, I. (1998). Postal self-exposure treatment of recurrent nightmares: Randomised controlled trial. *British Journal of Psychiatry, 172*, 257–262.

Busby, K., & De Koninck, J. (1980). Short-term effects of for self-regulation on personality dimensions and dream content. *Perceptual and Motor Skills, 50*, 751–765.

Butterfield, M. I., Becker, M. E., Connor, K. M., Sutherland, S., Churchill, L. E., & Davidson, J. R. T. (2001). Olanzapine in the treatment of post-traumatic stress disorder: A pilot study. *International Clinical Psychopharmacology, 16*, 197–203.

Buysse, D. J., Reynolds, C. F., Monk T. H., Berman S. R., & Kupfer D. J. (1989). The Pittsburgh sleep quality index: A new instrument for psychiatric practice and research. *Psychiatry Research, 28*, 193–213.

Cahill, S. P., Rauch, S. A., Hembree, E. A., & Foa, E. B. (2003). Effect of cognitive-behavioral treatments for PTSD on anger. *Journal of Cognitive Psychotherapy, 17*, 117–131.

Calhoun, P. S., Wiley, M., Dennis, M. F., Means, M. K., Edinger, J. D., & Beckham, J. C. (2007). Objective evidence of sleep disturbance in women with post-traumatic stress disorder. *Journal of Traumatic Stress, 20*, 1009–1018.

Carskadon, M. A., Dement, W. C., Mitler, M. M., Guilleminault, C., Zarcone, V. P., & Spiegel, R. (1976). Self-report versus sleep laboratory findings in 122 drug-free subjects with complaints of chronic insomnia. *American Journal of Psychiatry, 133*, 1382–1388.

Cartwright, R. D. (1979). The nature and function of repetitive dreams: A survey and speculation. *Psychiatry, 42*, 131–137.

Cartwright, R. D. (1991). Dreams that work: The relation of dream incorporation to adaptation to stressful events. *Dreaming, 1*, 3–9.

Cartwright, R. (2005). Dreaming as a mood regulation system. In: M. Kryger, T. Roth, & W. Dement (Eds), *Principles and practice of sleep medicine* (4th ed., pp. 565–572). Philadelphia, PA: W. B. Saunders.

Cartwright, R. D., Kravitz, H. M., Eastman, C. I., & Wood, E. (1991). REM latency and the recovery from depression: Getting over divorce. *American Journal of Psychiatry, 148*, 1530–1535.

Cartwright, R. D., & Lloyd, S. R. (1994). Early REM sleep: A compensatory change in depression? *Psychiatry Research, 51*, 245–252.

Cason, H. (1935). The nightmare dream. *Psychological Monographs, 209*, 1–51.

Cellucci, A. J., & Lawrence, P. S. (1978). The efficacy of systematic desensitization in reducing nightmares. *Journal of Behavior Therapy and Experimental Psychiatry, 9*, 109–114.

Chivers, L., & Blagrove, M. (1999). Nightmare frequency, personality and acute psychopathology. *Personality and Individual Differences, 27,* 843–851.

Clark, R. D., Canive, J. M., Calais, L. A., Qualls, C., Brugger, R. D., & Vosburgh, T. B. (1999). Cyproheptadine treatment of nightmares associated with posttraumatic stress disorder. *Journal of Clinical Psychopharmacology, 19,* 486–487.

Cloitre, M., Koenen, K. C., Cohen, L. R., & Han, H. (2002). Skills training in affective and interpersonal regulation followed by exposure: A phase-based treatment for PTSD related to childhood abuse. *Journal of Consulting and Clinical Psychology, 70,* 1067–1074.

Clum, G. A., Nishith, P., & Resick, P. A. (2001). Trauma-related sleep disturbance and self-reported physical health symptoms in treatment-seeking female rape victims. *Journal of Nervous and Mental Disease, 189,* 618–622.

Coalson, B. (1995). Nightmare help: Treatment of trauma survivors with PTSD. *Psychotherapy, 32,* 381–388.

Cohen, A. S., Barlow, D. H., & Blanchard, E. B. (1985). Psychophysiology of relaxation-associated panic attacks. *Journal of Abnormal Psychology, 94,* 96–101.

Cohen, L. R., Hien, D. A., & Batchelder, S. (2008). The impact of cumulative maternal trauma and diagnosis on parenting behavior. *Child Maltreatment, 13,* 27–38.

Coren, S. (1988). Prediction of insomnia from arousability predisposition scores: Scale development and cross-validation. *Behavior Research and Therapy, 26,* 415–420.

Coren, S. (1994). The prevalence of self-reported sleep disturbances in young adults. *International Journal of Neuroscience, 79,* 67–73.

Coyle, K., & Watts, F. N. (1991). The factorial structure of sleep dissatisfaction. *Behaviour Research and Therapy, 29,* 513–520.

Craske, M. G., & Barlow, D. H. (2001). Panic disorder and agoraphobia. In D. H. Barlow (Ed.), *Clinical handbook of psychological disorders* (pp. 1–59). New York: Guilford Press.

Craske, M. G., Barlow, D. H., & Meadows, E. (2000). *Master your own anxiety and panic: Therapist guide for anxiety, panic, and agoraphobia (MAP-3).* San Antonio, TX: Graywind/Psychological Corporation.

Craske, M. G., & Rowe, M. K. (1997). Nocturnal panic. *Clinical Psychology: Science and Practice, 4,* 153–174.

Cuddy, M. A., & Belicki, K. (1992). Nightmare frequency and related sleep disturbance as indicators of a history of sexual abuse. *Dreaming, 2,* 15–22.

Cukrowicz, K. C., Otamendi, A., Pinto, J. V., Bernert, R. A., Krakow, B., & Joiner, T. E. (2006). The impact of insomnia and sleep disturbances on depression and suicidality. *Dreaming, 16,* 1–10.

Dagan, Y., Lavie, P., & Bleich, A. (1991). Elevated awakening thresholds in sleep stage 3–4 in war-related post-traumatic stress disorder. *Biological Psychiatry, 30,* 618–622.

Daly, C. M., Doyle, M. E., Raskind, M., Raskind, E., & Daniels, C. (2005). Clinical case series: The use of Prazosin for combat-related recurrent nightmares among Operation Iraqi Freedom combat veterans. *Military Medicine, 170,* 513–515.

Dancu, C. V., Foa, E. B., & Smucker, M. R. (1993). *Treatment of chronic posttraumatic stress disorder in adult survivors of incest: Cognitive/behavioral interventions.* Paper presented at the annual meeting of the Association for the Advancement of Behavior Therapy, Atlanta, GA.

David, D., & Mellman, T. A. (1997). Dreams following Hurricane Andrew. *Dreaming, 7,* 209–214.

Davidson, J. R. T., Hughes, D., Blazer, D. G., & George, L. K. (1991). Post-traumatic stress disorder in the community: An epidemiological study. *Psychological Medicine, 21,* 713–721.

Davidson, J. R. T., Landerman L.R., Farfel G. M., & Clary C. M. *(2002).* Characterizing the effects of sertraline in post-traumatic stress disorder. *Psychological Medicine, 32,* 661–670.

Davis, J. L. (2003). *Exposure, relaxation, & rescripting therapy: Participant manual.* Tulsa, OK: University of Tulsa.

Davis, J. L., Byrd, P., Rhudy, J. L., & Wright, D. C. (2007). Characteristics of chronic nightmares in a trauma exposed clinical sample. *Dreaming, 17,* 187–198.

Davis, J. L., DeArellano, M., Falsetti, S. A., & Resnick, H. S. (2003). Treatment of nightmares following trauma: A case study. *Clinical Case Studies, 2,* 283–294.

Davis, J. L., & Wright, D. C. (2005). Case series utilizing Exposure, Relaxation, & Rescripting Therapy: Impact on nightmares, sleep quality, and psychological distress. *Behavioral Sleep Medicine, 3,* 151–157.

Davis, J. L., & Wright, D. C. (2006). Exposure, Relaxation, and Rescripting Therapy for trauma-related nightmares. *Journal of Trauma and Dissociation, 7,* 5–18.

Davis, J. L., & Wright, D. C. (2007). Randomized clinical trial for treatment of chronic nightmares in trauma-exposed adults. *Journal of Traumatic Stress, 20,* 123–133.

Davis, J. L., Wright, D., & Borntrager, C. (2001). *The Trauma-Related Nightmare Survey.* Tulsa, OK: University of Tulsa.

Davis, J. L., Wright, D. C., Byrd, P. M., & Rhudy, J. L. (2006). *Posttreatment clinical significance scale.* Unpublished measure. Tulsa, OK: University of Tulsa.

DeFazio, V. J., Rustin, S., & Diamond, A. (1975). Symptom development in Vietnam era veterans. *American Journal of Orthopyschiatry, 45,* 158–163.

de Jong, J. T. V. M., Komproe, I. H., Van Ommeren, M., El Masri, M., Araya, M., Khaled, N., et al. (2001). Lifetime events and posttraumatic stress disorder in 4 postconflict settings. *Journal of the American Medical Association, 286,* 555–562.

Derogatis, L. R. (1992). *SCL-90-R: Administration, scoring and procedures manual II for the revised version.* Towson, MD: Clinical Psychometric Research.

Devine, E. B., Hakim, Z., & Green, J. (2005). A systematic review of patient-reported outcome instruments measure sleep dysfunction in adults. *Pharmacoeconomics, 23,* 889–912.

Doghramji, P. P. (2004). Recognizing sleep disorders in a primary care setting. *Journal of Clinical Psychiatry, 65 (Suppl 16),* 23–26.

Domhoff, G. W. (2000). *The repetition principle in dreams: Is it a possible clue to a function of dreams?* Retrieved November 2007, from http://www.dreamresearch.net/Library/domhoff_2000b.html

Donovan, B. S., Padin-Rivera, E., Chapman, H., Strauss, M., & Murray, M. (2004). Development of the nightmare intervention and treatment evaluation (NITE) scale. *Journal of Trauma Practice, 3,* 49–69.

Dorrian, J., & Dinges, D. F. (2006). Sleep deprivation and its effects on cognitive performance. In T. L. Lee-Chiong (Ed.), *Sleep: A comprehensive handbook* (pp. 139–144). Hoboken, NJ: John Wiley & Sons, Inc.

Douglas, A. B., Bornstein, R., Nino-Murcia, G., Keenan, S., Miles, L., Zarcone, V. P., et al. (1994). The sleep disorders questionnaire 1: Creation and multivariate structure of SDQ. *Sleep, 17,* 160–167.

Drake, C. L., Roehrs, T., & Roth, T. (2003). Insomnia causes, consequences, and therapeutics: An overview. *Depression and Anxiety, 18,* 163–176.

Dunn, K. K., & Barrett, D. (1988). Characteristics of nightmare subjects and their nightmares. *Psychiatric Journal of the University of Ottawa, 13,* 91–93.

Ehlers, A., & Clark, D.M. (2000). A cognitive model of post-traumatic stress disorder. *Behaviour Research and Therapy, 38,* 319–345.

Elhai, J. D., Gray, M. J., Kashdan, T. B., & Franklin, C. L. (2005). Which instruments are most commonly used to assess traumatic event exposure and post-traumatic effects?: A survey of traumatic stress professionals. *Journal of Traumatic Stress, 18,* 541–545.

Elliott, A. C. (2001). Primary care assessment and management of sleep disorders. *Journal of the American Academy of Nursing Practitioners, 13,* 409–417.

Empson, J. (1989). *Sleep and dreaming.* Boston: Faber and Faber.

Erman, M. K. (1987). Dream anxiety attacks (nightmares). *Psychiatric Clinics of North America, 10,* 667–674.

Esposito, K., Benitz, A., Barza, L., & Mellman, T. (1999). Evaluation of dream content in combat-related PTSD. *Journal of Traumatic Stress, 12,* 681–687.

Falsetti, S. A. (1997). The decision-making process of choosing a treatment for patients with civilian trauma-related PTSD. *Journal of Cognitive and Behavioral Practice, 4,* 99–121.

Falsetti, S. A., & Resnick, H. S. (1997). *Multiple channel exposure therapy: Therapist manual.* Charleston, SC: Medical University of South Carolina.

Falsetti S. A., & Resnick, H. S. (2000). Treatment of PTSD using cognitive and cognitive behavioral therapies. *Journal of Cognitive Psychotherapy, 14,* 97–122.

Falsetti, S. A., Resnick, H. S., & Davis, J. L. (2005). Multiple channel exposure therapy: Combining cognitive behavioral therapies for the treatment of posttraumatic stress disorder with panic attacks. *Behavior Modification, 29,* 70–94.

Feeny, N. C., & Foa, E. B. (2006). Cognitive vulnerability to PTSD. In L. B. Alloy & J. H. Riskind (Eds.), *Cognitive vulnerability to emotional disorders* (pp. 285–301). Mahwah, NJ: Lawrence Erlbaum Associates Publishers.

Feeny, N. C., Hembree, E. A., & Zoellner, L. A. (2003). Myths regarding exposure therapy for PTSD. *Cognitive and Behavioral Practice, 10,* 85–90.

Feeny, N. C., Zoellner, L. A., & Foa, E. B. (2002). Treatment outcome for chronic PTSD among female assault victims with BPC: A preliminary examination. *Journal of Personality Disorders, 16,* 30–40.

Felitti, V. J., Anda, R. F., Nordenberg, D., Williamson, D. F., Spitz, A. M., Edwards, V., et al. (1998). Relationship of childhood abuse and household dysfunction to many of the leading causes of death in adults: The adverse childhood experience (ACE) study. *American Journal of Preventative Medicine, 14,* 245–258.

Finkelhor, D., Ormrod, R., Turner, H., & Hamby, S. (2005). The victimization of children and youth: A comprehensive, national survey. *Child Maltreatment, 10,* 5–25.

First, M. B., Spitzer, R. L., Gibbon, M., & Williams, J. B. W. (1996). Structured clinical interview for DSM-IV Axis I disorders, clinician version (SCID-CV). Washington, DC: American Psychiatric Press, Inc.

Foa, E. B., Cashman, L., Jaycox, L., & Perry, K. (1997). The validation of a self-report measure of posttraumatic stress disorder: The Posttraumatic Diagnostic Scale. *Psychological Assessment, 9,* 445–451.

Foa, E. B., Davidson, J. R. T., & Frances, A. (1999). The expert consensus guideline series: Treatment of posttraumatic stress disorder. *Journal of Clinical Psychiatry, 60* (supplement 60), 1–76.

Foa, E. B., Keane, T. M., & Friedman, M. J. (2000). *Effective treatments for PTSD.* New York: Guilford Press.

Foa, E. B., & Kozak, M. J. (1986). Emotional processing of fear: Exposure to corrective information. *Psychological Bulletin, 99,* 20–35.

Foa, E. B., & McNally, R. J. (1995). Mechanisms of change in exposure therapy. In R. Rapee (Ed.), *Current controversies in the anxiety disorders* (pp. 329–343). New York: Guilford Press.

Foa, E. B., & Meadows, E. A. (1997). Psychosocial treatments for post-traumatic stress disorder: A critical review. *Annual Review of Psychology, 48,* 449–480.

Foa, E. B., Molnar, C., & Cashman, L. (1995). Change in rape narratives during exposure therapy for posttraumatic stress disorder. *Journal of Traumatic Stress, 8,* 675–690.

Foa, E. B., Riggs, D. S., Dancu, C. V., & Rothbaum, B. O. (1993). Reliability and validity of a brief instrument for assessing post-traumatic stress disorder. *Journal of Traumatic Stress, 6,* 459–473.

Foa, E. B., Riggs, D. S., Massie, E. D., & Yarczower, M. (1995). The impact of fear activation and anger on the efficacy of exposure treatment for post-traumatic stress disorder. *Behavior Therapy, 26,* 487–499.

Foa, E. B., & Rothbaum, B. O. (1998). *Treating the trauma of rape.* New York: The Guilford Press.

Foa, E. B., Rothbaum, B. O., & Furr, J. M. (2003). Augmenting exposure therapy with other CBT procedures. *Psychiatric Annals, 33,* 47–53.

Foa, E. B., Rothbaum, B. O., Riggs, D. S., & Murdock, T. B. (1991). Treatment of post-traumatic stress disorder in rape victims: A comparison between cognitive-behavioral procedures and counseling. *Journal of Consulting and Clinical Psychology, 59,* 715–723.

Foa, E. B., Steketee, G. R., & Rothbaum, B. O. (1989). Behavioral/cognitive conceptualizations of post-traumatic stress disorder. *Behavior Therapy, 20,* 155–176.

Foa, E. B., Zoellner, L. A., Feeny, N. C., Hembree, E., & Alvarez-Conrad, J. (2002). Does imaginal exposure exacerbate PTSD symptoms? *Journal of Consulting and Clinical Psychology, 70,* 1022–1028.

Forbes, D., Creamer, M., & Biddle, D. (2001). The validity of the PTSD checklist as a measure of symptomatic change in combat-related PTSD. *Behavior Research and Therapy, 39,* 977–986.

Forbes, D., Phelps, A. J., & McHugh, A. F. (2001). Treatment of combat-related nightmares using imagery rehearsal: A pilot study. *Journal of Traumatic Stress, 14,* 433–442.

Forbes, D., Phelps, A. J., McHugh, A. F., Debenham, P., Hopwood, M., & Creamer, M. (2003). Imagery rehearsal in the treatment of post-traumatic nightmares in Australian veterans with chronic combat-related PTSD: 12-month follow-up. *Journal of Traumatic Stress, 16,* 509–513.

Ford, D. E., & Kamerow, D. B. (1989). Epidemiologic study of sleep disturbances and psychiatric disorders: An opportunity for prevention? *Journal of the American Medical Association, 262,* 1479–1484.

Foy, D. W., Kagan, B., McDermott, C., Leskin, G., Sipprelle, R. C., & Paz, G. (1996). Practical parameters in the use of flooding for treating chronic PTSD. *Clinical Psychology and Psychotherapy, 2,* 169–175.

Freed, S., Craske, M. G., & Greher, M. R. (1999). Nocturnal panic and trauma. *Depression and Anxiety, 9,* 141–145.

Freud, S. (1955). Beyond the pleasure principle. In J. Strachey (Ed. and Trans.), *The standard edition of the complete psychological works of Sigmund Freud* (Vol. 18). London: Hogarth Press. (Original work published 1920)

Freud, S. (1900/1955). *The interpretation of dreams.* New York: Basic Books.

Gallop, D. (1990). *Aristotle on Sleep and Dreams.* Peterborough, Ontario: Broadview Press Ltd.

Germain, A., Hall, M., Krakow, B., Shear, M. K., & Buysse, D. J. (2005). A brief sleep scale for post-traumatic stress disorder: Pittsburgh sleep quality index addendum for PTSD. *Anxiety Disorders, 19,* 233–244.

Germain, A., Hall, M., Shear, M. K., Nofzinger, E. A., & Buysse, D. J. (2006). Ecological study of sleep disruption in PTSD: A pilot study. *Annals of the New York Academy of Sciences, 1071,* 438–441.

Germain, A., Krakow, B., Faucher, B., Zadra, A., Nielsen, T., Hollifield, M., et al. (2004). Increased mastery elements associated with imagery rehearsal treatment for nightmares in sexual assault survivors with PTSD. *Dreaming, 14,* 195–206.

Germain, A., & Nielsen, T. (2003a). Impact of imagery rehearsal treatment on distressing dreams, psychological distress, and sleep parameters in nightmare patients. *Behavioral Sleep Medicine, 1,* 140–154.

Germain, A., & Nielsen, T. A. (2003b). Sleep pathophysiology in post-traumatic stress disorder and idiopathic nightmare sufferers. *Biological Psychiatry, 54,* 1092–1098.

Germain, A., Shear, M. K., Hall, M., & Buysse, D. J. (2007). Effects of a brief behavioral treatment for PTSD-related sleep disturbances: A pilot study. *Behaviour Research and Therapy, 45,* 627–632.

Gidron, Y., Peri, T., Connolly, J. F., & Shalev, A. Y. (1996). Written disclosure in post-traumatic stress disorder: Is it beneficial for the patient? *Journal of Nervous and Mental Disease, 184,* 505–507.

Giles, D. E., Kupfer, D. J., Rush, A. J., & Roffwarg, H. P. (1998). Controlled comparison of electrophysiological sleep in families of probands with unipolar depression. *American Journal of Psychiatry, 155,* 192–199.

Gill, J. M., & Page, G. G. (2006). Psychiatric and physical health ramifications of traumatic events in women. *Issues in Mental Health Nursing, 27,* 711–734.

Golding, J. M., Stein, J. A., Siegel, J. M., Burnam, M. A., & Sorenson, S. B. (1988). Sexual assault history and use of health and mental health services. *American Journal of Community Psychology, 6,* 625–644.

Goldstein, G., van Kammen, W., Shelly, C., Miller, D. J., & van Kammen, D. P. (1987). Survivors of imprisonment in the pacific theater during World War II. *American Journal of Psychiatry, 144,* 1210–1213.

Goodman, L. A., Koss, M. P., & Russo, N. F. (1993). Violence against women: Physical and mental health effects. Part I: Research findings. *Applied and Preventative Psychology, 2,* 79–89.

Gray, M. J., Litz, B. T., Hsu, J. L., & Lombardo, T. W. (2004). Psychometric properties of the life events checklist. *Assessment, 11*, 330–341.

Gray, M. J., & Slagle, D. M. (2006). Selecting a potentially traumatic event screening measure: Practical and psychometric considerations. *Journal of Trauma Practice, 5*, 1–20.

Green, B. (1993). Disasters and post-traumatic stress disorder. In J. R. T. Davidson & E. B. Foa (Eds.), *Post-traumatic stress disorder: DSM-IV and beyond.* Washington DC: American Psychiatric Press.

Greenberg, R., Pillard, R., & Pearlman, C. (1972). The effect of dream (stage REM) deprivation on adaptation to stress. *Psychosomatic Medicine, 34*, 257–262.

Grunert, B. K., Weis, J. M., Smucker, M. R., & Christianson, H. F. (2007). Imagery rescripting and reprocessing therapy after failed prolonged exposure for posttraumatic stress disorder following industrial injury. *Journal of Behavior Therapy and Experimental Psychiatry, 38*, 317–328.

Guerrero, J., & Crocq, M. (1994). Sleep disorders in the elderly: Depression and post-traumatic stress disorder. *Journal of Psychosomatic Research, 38*, 141–150.

Guilleminault, C. (1982). *Sleeping and waking disorders: Indications and techniques.* Menlo Park: Addison-Wesley Publishing Co.

Guy, W. (1976). Clinical Global Impressions. In: ECDEU Assessment Manual for Psychopharmacology, revised (DHEW Publ No ADM 76-338) (pp. 218–222). Rockville, MD: National Institute of Mental Health.

Hackmann, A., & Holmes, E. A. (2004). Reflecting on imagery: A clinical perspective and overview of the special issue of *Memory* on mental imagery and memory in psychopathology. *Memory, 12*, 389–402.

Hall, C., & Van de Castle, R. I. (1966). *The content analysis of dreams.* New York: Appleton-Century-Crofts.

Halliday, G. (1987). Direct psychological therapies for nightmares: A review. *Clinical Psychology Review, 7*, 501–523.

Halliday, G. (1995). Treating nightmares in children. In C. E. Schaefer (Ed.), *Clinical handbook of sleep disorders in children* (pp. 149–176). Northvale, NJ: Jason Aronson.

Halligan, S. L., & Yehuda, R. (2000). Risk factors for PTSD. *PTSD Research Quarterly, 11*, 1–7.

Harding, T. W., de Arango, M. V., Baltazar, J., Climent, C. E., Ibrahim, H. H., Ladrido-Ignacio, L., et al. (1980). Mental disorders in primary health care: A study of their frequency and diagnosis in four developing countries. *Psychological Medicine, 10*, 231–241.

Hartmann, E. (1984). *The nightmare: The psychology and biology of terrifying dreams.* New York: Basic Books, Inc.

Hartmann, E. (1989). Boundaries of dreams, boundaries of dreamers: Thin and thick boundaries as a new personality measure. *Psychiatric Journal of the University of Ottawa, 14*, 557–560.

Hartmann, E. (1991). Dreams that work or dreams that poison? What does dreaming do? An editorial essay. *Dreaming, 1*, 23–25.

Hartmann, E. (1995). Dreaming connects: A hypothesis on the nature and function of dreaming based on dreams following trauma. *Sleep Research, 24*, 147.

Hartmann, E. (1996). Who develops PTSD nightmares and who doesn't. In D. Barrett (Ed.), *Trauma and dreams* (pp. 100–113). Cambridge, MA: Harvard University Press.

Hartmann, E. (1998a). *Dreams and nightmares: The origin and meaning of dreams.* Cambridge, MA: Perseus Publishing.

Hartmann, E. (1998b). Nightmare after trauma as paradigm for all dreams: A new approach to the nature and functions of dreaming. *Psychiatry, 61,* 223–238.

Hartmann, E., Mitchell, W., Brune, P., & Greenwald, D. (1984). Childhood nightmares but not childhood insomnia may predict adult psychopathology. *Sleep Research, 13,* 117.

Hartmann, E., Russ, D., Oldfield, M., Sivan, I., & Cooper, S. (1987). Who has nightmares? The personality of the lifelong nightmare sufferer. *Archives of General Psychiatry, 44,* 49–56.

Hartmann, E., Russ, D., van der Kolk, B., Falke, R., & Oldfield, M. (1981). A preliminary study of the personality of the nightmare sufferer: Relationship to schizophrenia and creativity? *American Journal of Psychiatry, 138,* 794–797.

Hartmann, E., Zborowski, M., Rosen, R., & Grace, N. (2001). Contextualizing images in dreams: More intense after abuse and trauma. *Dreaming, 11,* 115–126.

Harvey, A. G. (2000). Pre-sleep cognitive activity: A comparison of sleep-onset insomniacs and good sleepers. *British Journal of Clinical Psychology, 39,* 275–286.

Harvey, A. G. (2002). A cognitive model of insomnia. *Behaviour Research and Therapy, 40,* 869–893.

Harvey, A. G., & Bryant, R. A. (1998). The relationship between acute stress disorder and posttraumatic stress disorder: A prospective evaluation of motor vehicle accident survivors. *Journal of Consulting and Clinical Psychology, 66,* 507–512.

Harvey, A. G., Jones, C., & Schmidt, D. A. (2003). Sleep and posttraumatic stress disorder: A review. *Clinical Psychology Review, 23,* 377–407.

Haynes, S. N., & Mooney, D. K. (1975). Nightmares: Etiological, theoretical, and behavioral treatment considerations. *Psychological Record, 25,* 225–236.

Hays, R. D., & Stewart, A. L. (1992). Sleep measures. In A. Stewart & J. E. Ware (Eds.), *Measuring functioning and well-being: The medical outcome study approach.* Durham, NC: Duke University Press.

Hearne, K. M. T. (1991). A questionnaire and personality study of nightmare sufferers. *Journal of Mental Imagery, 15,* 55–64.

Hedges, D. W., & Woon, F. L. M. (2007). Structural magnetic resonance imaging findings in post-traumatic stress disorder and their responses to treatment: A systematic review. *Current Psychiatry Reviews, 3,* 85–93.

Hefez, A., Metz, L., & Lavie, P. (1987). Long-term effects of extreme situational stress on sleep and dreaming. *American Journal of Psychiatry, 144,* 344–347.

Heide, F. J., & Borkovec, T. D. (1983). Relaxation-induced anxiety: Paradoxical anxiety enhancement due to relaxation training. *Journal of Consulting and Clinical Psychology, 51,* 171–182.

Heide, F. J., & Borkovec, T. D. (1984). Relaxation-induced anxiety: Mechanisms and theoretical implications. *Behaviour Research and Therapy, 22,* 1–12.

Heltzer, J. E., Robins, L. M., & McEvoy, L. (1987). Post-traumatic stress disorder in the general population: Findings of the Epidemiological Catchment Area survey. *New England Journal of Medicine, 317,* 1630–1634.

Hembree, E. A., Cahill, S. P., & Foa, E. B. (2004). Impact of personality disorders on treatment outcome for female assault survivors with chronic post-traumatic stress disorder. *Journal of Personality Disorders, 18,* 117–127.

Hembree, E. A., Foa, E. B., Dorfan, N. M., Street, G. P., Kowalski, J., & Tu, X. (2003). Do patients drop out prematurely from exposure therapy for PTSD? *Journal of Traumatic Stress, 16,* 555–562.

Hersen, M. (1971). Personality characteristics of nightmare sufferers. *Journal of Nervous and Mental Disease, 153,* 27–31.

Hobson, J. A., & McCarley, R. W. (1977). The brain as a dream state generator: An activation-synthesis hypothesis of the dream process. *American Journal of Psychiatry, 134,* 1335–1348.

Hobson, J. A., Stickgold, R., & Pace-Schott, E. F. (1998). The neuropsychology of REM sleep dreaming. *NeuroReport, 9,* R1–R14.

Horne, J. A., & Pettitt, A. N. (1985). High incentive effects on vigilance performance during 72 hours of total sleep deprivation. *Acta Psychologica, 58,* 123–139.

Horowitz, M. J. (1975). Intrusive and repetitive thoughts after experimental stress. *Archives of General Psychiatry, 32,* 1457–1463.

Horowitz, M. J., & Wilner, N. (1976). Stress films, emotion, and cognitive response. *Archives of General Psychiatry, 33,* 1339–1344.

Horowitz, M. J. (1983). *Image formation and psychotherapy* (rev ed.). New York: Jason Aronson.

Horowitz, M. J., Wilner, N., & Kaltreider, N. (1980). Signs and symptoms of post traumatic stress disorder. *Archives of General Psychiatry, 37,* 85–92.

Hublin, C., Kaprio, J., Partinen, M., & Koskenvuo, M. (1999). Nightmares: Familial aggregation and association with psychiatric disorders in a nationwide twin cohort. *American Journal of Medical Genetics, 88,* 329–336.

Hublin, C., Kaprio, J., Partinen, M., & Koskenvuo, M. (2001). Parasomnias: Co-occurrence and genetics. *Psychiatric Genetics, 11,* 65–70.

Inman, D. J., Silver, S. M., & Doghramji, K. (1990). Sleep disturbance in post-traumatic stress disorder: A comparison with non-PTSD insomnia. *Journal of Traumatic Stress, 3,* 429–437.

Irwin, C., Falsetti, S. A., Lydiard, R. B., Ballenger, J. C., Brock, C. D., & Brener, W. (1996). Comorbidity of post-traumatic stress disorder and irritable bowel syndrome. *Journal of Clinical Psychiatry, 57,* 576–578.

Irwin, K. L., Edlin, B. R., Wong, L., Faruque, S., McCoy, H. V., Word, C., et al. (1995). Urban rape survivors: Characteristics and prevalence of human immunodeficiency virus and other sexually transmitted infections. *Obstetrics and Gynecology, 85,* 330–336.

Jacobs-Rebhun, S., Schnurr, P. P., Friedman, M. J., Peck, R., Brophy, M., & Fuller, D. (2000). Posttraumatic stress disorder and sleep difficulty. *American Journal of Psychiatry, 157,* 1525–1526.

Janoff-Bulman, R. (1989). Assumptive worlds and the stress of traumatic events: Applications of the schema construct. *Social Cognition, 7,* 113–136.

Janoff-Bulman, R., & Frieze, I. H. (1983). A theoretical perspective for understanding reactions to victimization. *Journal of Social Issues, 39,* 1–17.

Jaycox, L. H., & Foa, E. B. (1996). Obstacles in implementing exposure therapy for PTSD: Case discussions and practical solutions. *Clinical Psychology and Psychotherapy, 3,* 176–184.

Johnson, D. R., Rosenheck, R., Fontana, A., Lubin, H., Charney, D., & Southwick, S.

(1996). Outcome of intensive treatment for combat-related posttraumatic stress disorder. *American Journal of Psychiatry, 153,* 771–777.

Kales, A., Soldatos, C. R., Caldwell, A. B., Charney, D. S., Kales, J. D., Markel, D., et al. (1980). Nightmares: Clinical characteristics and personality patterns. *American Journal of Psychiatry, 137,* 1197–1201.

Kaminer, H., & Lavie, P. (1991). Sleep and dreaming in holocaust survivors: Dramatic decrease in dream recall in well-adjusted survivors. *Journal of Nervous and Mental Disease, 179,* 664–669.

Kazdin, A. E. (2003). *Research design in clinical psychology* (4th ed.). Boston: Allyn and Bacon.

Keane, T., Fairbank, J., Caddell, J., & Zimering, R. (1989). Implosive (flooding) therapy reduces symptoms of PTSD in Vietnam combat veterans. *Behavior Therapy, 20,* 245–260.

Keane, T., Fairbank, J., Caddell, J., Zimering, R., Taylor, K., & Mora, C. (1989). Clinical evaluation of a measure to assess combat exposure. *Psychological Assessment, 1,* 53–55.

Kellner, R., Neidhardt, J., Krakow, B., & Pathak, D. (1992). Changes in chronic nightmares after one session of desensitization or rehearsal instructions. *American Journal of Psychiatry, 149,* 659–663.

Kendall, P. C. (1998). Directing misperceptions: Researching the issues facing manual-based treatments. *Clinical Psychology Science and Practice, 5,* 396–399.

Kessler, R. C., Sonnega, A., Bromet, E., Hughes, M., & Nelson, C. B. (1995). Posttraumatic stress disorder in the National Comorbidity Survey. *Archives of General Psychiatry, 52,* 1048–1060.

Khassawneh, B. Y. (2006). Periodic limb movement disorder. In T. L. Lee-Chiong (Ed.), *Sleep: A comprehensive handbook* (pp. 483–486). Hoboken, NJ: John Wiley & Sons, Inc.

Kilpatrick, D. G., Acierno, R., Resnick, H. S., Saunders, B. E., & Best, C. L. (1997). A 2-year longitudinal analysis of the relationship between violent assault and substance use in women. *Journal of Consulting and Clinical Psychology, 65,* 834–847.

Kilpatrick, D. G., Saunders, B. E., Amick-McMullan, A., Best, C. L. , Veronen, L. J., & Resnick, H. S. (1989). Victim and crime factors associated with the development of crime-related post-traumatic stress disorder. *Behavior Therapy, 20,* 199–214.

Kilpatrick, D. G., Saunders, B. E., & Smith D. W. (2002). Research in brief: Youth victimization: Prevalence and implications (NCJ 194972). Washington, DC: U.S. Department of Justice, National Institute of Justice.

Kilpatrick, D. G., Veronen, L. J., & Best, C. L. (1985). Factors predicting psychological distress among rape victims. In: C. R. Figley (Ed.), *Trauma and its wake: The study and treatment of post-traumatic stress disorder* (pp. 113–141). New York: Brunner/Mazel, Inc.

Kilpatrick, D. G., Veronen, L. J., & Resick, P. A. (1982). Psychological sequelae to rape: Assessment and treatment strategies. In D. M. Doleys, R. I. Meredity, & A. R. Ciminero (Eds.), *Behavioral medicine: Assessment and treatment strategies.* New York: Plenum.

Kimerling, R., & Calhoun, K. S. (1994). Somatic symptoms, social support, and treatment seeking among sexual assault victims. *Journal of Consulting and Clinical Psychology, 62,* 333–340.

Klein, E., Koren, D., Arnon, I., & Lavie, P. (2002). No evidence of sleep disturbance in post-traumatic stress disorder: A polysomnographic study in injured victims of traffic accidents. *Israel Journal of Psychiatry and Related Sciences, 39,* 3–10.

Klink, M., & Quan, S. F. (1987). Prevalence of reported sleep disturbances in a general adult population and their relationship to obstructive airways diseases. *Chest, 91,* 540–546.

Kobayashi, I., Boarts, J. M., & Delahanty, D. L. (2007). Polysomnographically measured sleep abnormalities in PTSD: A meta-analytic review. *Psychophysiology, 44,* 1–10.

Koopman, C., Ismailji, T., Holmes, D., Classen, C. C., Palesh, O., & Wales, T. (2005). The effects of expressive writing on pain, depression, and post-traumatic stress disorder symptoms in survivors of intimate partner violence. *Journal of Health Psychology, 10,* 211–221.

Koren, D., Arnon, I., & Klein, E. (1999). Acute stress response and posttraumatic stress disorder in traffic accident victims: A one-year prospective, follow-up study. *American Journal of Psychiatry, 156,* 367–373.

Koren, D., Arnon, I., Lavie, P., & Klein, E. (2002). Sleep complaints as early predictors of posttraumatic stress disorder: A 1-year prospective study of injured survivors of motor vehicle accidents. *American Journal of Psychiatry, 159,* 855–857.

Krakow, B. (2004). Imagery rehearsal therapy for chronic posttraumatic nightmares: A mind's eye view. In R. I. Rosner, W. J. Lyddon, & A. Freeman (Eds.), *Cognitive therapy and dreams* (pp. 89–109). New York: Springer Publishing.

Krakow, B. (2006). Nightmare complaints in treatment-seeking patients in clinical sleep medicine settings: Diagnostic and treatment implications. *Sleep, 29,* 1313–1319.

Krakow, B., Artar, A., Warner, T. D., Melendrez, D., Johnston, L., Hollifield, M., et al. (2000). Sleep disorder, depression, and suicidality in female sexual assault survivors. *Crisis, 21,* 163–170.

Krakow, B., Germain, A., Tandberg, D., Koss, M., Schrader, R., Hollifield, M., et al. (2000). Sleep breathing and sleep movement disorders masquerading as insomnia in sexual-assault survivors. *Comprehensive Psychiatry, 41,* 49–56.

Krakow, B., Haynes, P. L., Warner, T. D., Melendrez, D., Sisley, B. N., Johnston, L., et al. (2007). Clinical sleep disorder profiles in a large sample of trauma survivors: An interdisciplinary view of posttraumatic sleep disturbance. *Sleep and Hypnosis, 9,* 6–15.

Krakow, B., Hollifield, M., Johnston, L., Koss, M., Schrader, R., Warner, T. D., et al. (2001). Imagery rehearsal therapy for chronic nightmares in sexual assault survivors with post-traumatic stress disorder: A randomized controlled trial. *Journal of the American Medical Association, 286,* 537–545.

Krakow, B., Hollifield, M., Schrader, R., Koss, M., Tandberg, D., Lauriello, J., et al. (2000). A controlled study of imagery rehearsal for chronic nightmares in sexual assault survivors with PTSD: A preliminary report. *Journal of Traumatic Stress, 13,* 589–609.

Krakow, B., Johnston, L., Melendrez, D., Hollifield, M., Warner, T. D., Chavez-Kennedy, D., et al. (2001). An open-label trial of evidence-based cognitive behavior therapy for nightmares and insomnia in crime victims with PTSD. *American Journal of Psychiatry, 158,* 2043–2047.

Krakow, B., Kellner, R., Neidhardt, J., Pathak, D., & Lambert, L. (1993). Imagery re-hearsal treatment of chronic nightmares: With a thirty-month follow-up. *Journal of Behaviour Therapy and Experimental Psychiatry, 24,* 325–330.

Krakow, B., Kellner, R., Pathak, D., & Lambert, L. (1995). Imagery rehearsal treatment for chronic nightmares. *Behaviour Research and Therapy, 33,* 837–843.

Krakow, B., Kellner, R., Pathak, D., & Lambert, L. (1996). Long term reduction of nightmares with imagery rehearsal treatment. *Behavioural and Cognitive Psychotherapy, 24,* 135–148.

Krakow, B., Lowry, C., Germain, A., Gaddy, L., Hollifeld, M., Koss, M., et al. (2000). A retrospective study on improvements in nightmares and post-traumatic stress disorder following treatment for co-morbid sleep-disordered breathing. *Journal of Psychosomatic Research, 49,* 291–298.

Krakow, B., Melendrez, D., Johnston, L. G., Clark, J. O., Santana, E., Warner, T. D., et al. (2002). Sleep dynamic therapy for Cerro Grande fire evacuees with post-traumatic stress symptoms: A preliminary report. *Journal of Clinical Psychiatry, 63,* 673–684.

Krakow, B., Melendrez, D., Johnston, L. G., Warner, T. D., Clark, J. O., Pacheco, M., et al. (2002). Sleep-disordered breathing, psychiatric distress, and quality of life impairment in sexual assault survivors. *Journal of Nervous and Mental Disease, 190,* 442–452.

Krakow, B., Melendrez, D., Pedersen, B., Johnston, L., Hollifield, M., Germain, A., et al. (2001). Complex insomnia: Insomnia and sleep-disordered breathing in a consecutive series of crime victims with nightmares and PTSD. *Biological Psychiatry, 49,* 948–953.

Krakow, B., Melendrez, D., Warner, T. D., Clark, J. O., Sisley, B. N., Dorin, R., et al. (2006). Signs and symptoms of sleep-disordered breathing in trauma survivors. *Journal of Nervous and Mental Disease, 194,* 433–438.

Krakow, B., Sandoval, D., Schrader, R., Keuhne, B., McBride, L., Yau, C. L., et al. (2001). Treatment of chronic nightmares in adjudicated adolescent girls in a residential facility. *Journal of Adolescent Health, 29,* 94–100.

Krakow, B., & Zadra, A. (2006). Clinical management of chronic nightmares: Imagery rehearsal therapy. *Behavioral Sleep Medicine, 4,* 45–70.

Kramer, M. (1979). Dream disturbances. *Psychiatric Annals, 9,* 50–68.

Kramer, M. (1991). The nightmare: A failure in dream function. *Dreaming, 1,* 277–285.

Kramer, M., & Kinney, L. (1988). Sleep patterns in trauma victims with disturbed dreaming. *Psychiatric Journal of the University of Ottawa, 13,* 12–16.

Kramer, M., & Kinney, L. (2003). Vigilance and avoidance during sleep in US Vietnam veterans with post-traumatic stress disorder. *Journal of Nervous and Mental Disease, 191,* 685–687.

Kramer, M., Shoen, L., & Kinney, L. (1984). The dream experience in dream-disturbed Vietnam veterans. In B. A. van der Kolk (Ed.), *Post traumatic stress disorders: Psychological and biological sequelae* (pp. 81–95). Washington DC: American Psychiatric Association.

Kramer, M., Shoen, L., & Kinney, L. (1987). Nightmares in Vietnam veterans. *Journal of the American Academy of Psychoanalysis, 15,* 67–81.

Krystal, A. D., & Davidson, J. R. T. (2007). The use of prazosin for the treatment of trauma nightmares and sleep disturbance in combat veterans with post-traumatic stress disorder. *Biological Psychiatry, 61,* 925–927.

Kuch, K., & Cox, B. J. (1992). Symptoms of PTSD in 124 survivors of the Holocaust. *American Journal of Psychiatry, 149,* 337–340.

Kulka, R. A., Schlenger, W. E., Fairbank, J. A., Hough, R. L., Jordan, B. K., Marmar, C.R., & Weiss, D. S. (1990). *Trauma and the Vietnam war generation: Report of findings from the National Vietnam Veterans Readjustment Study.* Philadelphia: Brunner/Mazel.

Kushida, C. A., Littner, M. R., Morgenthaler, T., Alessi, C. A., Bailey, D., Coleman, J., et al. (2005). Practice parameters for the indications for polysomnography and related procedures: An update for 2005. *Sleep, 28,* 499–521.

Lambert, M., & Barley, D. (2001). Research summary on the therapeutic relationship and psychotherapy outcome. *Psychotherapy, 38,* 357–361.

Lang, P. J. (1968). Fear reduction and fear behavior: Problems in treating a construct. In J. M. Shlien (Ed.), *Research in psychotherapy, vol I.* (pp. 90–102). Washington, DC: American Psychological Association.

Lang, P. J., Cuthbert, B. N., & Bradley, M. M. (1998). Measuring emotion in therapy: Imagery, activation, and feeling. *Behavior Therapy, 29,* 665–674.

Lang, P. J., Melamed, B. G., & Hart, J. (1970). A psychophysiological analysis of fear modification using an automated desensitization procedure. *Journal of Abnormal Psychology, 76,* 220–234.

Laor, N., Wolmer, L., Wiener, Z., Reiss, A., Muller, U., Weizman, R., et al. (1998). The function of image control in the psychophysiology of posttraumatic stress disorder. *Journal of Traumatic Stress, 11,* 679–696.

Laor, N., Wolmer, L., Wiener, Z., Weizman, R., Toren, P., & Ron, S. (1999). Image control and symptom expression in posttraumatic stress disorder. *Journal of Nervous and Mental Disease, 187,* 673–679.

Largo-Marsh, L., & Spates, C. R. (2002). The effects of writing therapy in comparison to EMD/R on traumatic stress: The relationship between hypnotizability and client expectancy to outcome. *Professional Psychology: Research and Practice, 33,* 581–586.

Lavie, P. (2001). Sleep disturbances in the wake of traumatic events. *New England Journal of Medicine, 345,* 1825–1832.

Lavie, P., & Hertz, G. (1979). Increased sleep motility and respiration rates in combat neurotic patients. *Biological Psychiatry, 14,* 983–987.

Lavie, P., Katz, N., Pillar, G., & Zinger, Y. (1998). Elevated awaking thresholds during sleep: Characteristics of chronic war-related post-traumatic stress disorder patients. *Biological Psychiatry, 44,* 1060–1065.

Lawrence, J. W., Fauerbach, J., & Munster, A. (1996). Early avoidance of traumatic stimuli predicts chronicity of intrusive thoughts following burn injury. *Behavioral Research and Therapy, 34,* 643–646.

Lawyer, S. R., Resnick, H. S., Galea, S., Ahern, J., Kilpatrick, D. G., & Vlahov, D. (2006). Predictors of peritraumatic reactions and PTSD following the September 11th terrorist attacks. *Psychiatry, 69,* 130–141.

Lebowitz, L., & Newman, E. (1996). The role of cognitive-affective themes in the assessment and treatment of trauma reaction. *Clinical Psychology and Psychotherapy: An International Journal of Theory and Practice, 3,* 196–207.

Leskin, G. A., Woodward, S. H., Young, H. E., & Sheikh, J. I. (2002). Effects of comorbid diagnoses on sleep disturbance in PTSD. *Journal of Psychiatric Research, 36,* 449–452.

Leuger, R. J. (2001). Imagery techniques in cognitive behavior treatments of anxiety and trauma. In A. A. Sheikh (Ed.), *Handbook of therapeutic imagery techniques* (pp. 75–84). Amityville, NY: Baywood Publishing Company, Inc.

Levin, R., & Fireman, G. (2002a). Phenomenal qualities of nightmare experience in a prospective study of college students. *Dreaming, 12,* 109–120.

Levin, R., & Fireman, G. (2002b). Nightmare prevalence, nightmare distress, and self-reported psychological disturbance. *Sleep, 25,* 205–212.

Levin, R., Galin, J., & Zywiak, B. (1991). Nightmares, boundaries, and creativity. *Dreaming, 1,* 63–74.

Levin, R., & Nielsen, T. A. (2007). Disturbed dreaming, posttraumatic stress disorder, and affect distress: A review and neurocognitive model. *Psychological Bulletin, 133,* 482–528.

Lichstein, K. L., & Rosenthal, T. L. (1980). Insomniacs' perceptions of cognitive versus somatic determinants of sleep disturbance. *Journal of Abnormal Psychology, 89,* 105–107.

Lidz, T. (1946). Nightmares and the combat neuroses. *Journal of the Biology and the Pathology of Interpersonal Relations, 9,* 37–49.

Lindauer, R. J., Vlieger, E. J., Jalink, M., Olff, M., Carlier, I. V., Majoie, C. B., et al. (2005). Effects of psychotherapy on hippocampal volume in out-patients with post-traumatic stress disorder: A MRI investigation. *Psychological Medicine, 35,* 1421–1431.

Littleton, H. (2007). An evaluation of the coping patterns of rape victims: Integration with a schema-based information-processing model. *Violence Against Women, 13,* 789–801.

Littner, M., Kushida, C. A., Anderson, W. M., Bailey, D., Berry, R. B., Davila, D. G., et al. (2003). Practice parameters for the role of actigraphy in the study of sleep and circadian rhythms: An update for 2002. *Sleep, 26,* 337–341.

Litz, B. T., Blake, D. D., Gerardi, R. G., & Keane, T. M. (1990). Decision making guidelines for the use of direct therapeutic exposure in the treatment of post-traumatic stress disorder. *Behavior Therapist, 13,* 91–93.

Litz, B. T., & Keane, T. M. (1989). Information processing in anxiety disorders: Application to the understanding of post-traumatic stress disorder. *Clinical Psychology Review, 9,* 243–257.

Lueger, R. J. (2001). Imagery techniques in cognitive behavior treatments of anxiety and trauma. In A. A. Sheikh (Ed.), *Handbook of therapeutic imagery techniques* (pp. 75–84). Amityville, NY: Baywood Publishing Company, Inc.

Maher, M. J., Rego, S. A., & Asnis, G. M. (2006). Sleep disturbances in patients with post-traumatic stress disorder: Epidemiology, impact and approaches to management. *CNS Drugs, 20,* 568–590.

Mahowald, M. W., & Bornemann, M. A. C. (2005). NREM sleep-arousal parasomnias. In M. H. Kryger, T. Roth, & W. C. Dement (Eds.), *Principles and practices of sleep medicine* (4th ed., pp. 889–896). Philadelphia: Elsevier Sanders.

Maquet, P., Péters, J., & Aerts, J. (1996). Functional neuroanatomy of human rapid-eye-movement sleep and dreaming. *Nature, 383,* 163–166.

Marks, I. (1978). Rehearsal relief of a nightmare. *British Journal of Psychiatry, 133,* 461–465.

Marks, I. (1987). Nightmares. *Integrative Psychiatry, 5,* 71–81.

Mastin, D., Bryson, J., & Corwyn, R. (2006). Assessment of sleep hygiene using the sleep hygiene index. *Journal of Behavioral Medicine, 29,* 223–227.

Mazzoni, G. A. L., & Loftus, E. F. (1998). Dream interpretation can change beliefs about the past. *Psychotherapy, 35,* 177–187.

McCall, W. V., & Edinger, J. D. (1992). Subjective total insomnia: An example of sleep state misperception. *Sleep, 15,* 71–73.

McCann, I. L., Sakheim, D. K., & Abrahamson, D. J. (1988). Trauma and victimization: A model of psychological adaptation. *Counseling Psychologist, 16,* 531–594.

McGuigan, W. M., & Middlemiss, W. (2005). Sexual abuse in childhood and interpersonal violence in adulthood. *Journal of Interpersonal Violence, 20*, 1271–1287.

Mehra, R., & Strohl, K. P. (2006). Evaluation of sleep disordered breathing: Polysomnography. In T. L. Lee-Chiong (Ed.), *Sleep: A comprehensive handbook* (pp. 303–315). Hoboken, NJ: John Wiley & Sons, Inc.

Mellman, T. A. (1997). Psychobiology of sleep disturbances in post-traumatic stress disorder. *Annals of the New York Academy of Science, 821*, 142–149.

Mellman, T. A. (2000). Sleep and the pathogenesis of PTSD. In A. Shalev, R. Yehuda, & A. C. McFarlane (Eds.), *International handbook of human response to trauma* (pp. 299–306). New York: Plenum Publishing Company.

Mellman, T. A. (2006). Sleep and anxiety disorders. *Psychiatric Clinics of North America, 29*, 1047–1058.

Mellman, T. A., David, D., Bustamante, V., Torres, J., & Fins, A. (2001). Dreams in the acute aftermath of trauma and their relationship to PTSD. *Journal of Traumatic Stress, 14*, 241–247.

Mellman, T. A., David, D., Kulick-Bell, R., Hebding, J., & Nolan, B. (1995). Sleep disturbance and its relationship to psychiatric morbidity after Hurricane Andrew. *American Journal of Psychiatry, 152*, 1659–1663.

Mellman, T. A., & Hipolito, M. M. S. (2006). Sleep disturbances in the aftermath of trauma and post-traumatic stress disorder. *CNS Spectrums, 11*, 611–615.

Mellman, T. A., Kulick-Bell, R., Ashlock, L. E., & Nolan, B. (1995). Sleep events among veterans with combat-related post-traumatic stress disorder. *American Journal of Psychiatry, 152*, 110–115.

Mellman, T. A., Kumar, A., Kulick-Bell, R., Kumar, M., & Nolan, B. (1995). Nocturnal/daytime urine noradrenergic measures and sleep in combat-related PTSD. *Biological Psychiatry, 38*, 174–179.

Miller, W. R., & DiPilato, M. (1983). Treatment of nightmares via relaxation and desensitization: A controlled evaluation. *Journal of Clinical and Consulting Psychology, 51*, 870–877.

Monk, R. H., Reynolds, C. F., Kupfer, D. J., Buysse, D. J., Coble, P. A., Hayes, A. J., et al. (1994). The Pittsburgh sleep diary. *Journal of Sleep Research, 3*, 111–120.

Moore, B. A., & Krakow, B. (2007). Imagery rehearsal therapy for acute post-traumatic nightmares among combat soldiers in Iraq. *American Journal of Psychiatry, 164*, 683–684.

Morin, C. M. (1993). *Insomnia: Psychological assessment and management*. NY: Guilford Press.

Morin, C. M. (2005). Psychological and behavioral treatments for primary insomnia. In M. H. Kryger, T. Roth, & W. C. Dement (Eds.), *Principles and practices of sleep medicine* (4th ed., pp. 726–737). Philadelphia: Elsevier Sanders.

Morin, C. M., Blais, F., & Savard, J. (2002). Are changes in beliefs and attitudes about sleep related to sleep improvements in the treatment of insomnia? *Behaviour Research and Therapy, 40*, 741–752.

Morin, C. M., Culbert, J. P., & Schwartz, S. M. (1994). Nonpharmacological interventions for insomnia: A meta-analysis of treatment efficacy. *American Journal of Psychiatry, 151*, 1172–1180.

Morin, C. M., Rodrigui, S., & Ivers, H. (2003). Role of stress, arousal, and coping skills in primary insomnia. *Psychosomatic Medicine, 65*, 259–267.

Morin, C. M., Stone, J., Trinkle, D., Mercer, J., & Remsberg, S. (1993). Dysfunctional beliefs and attitudes about sleep among older adults with and without insomnia complaints. *Psychology and Aging, 8,* 463–467.

Morriss, R., Sharpe, M., Sharpley, A. L., Cowen, P. J., Hawton, K., & Morris, J. (1993). Abnormalities of sleep in patients with the chronic fatigue syndrome. *British Medical Journal, 306,* 1161–1164.

Morriss, R. K., Wearden, A. J., & Battersby, L. (1997). The relationship of sleep difficulties to fatigue, mood and disability in chronic fatigue syndrome. *Journal of Psychosomatic Research, 42,* 597–605.

Mowrer, O. H. (1947). On the dual nature of learning: A re-interpretation of "conditioning" and "problem-solving." *Harvard Educational Review, 17,* 102–148.

Mowrer, O. H. (1960). *Learning theory and behavior.* New York: John Wiley & Sons, Inc.

Mullen, P. E., Martin, J. L., & Anderson, J. C. (1996). The long-term impact of the physical, emotional, and sexual abuse of children: A community study. *Child Abuse & Neglect, 20,* 7–21.

Mundt, J. C., Marks, I. M., Shear, M. K., & Greist, J. M. (2002). The work and social adjustment scale: A simple measure of impairment in functioning. *British Journal of Psychiatry, 180,* 461–464.

Nadar, K. (1996). Children's traumatic dreams. In D. Barrett (Ed.), *Trauma and dreams* (pp. 9–24). Cambridge, MA: Harvard University Press.

National Institutes of Health. (2004). *Frontiers of knowledge in sleep & sleep disorders: Opportunities for improving health and quality of life.* Retrieved January 2, 2008, from www.nhlbi.nih.gov/meetings/slp_front.htm

Neidhardt, E. J., Krakow, B., Kellner, R., & Pathak, D. (1992). The beneficial effects of one treatment session and recording of nightmares on chronic nightmare sufferers. *Sleep, 15,* 470–473.

Neria, Y., Gross, R., Litz, B., Maguen, S., Insel, B., Seirmarco, G., et al. (2007). Prevalence and psychological correlates of complicated grief among bereaved adults 2.5–3.5 years after September 11th attacks. *Journal of Traumatic Stress, 20,* 251–262.

Newman, E., Riggs, D. S., & Roth, S. (1997). Thematic resolution, PTSD, and complex PTSD: The relationship between meaning and trauma-related diagnoses. *Journal of Traumatic Stress, 10,* 197–213.

Neylan, T. C., Marmar, C. R., Metzler, T. J., Weiss, D. S., Zatzick, D. F., Delucchi, K. L., et al. (1998). Sleep disturbances in the Vietnam generation: Findings from a nationally representative sample of male Vietnam veterans. *American Journal of Psychiatry, 155,* 929–933.

Neylan, T. C., Otte, C., Yehuda, R., & Marmar, C. R. (2006). Neuroendocrine regulation of sleep disturbances in PTSD. *Annals of the New York Academy of Sciences, 1071,* 203–215.

Nguyen, T. T., Madrid, S., Marquez, H., & Hicks, R. A. (2002). Nightmare frequency, nightmare distress, and anxiety. *Perceptual and Motor Skills, 95,* 219–225.

Nicassio, P. M., Mendlowitz, D. R., Fussell, J. J., & Petras, L. (1985). The phenomenology of the pre-sleep state: The development of the pre-sleep arousal scale. *Behaviour Research and Therapy, 23,* 263–271.

Nielsen, T. A. (2005). Disturbed dreaming in medical conditions. In M. H. Kryger, T. Roth, & W. C. Dement (Eds.), *Principles and practices of sleep medicine* (4th ed., pp. 936–945). Philadelphia: Elsevier Sanders.

Nielsen, T. A., Deslauriers, D., & Baylor, G. W. (1991). Emotions in dream and waking event reports. *Dreaming, 1,* 287–300.

Nielsen, T. A., Laberge, L., Paquet, J., Tremblay, R. E., Vitaro, F., & Montplaisir, J. (2000). Development of disturbing dreams during adolescence and their relation to anxiety symptoms. *Sleep, 23,* 727–736.

Nielsen, T. A., Stenstrom, P., & Levin, R. (2006). Nightmare frequency as a function of age, gender, and September 11, 2001: Findings from an Internet questionnaire. *Dreaming, 16,* 145–158.

Nielsen, T. A., & Zadra, A. (2005). Nightmares and other common dream disturbances. In M. H. Kryger, T. Roth, & W. C. Dement (Eds.), *Principles and practices of sleep medicine* (4th ed., pp. 926–935). Philadelphia: Elsevier Sanders.

Norris, F. H. (1992). Epidemiology of trauma: Frequency and impact of different potentially traumatic events on different demographic groups. *Journal of Consulting and Clinical Psychology, 60,* 409–418.

North, C. S., Nixon, S. J., Shariat, S., Mallonee, S., McMillen, J. C., Spitznagel, E. L., et al. (1999). Psychiatric disorders among survivors of the Oklahoma City bombing. *Journal of the American Medical Association, 282,* 755–762.

Ohayon, M. M., & Shapiro, C. M. (2000). Sleep disturbances and psychiatric disorders associated with post-traumatic stress disorder in the general population. *Comprehensive Psychiatry, 41,* 469–478.

Olff, M., de Vries, G., Guzelcan, Y., Assies, J., & Gersons, B. P. R. (2007). Changes in cortisol and DHEA plasma levels after psychotherapy for PTSD. *Psychoneuroendocrinology, 32,* 619–626.

Opalic, P. (2000). Research of the dreams of the traumatized subjects. *Psihijatrija Danas, 32,* 129–147.

Orr, S. P., & Roth, W. T. (2000). Psychophysiological assessment: Clinical applications for PTSD. *Journal of Affective Disorders, 61,* 225–240.

Pagel, J. F. (2000). Nightmares and disorders of dreaming. *American Family Physician, 61,* 2037–2042.

Parrott, A. C., & Hindmarch, I. (1978). Factor analysis of a sleep evaluation questionnaire. *Psychological Medicine, 8,* 325–329.

Partinen, M., & Gislason, T. (1995). Basic Nordic sleep questionnaire (BNSQ): A quantitated measure of subjective sleep complaints. *Journal of Sleep Research, 4,* 150–155.

Peirce, J. T. (2006). Efficacy of imagery rehearsal treatment related to specialized populations: A case study and brief report. *Dreaming, 16,* 280–285.

Pennebaker, J. W., & Graybeal, A. (2001). Patterns of natural language use: Disclosure, personality, and social integration. *Current Directions in Psychological Science, 10,* 90–93.

Pennebaker, J. W., Kiecolt-Glaser, J. K., & Glaser, R. (1988). Disclosure of traumas and immune function: Health implications for psychotherapy. *Journal of Consulting and Clinical Psychology, 56,* 239–245.

Pennebaker, J. W., Mayne, T. J., & Francis, M. E. (1997). Linguistic predictors of adaptive bereavement. *Journal of Personality and Social Psychology, 72,* 863–871.

Pennington, H., Davis, J. L., & Rhudy, J. L. (2008). *Imagery vividness in chronic nightmare sufferers.* Unpublished manuscript, University of Tulsa.

Perlis, M. L., & Lichstein, K. L. (Eds.). (2003). *Treating sleep disorders: Principles and practices of behavioral sleep medicine.* Hoboken, NJ: John Wiley & Sons, Inc.

Peskind, E. R., Bonner, L. T., Hoff, D. G., & Raskind, M. A. (2003). Prazosin reduces trauma-related nightmares in older men with chronic post-traumatic stress disorder. *Journal of Geriatric Psychiatry and Neurology, 61,* 165–171.

Petrie, K. J., Booth, R. J., & Pennebaker, J. W. (1998). The immunological effects of thought suppression. *Journal of Personality and Social Psychology, 75,* 1264–1272.

Pfeffer, C. R., Altemus, M., Heo, M., & Jiang, H. (2007). Salivary cortisol and psychopathology in children bereaved by the September 11, 2001 terror attacks. *Biological Psychiatry, 61,* 957–965.

Phelps, A. J., Forbes, D., & Creamer, M. (2008). Understanding posttraumatic nightmares: An empirical and conceptual review. *Clinical Psychology Review, 28,* 338–355.

Pietrowsky, R., & Köthe, M. (2003). Personal boundaries and nightmare consequences in frequent nightmare sufferers. *Dreaming, 13,* 245–254.

Pillar, G., Malhotra, A., & Lavie, P. (2000). Post-traumatic stress disorder and sleep—what a nightmare! *Sleep Medicine Reviews, 4,* 183–200.

Pitman, R. K., Altman, B., Greenwald, E., Longpre, R. E., Macklin, M. L., Poire, R. E., & Steketee, G. S. (1991). Psychiatric complications during flooding therapy for post-traumatic stress disorder. *Journal of Clinical Psychiatry, 52,* 17–20.

Raskind, M. A., Peskind, E. R., Hoff, D. J., Hart, K. L., Holmes, H. A., Warren, D., et al. (2007). A parallel group placebo controlled study of prazosin for trauma-related nightmares and sleep disturbances in combat veterans with post-traumatic stress disorder. *Biological Psychiatry, 61,* 928–934.

Raskind, M. A., Peskind, E. R., Kanter, E. D., Petrie, E. C., Radant, A., Thompson, C. E., et al. (2003). Reduction of nightmares and other PTSD symptoms in combat veterans by prazosin: A placebo-controlled study. *American Journal of Psychiatry, 160,* 371–373.

Raskind, M. A., Thompson, C., Petrie, E. C., Dobie, J. D., Rein, R. J., Hoff, D. J., et al. (2002). Prazosin reduces nightmares in combat veterans with post-traumatic stress disorder. *Journal of Clinical Psychiatry, 63,* 565–568.

Rauch, S. A. M., Foa, E. B., Furr, J. M., & Filip, J. C. (2004). Imagery vividness and perceived anxious arousal in prolonged exposure treatment for PTSD. *Journal of Traumatic Stress, 17,* 461–465.

Resick, P. A., Falsetti, S. A., Resnick, H. S., & Kilpatrick, D. G. (1991). *The modified PTSD symptom scale—Self-report.* St. Louis, MO: University of Missouri & Charleston, SC: National Crime Victims Research and Treatment Center, Medical University of South Carolina.

Resick, P. A., & Schnicke, M. K. (1993). *Cognitive processing therapy for rape victims: A treatment manual.* Newbury Park, CA: Sage.

Resnick, H. S., Acierno, R., & Kilpatrick, D. G. (1997). Health impact of interpersonal violence 2: Medical and mental health outcomes. *Behavioral Medicine, 23,* 65–78.

Resnick, H. S., Best, C. L., Kilpatrick, D. G., Freedy, J. R., & Falsetti, S. A. (1993). *Trauma Assessment for Adults—Self-Report Version. Unpublished Scale.* Charleston, SC: National Crime Victims Research and Treatment Center, Medical University of South Carolina.

Resnick, H. S., Kilpatrick, D. G., Dansky, B. S., Saunders, B. E., & Best, C. L. (1993). Prevalence of civilian trauma and posttraumatic stress disorder in a representative national sample of women. *Journal of Consulting and Clinical Psychology, 61,* 984–991.

Revonsuo, A. (2000). The reinterpretation of dreams: An evolutionary hypothesis of function of dreaming. *Behavioral and Brain Sciences, 23,* 877–901.

Rhudy, J. L., Davis, J. L., Williams, A. E., McCabe, K. M., & Byrd, P. M. (2008). Physiological- emotional reactivity to nightmare-related imagery in trauma-exposed persons with chronic nightmares. *Behavioral Sleep Medicine, 6,* 158–177.

Rhudy, J. L., Davis, J. L., Williams, A. E., McCabe, K. M., Bartley, E. J., Byrd, P. M., & Pruiksma, K. E. (under review). Cognitive-behavioral treatment reduces physiological-emotional reactions to nightmare imagery in trauma-exposed persons suffering from chronic nightmares.

Riggs, D. S., Rothbaum, B. O., & Foa, E. B. (1995). A prospective examination of symptoms of posttraumatic stress disorder in vicitms of nonsexual assault. *Journal of Interpersonal Violence, 10,* 201–214.

Robert, G., & Zadra, A. (2008). Measuring nightmare and bad dream frequency: impact of retrospective and prospective instruments. *Journal of Sleep Research, 17,*132–139.

Roberts, J., & Lennings, C. J. (2006). Personality, psychopathology and nightmares in young people. *Personality and Individual Differences, 41,* 733–744.

Roehrs, T., & Roth, T. (2001). Sleep, sleepiness, and alcohol use. *Alcohol Research and Health, 25,* 101–109.

Rogers, A. E. (1997). Nursing management of sleep disorders: Part I—assessment. *ANNA Journal, 24,* 666–671.

Rosen, J., Reynolds, C. F., Yeager, A. L., Houck, P. R., & Hurwitz, L. F. (1991). Sleep disturbances in survivors of the Nazi Holocaust. *American Journal of Psychiatry, 148,* 62–66.

Ross, R. J., Ball, W. A., Sullivan, K. A., & Caroff, S. N. (1989). Sleep disturbance as the hallmark of post-traumatic stress disorder. *American Journal of Psychiatry, 146,* 697–707.

Roszell, D. K., McFall, M. E., & Malas, K. L. (1991). Frequency of symptoms and concurrent psychiatric disorder in Vietnam veterans with chronic PTSD. *Hospital and Community Psychiatry, 42,* 293–296.

Roth, S., & Newman, E. (1991). The process of coping with trauma. *Journal of Traumatic Stress, 4,* 279–297.

Roth, T., Zammit, G., Kushida, C., Doghramji, K., Mathias, S. D., Wong, J. M., et al. (2002). A new questionnaire to detect sleep disorders. *Sleep Medicine, 3*(2), 99–108.

Rothbaum, B. O., & Mellman, T. A. (2001). Dreams and exposure therapy in PTSD. *Journal of Traumatic Stress, 14,* 481–490.

Rowling, J. K. (1999). *Harry Potter and the prisoner of Azkaban.* New York: Scholastic Press.

Rusch, M. D., Grunert, B. K., Mendelsohn, R. A., & Smucker, M. R. (2000). Imagery rescripting or recurrent, distressing images. *Cognitive and Behavioral Practice, 7,* 173–182.

Saakvitne, K. W., & Pearlman, L. A. (1996). *Transforming the pain: A workbook on vicarious traumatization.* New York: W. W. Norton and Company.

Sadeh, A., Hayden, R. M., McGuire, J. P. D., Sachs, H., & Civita, R. (1994). Somatic, cognitive, and emotional characteristics of abused children hospitalized in a psychiatric hospital. *Child Psychiatry and Human Development, 24,* 191–200.

Sadeh, A., McGuire, J. P. D., Sachs, H., Seifer, R., Tremblay, A., Civita, R., et al. (1995). Sleep and psychological characteristics of children on a psychiatric inpatient unit. *Journal of the American Academy of Child and Adolescent Psychiatry, 34,* 813–819.

Salvio, M., Wood, J. M., Schwartz, J., & Eichling, P. S. (1992). Nightmare prevalence in the health elderly. *Psychology and Aging, 7,* 324–325.

Schnider, K. R., Elhai, J. D., & Gray, M. J. (2007). Coping style predicts posttraumatic stress and complicated grief symptom severity among college students reporting a traumatic loss. *Journal of Counseling Psychology, 54,* 344–350.

Schnurr, P. P., & Green, B. L. (Eds.). (2003). *Trauma and health: Physical health consequences of exposure to extreme stress.* Washington, DC: American Psychological Association.

Schnurr, P. P., & Green, B. L. (2004). Understanding relationships among trauma, posttraumatic stress disorder, and health outcomes. *Advances in Mind-Body Medicine, 20* 18–29.

Schoutrop, M. J. A., Lange, A., Hanewald, G., Davidovich, U., & Salomon, H. (2002). Structured writing and processing major stressful events: A controlled trial. *Psychotherapy and Psychosomatics, 71,* 151–157.

Schredl, M. (2003). Effects of state and trait factors on nightmare frequency. *European Archives of Psychiatry and Clinical Neuroscience, 253,* 241–247.

Schreuder, B. J. N., Igreja, V., van Dijk, J., & Kleijn, W. (2001). Intrusive re-experiencing of chronic strife or war. *Advances in Psychiatric Treatment, 7,* 102–108.

Schreuder, B. J. N., Kleijn, W. C., & Rooijmans, H. G. M. (2000). Nocturnal re-experiencing more than forty years after war trauma. *Journal of Traumatic Stress, 13,* 453–463.

Schreuder, B. J. N., van Egmond, M., Kleijn, W. C., & Visser, A. T. (1998). Daily reports of posttraumatic nightmares and anxiety dreams in Dutch war victims. *Journal of Anxiety Disorders, 12,* 511–524.

Scientific Advisory Committee of the Medical Outcomes Trust. (2002). Assessing health status and quality-of-life instruments: Attributes and review criteria. *Quality of Life Research, 11,* 193–205.

Scurfield, R. M., Kenderdine, S. K., & Pollard, R. J. (1990). Inpatient treatment for war-related post-traumatic stress disorder: Initial findings on a longer-term outcome study. *Journal of Traumatic Stress, 3,* 185–201.

Seligman, M. E. P., & Yellen, A. (1987). What is a dream? *Behavioral Research and Therapy, 25,* 1–24.

Sheehan, P. W. (1967). A shortened form of Betts' questionnaire upon mental imagery. *Journal of Clinical Psychology, 23,* 386–389.

Sheikh, J. I., Woodward, S. H., & Leskin, G. A. (2003). Sleep in post-traumatic stress disorder and panic: Convergence and divergence. *Depression and Anxiety, 18,* 187–197.

Shen, J., Chung, S. A., Kayumov, L., Moller, H., Hossain, N., Wang, X., et al. (2006). Polysomnographic and symptomatological analyses of major depressive disorder patients treated with mirtazapine. *Canadian Journal of Psychiatry, 51,* 27–34.

Skinner, H. A. (1982). The drug abuse screening test. *Addictive Behaviors, 7,* 363–371.

Smith, D. W., Davis, J. L., & Fricker-Elhai, A. E. (2004). How does trauma beget trauma? Cognitions about risk in women with sexual abuse histories. *Child Maltreatment, 9,* 292–303.

Smith, L. J., Nowakowski, S., Soeffing, J. P., Orff, H. J., & Perlis, M. L. (2003). The measurement of sleep. In M. L. Perlis & K. L. Lichstein (Eds.), *Treating sleep disorders: Principles and practice of behavioral sleep medicine* (pp. 29–73). Hoboken, NJ: John Wiley & Sons, Inc.

Smucker, M. R., Dancu, C., Foa, E. B., & Niederee, J. L. (2002). Imagery rescripting: A new treatment for survivors of childhood sexual abuse suffering from posttraumatic stress. In R. L. Leahy & E. T. Dowd (Eds.), *Clinical advances in cognitive psychotherapy: Theory and application* (pp. 294–310). New York: Springer Publishing.

Smucker, M. R., & Niederee, J. (1995). Treating incest-related PTSD and pathogenic schemas through imaginal exposure and rescripting. *Cognitive and Behavioral Practice, 2*, 63–93.

Solomon, S. D., & Davidson, J. R. T. (1997). Trauma: Prevalence, impairment, service use, and cost. *Journal of Clinical Psychiatry, 58*(Suppl.), 5–11.

Spadafora, A., & Hunt, H. T. (1990). The multiplicity of dreams: Cognitive-affective correlates of lucid, archetypal, and nightmare dreaming. *Perceptual and Motor Skills, 71*, 627–644.

Spielman, A. J., Caruso, L. S., & Glovinsky, P. B. (1987). A behavioral perspective on insomnia treatment. *Psychiatric Clinics of North America, 10*, 541–553.

Spoormaker, V. I., Schredl, M., & van den Bout, J. (2006). Nightmares: From anxiety symptom to sleep disorder. *Sleep Medicine Reviews, 10*, 19–31.

Spoormaker, V. I., van den Bout, J., & Meijer, E. J. G. (2003). Lucid dreaming treatment for nightmares: A series of cases. *Dreaming, 13*, 181–186.

Spoormaker, V. I., Verbeek, I., Bout, J. van den, & Klip, E. C. (2005). Initial validation of the SLEEP-50 questionnaire. *Behavioral Sleep Medicine, 3*, 227–246.

Stapleton, J. A, Asmundson, G. J. G, Woods, M., Taylor, S., & Stein, M. B. (2006). Health care utilization by United Nations peacekeeping veterans with co-occurring, self-reported, post-traumatic stress disorder and depression symptoms versus those without. *Military Medicine, 171*, 562–566.

Stapleton, J. A., Taylor, S., & Asmundson, G. J. G. (2006). Effects of three PTSD treatments on anger and guilt: Exposure therapy, eye movement desensitization and reprocessing, and relaxation training. *Journal of Traumatic Stress, 19*, 19–28.

Stein, M. B., Kline, N. A., & Matloff, J. L. (2002). Adjunctive olanzapine for SSRI-resistant combat-related PTSD: A double-blind, placebo-controlled study. *American Journal of Psychiatry, 159*, 1777–1779.

Stickgold, R. (2005). Why we dream. In M. Kryger, T. Roth, & W. Dement (Eds.), *Principles and practices of sleep medicine* (4th ed., pp. 579–587). Philadelphia: Elsevier Saunders.

Stutman, R. K., & Bliss, E. L. (1985). Posttraumatic stress disorder, hypnotizability, and imagery. *American Journal of Psychiatry, 142*, 741–743.

Tan, V. L., & Hicks, R. A. (1995). Type A-B behavior and nightmare types among college students. *Perceptual and Motor Skills, 81*, 15–19.

Taylor, R., & Raskind, M. A. (2002). The alpha1-adrenergic antagonist prazosin improves sleep and nightmares in civilian trauma post-traumatic stress disorder. *Journal of Clinical Psychopharmacology, 22*, 82–85.

Terr, L. C. (1979). Children of Chowchilla: A study of psychic trauma. *Psychoanalytic Study of Children, 34*, 552–623.

Terr, L. C. (1983). Chowchilla revisited: The effects of psychic trauma four years after a school-bus kidnapping. *American Journal of Psychiatry, 140,* 1543–1550.

Thompson, K. E., Hamilton, M., & West, J. A. (1995). Group treatment for nightmares in veterans with combat-related PTSD. *National Centre for PTSD Clinical Quarterly,* 13–17.

Tolin, D. F., & Foa, E. B. (2006). Sex differences in trauma and post-traumatic stress disorder: A quantitative review of 25 years of research. *Psychological Bulletin, 132,* 959–992.

Trajanovic, N. N., Radivojevic, V., Kaushansky, Y., & Shapiro, C. M. (2007). Positive sleep state misperception—A new concept of sleep misperception. *Sleep Medicine, 8,* 111–118.

Ullman, S. E., Townsend, S. M., Filipas, H. H., & Starzynski, L. L. (2007). Structural models of the relations of assault severity, social support, avoidance coping, self-blame, and PTSD among sexual assault survivors. *Psychology of Women Quarterly, 31,* 23–37.

van der Kolk, B., Blitz, R., Burr, W., Sherry, S., & Hartmann, E. (1981). Characteristics of nightmares among veterans with and without combat experiences. *Sleep Research, 10,* 179.

van der Kolk, B., Blitz, R., Burr, W., Sherry, S., & Hartmann, E. (1984). Nightmares and trauma: A comparison of nightmares after combat with lifelong nightmares in veterans. *American Journal of Psychiatry, 141,* 187–190.

van der Kolk, B., & Goldberg, H. L. (1983). Aftercare of schizophrenic patients: Psychopharmacology and consistency of therapists. *Hospital and Community Psychiatry, 4,* 340–343.

van Liempt, S., Vermetten, E., Geuze, E., & Westenberg, H. (2006). Pharmacotherapeutic treatment of nightmares and insomnia in post-traumatic stress disorder: An overview of the literature. *Annals of the New York Academy of Sciences, 1071,* 502–507.

van Minnen, A., Arntz, A., & Keijsers, G. P. J. (2002). Prolonged exposure in patients with chronic PTSD: Predictors of treatment outcome and dropout. *Behaviour Research and Therapy, 40,* 439–457.

Vaughan, K., & Tarrier, N. (1992). The use of image habituation training with post-traumatic stress disorders. *British Journal of Psychiatry, 161,* 658–664.

Vgontzas, A. N., & Kales, A. (1999). Sleep and its disorders. *Annual Review of Medicine, 50,* 387–400.

Walker, E. A., & Stenchever, M. A. (1993). Sexual victimization and chronic pelvic pain. *Obstetrics and Gynecology Clinic of North America, 20,* 795–807.

Wang, S., Wilson, J. P., & Mason, J. W. (1996). Stages of decompensation in combat-related post-traumatic stress disorder: A new conceptual model. *Integrative Physiological & Behavioral Science, 31,* 237–253.

Ware, J. E., Jr., & Sherbourne, C. D. (1992). The MOS 36-item short-form health survey (SF-36). I. Conceptual framework and item selection. *Medical Care, 30*(6), 473–483.

Weathers F., Huska J., & Keane T. (1991). *The PTSD checklist military version (PCL-M).* Boston: National Center for PTSD.

Weiss, D. S. (2007). Conundrums in a theory of disturbed dreaming: Comment on Levin and Nielsen. *Psychological Bulletin, 133,* 529–532.

Wilmer, H. A. (1996). The healing nightmare: War dreams of Vietnam veterans. In D. Barrett (Ed.), *Trauma and dreams* (pp. 86–99). Cambridge, MA: Harvard University Press.

Wilson, A. E., Calhoun, K. S., & Bernat, J. A. (1999). Risk recognition and trauma-related symptoms among sexually revictimized women. *Journal of Consulting and Clinical Psychology, 67,* 705–710.

Wind, T. W., & Silvern, L. E. (1992). Type and extent of child abuse as predictors of adult functioning. *Journal of Family Violence, 7,* 261–281.

Wittmann, L., Schredl, M., & Kramer, M. (2007). Dreaming in post-traumatic stress disorder: A critical review of phenomenology, psychophysiology and treatment. *Psychotherapy and Psychosomatics, 76,* 25–39.

Wolpe J. (1958). *Psychotherapy by reciprocal inhibition.* Stanford, CA: Stanford University Press.

Wood, J. M., & Bootzin, R. R. (1990). The prevalence of nightmares and their independence from anxiety. *Journal of Abnormal Psychology, 99,* 64–68.

Woodward, S. H. (1995). Neurobiological perspectives on sleep in post-traumatic stress disorder. In M. J. Friedman, D. S. Charney, & A. Y. Deutch (Eds.), *Neurobiological and clinical consequences of stress: From normal adaptation to PTSD* (pp. 315–333). Philadelphia: Lippincott-Raven Publishers.

Woodward, S. H., Bliwise, D. L., Friedman, M. J., & Gusman, F. D. (1996). First night effects in post-traumatic stress disorder inpatients. *Sleep, 19,* 312–317.

Woodward, S. H., Stegman, W. K., Pavao, J. R., Arsenault, N. J., Hartl, T. L., Krescher, K. D., et al. (2007). Self-selection bias in sleep and psychophysiological studies of post-traumatic stress disorder. *Journal of Traumatic Stress, 20,* 619–623.

World Health Organization. (2007). International statistical classification of diseases and related health problems (10th Revision, Version for 2007). Retrieved February 1, 2008 from *http://www.who.int/classifications/icd/en/.*

Yehuda, R., & McFarlane, A. C. (1997). *Psychobiology of posttraumatic stress disorder.* New York: New York Academy of Sciences.

Yoo, S., Gujar, N., Hu, P., Jolesz, F. A., & Walker, M. P. (2007). The human emotional brain without sleep—a prefrontal amygdala disconnect. *Current Biology, 17,* R877–R878.

Youakim, J. M., Doghramji, K., & Schutte, S. L. (1998). Post-traumatic stress disorder and obstructive sleep apnea syndrome. *Psychosomatics, 39,* 168–171.

Zadra, A., & Donderi, D. C. (2000). Nightmares and bad dreams: Their prevalence and relationship to well-being. *Journal of Abnormal Psychology, 109,* 273–281.

Zadra, A. L., & Pihl, R. O. (1997). Lucid dreaming as a treatment for recurrent nightmares. *Psychotherapy and Psychosomatics, 66,* 50–55.

Zadra, A., Pilon, M., & Donderi, D. C. (2006). Variety and intensity of emotions in nightmares and bad dreams. *Journal of Nervous and Mental Disease, 194,* 249–254.

Zayfert, C., & Becker, C. B. (2007). *Cognitive-behavioral therapy for PTSD: A case formulation approach.* New York: Guilford Press.

Zayfert, C., & DeViva, J. C. (2004). Residual insomnia following cognitive behavioral therapy for PTSD. *Journal of Traumatic Stress, 17,* 69–73.

Ziarnowski, A. P., & Broida, D. C. (1984). Therapeutic implications of the nightmares of Vietnam combat veterans. *VA Practitioner, 1,* 63–68.

Zoellner, L. A., Feeny, N. C., Cochran, B., & Pruitt, L. (2003). Treatment choice for PTSD. *Behaviour Research and Therapy, 41,* 879–886.

Index

SPRINGER PUBLISHING COMPANY

Healing Crisis and Trauma with Mind, Body, and Spirit

Barbara Rubin Wainrib, EdD

Learning new skills to address the injuries incurred by sudden trauma and unpredictable lives is essential. This book is written for those persons in the "helping professions." It is also written for those who have a sufficient understanding of psychology and a sufficient awareness of our current world, and want to gain some knowledge about being helpful.

This book offers the educator and the practitioner training methods, exercises, and intervention techniques applicable to the gamut of experiences that we currently encounter. It also will introduce readers to newer concepts and their applications such as role play, spirituality, the role of animals in healing, and the concept of forgiveness. Throughout the book, whether it is in those who represent the highly resilient or those who continue to struggle, a strengths perspective is emphasized. Finally, this book describes the "Phoenix Phenomenon", a concept Wainrib developed during the course of her teaching and practice, which articulates and illustrates an inherent ability to use resilience in the process of converting pain into growth.

Partial Contents:

- Understanding Crisis Intervention and Trauma
- Understanding Trauma and its Impact
- Mass Trauma, Past and Present
- Women and Trauma
- Trauma from Within: Life Threatening Illness
- Resilience and the Phoenix Phenomenon
- Trauma and the Mind
- Trauma and the Body
- Spirituality and Trauma
- New Sources of Healing
- Forgiveness
- Final Thoughts

2006 · 184 pp · Softcover · 978-0-8261-3245-1

11 West 42nd Street, New York, NY 10036-8002 • Fax: 212-941-7842
Order Toll-Free: 877-687-7476 • Order Online: www.springerpub.com

SPRINGER / PUBLISHING COMPANY

Healing the Heart of Trauma and Dissociation with EMDR and Ego State Therapy

Carol Forgash, LCSW, BCD
Margaret Copeley, MEd, Editors

"This book pioneers the integration of EMDR with ego state techniques and opens new and exciting vistas for the practitioners of each."

—From the Foreword by **John G. Watkins, PhD,** founder of ego state therapy

HEALING
THE **HEART** OF
TRAUMA AND
DISSOCIATION
with **EMDR** and
Ego State Therapy

Editors — Carol Forgash
Margaret Copeley

The powerful benefits of EMDR in treating PTSD have been solidly validated. In this groundbreaking new work nine master clinicians show how complex PTSD involving dissociation and other challenging diagnoses can be treated safely and effectively. They stress the careful preparation of clients for EMDR and the inclusion of ego state therapy to target the dissociated ego states that arise in response to severe and prolonged trauma.

Special Features

- Key aspects of this new approach to EMDR

- The first definitive look at the use of EMDR to treat dissociation and the dissociative disorders

- Opens a window into the psyches of clients whose healing depends on their therapists' enlistment of integrative interventions

- Provides practical applications for a full range of mental health practitioners: psychiatrists, psychologists, social workers, nurses, and counselors

- Clearly outlines the phased treatment that extends the EMDR preparation phase to create safety and stability for complex trauma clients

- Provides cutting edge information for graduate students in the mental health fields

2007 · 384 pp · Hardcover · 978-0-8261-4696-0

11 West 42nd Street, New York, NY 10036-8002 • Fax: 212-941-7842
Order Toll-Free: 877-687-7476 • Order Online: www.springerpub.com